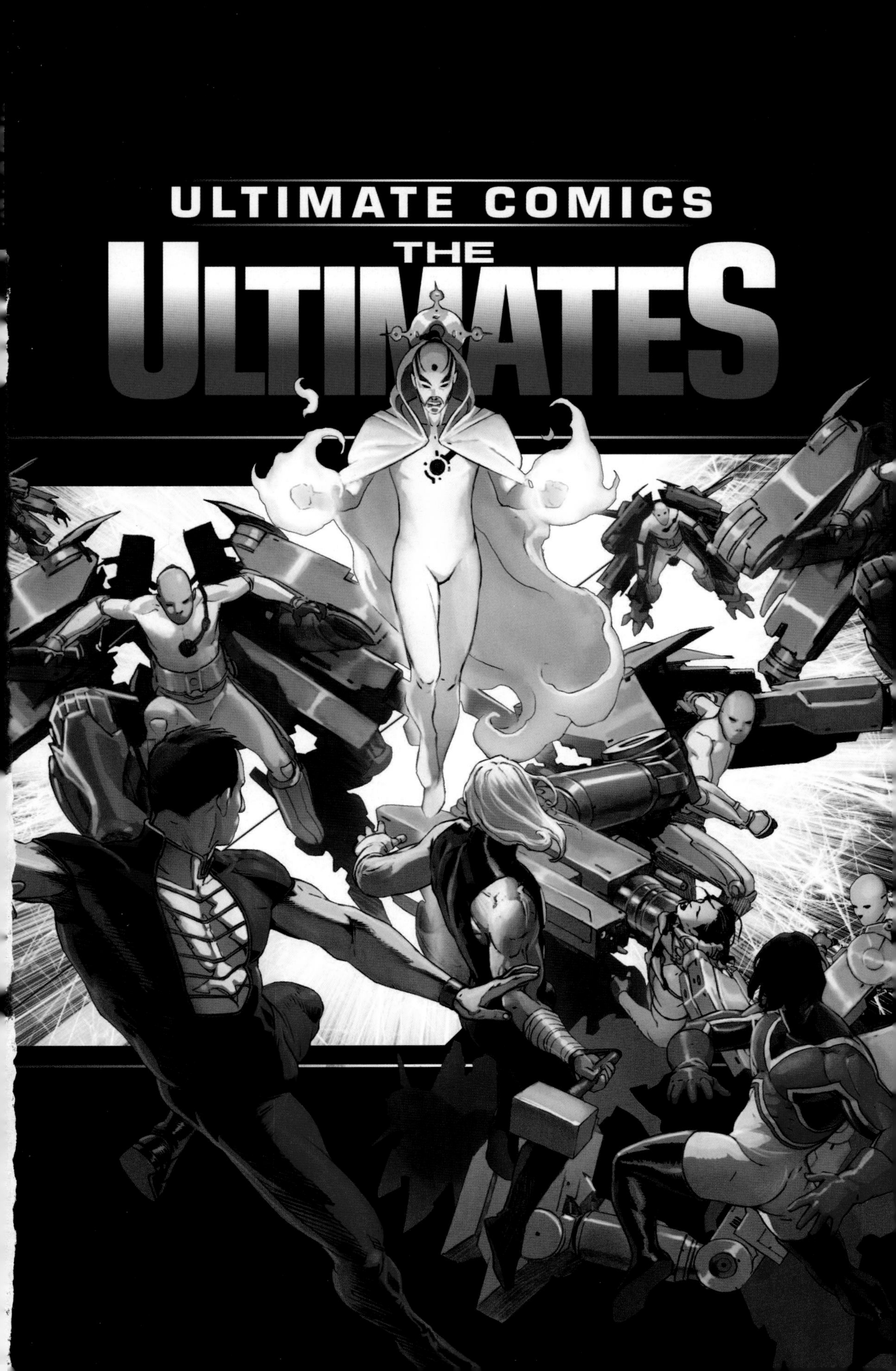
ULTIMATE COMICS
THE ULTIMATES

THE ULTIMATES

WRITER: **JONATHAN HICKMAN**

ARTIST: **ESAD RIBIC**

WITH **BRANDON PETERSON** (#5-6)

COLORIST: **DEAN WHITE**

WITH **JOSE VILLARRUBIA** & **JIM CHARALAMPIDIS** (#5)

AND **JOHN RAUCH** & **EDGAR DELGADO** (#6)

LETTERER: **VC'S CLAYTON COWLES**

COVER ART: **KAARE ANDREWS**

ASSISTANT EDITOR: **JON MOISAN**

ASSOCIATE EDITOR: **SANA AMANAT**

SENIOR EDITOR: **MARK PANICCIA**

COLLECTION EDITOR: **JENNIFER GRÜNWALD**

ASSISTANT EDITORS: **ALEX STARBUCK** & **NELSON RIBEIRO**

EDITOR, SPECIAL PROJECTS: **MARK D. BEAZLEY**

SENIOR EDITOR, SPECIAL PROJECTS: **JEFF YOUNGQUIST**

SENIOR VICE PRESIDENT OF SALES: **DAVID GABRIEL**

SVP OF BRAND PLANNING & COMMUNICATIONS: **MICHAEL PASCIULLO**

BOOK DESIGNER: **RODOLFO MURAGUCHI**

EDITOR IN CHIEF: **AXEL ALONSO**

CHIEF CREATIVE OFFICER: **JOE QUESADA**

PUBLISHER: **DAN BUCKLEY**

EXECUTIVE PRODUCER: **ALAN FINE**

ULTIMATE COMICS ULTIMATES BY JONATHAN HICKMAN VOL. 1. Contains material originally published in magazine form as ULTIMATE COMICS ULTIMATES #1-6. First printing 2012. Hardcover ISBN# 978-0-7851-5717-5. Softcover ISBN# 978-0-7851-5718-2. Published by MARVEL WORLDWIDE, INC., a subsidiary of MARVEL ENTERTAINMENT, LLC. OFFICE OF PUBLICATION: 135 West 50th Street, New York, NY 10020. Copyright © 2011 and 2012 Marvel Characters, Inc. All rights reserved. Hardcover: $24.99 per copy in the U.S. and $27.99 in Canada (GST #R127032852). Softcover: $19.99 per copy in the U.S. and $21.99 in Canada (GST #R127032852). Canadian Agreement #40668537. All characters featured in this issue and the distinctive names and likenesses thereof, and all related indicia are trademarks of Marvel Characters, Inc. No similarity between any of the names, characters, persons, and/or institutions in this magazine with those of any living or dead person or institution is intended, and any such similarity which may exist is purely coincidental. **Printed in the U.S.A.** ALAN FINE, EVP - Office of the President, Marvel Worldwide, Inc. and EVP & CMO Marvel Characters B.V.; DAN BUCKLEY, Publisher & President - Print, Animation & Digital Divisions; JOE QUESADA, Chief Creative Officer; DAVID BOGART, SVP of Business Affairs & Talent Management; TOM BREVOORT, SVP of Publishing; C.B. CEBULSKI, SVP of Creator & Content Development; DAVID GABRIEL, SVP of Publishing Sales & Circulation; MICHAEL PASCIULLO, SVP of Brand Planning & Communications; JIM O'KEEFE, VP of Operations & Logistics; DAN CARR, Executive Director of Publishing Technology; SUSAN CRESPI, Editorial Operations Manager; ALEX MORALES, Publishing Operations Manager; STAN LEE, Chairman Emeritus. For information regarding advertising in Marvel Comics or on Marvel.com, please contact John Dokes, SVP Integrated Sales and Marketing, at jdokes@marvel.com. For Marvel subscription inquiries, please call 800-217-9158. **Manufactured between 1/16/2012 and 2/13/2012 (hardcover), and 1/16/2012 and 8/13/2012 (softcover), by R.R. DONNELLEY, INC., SALEM, VA, USA.**

10 9 8 7 6 5 4 3 2 1

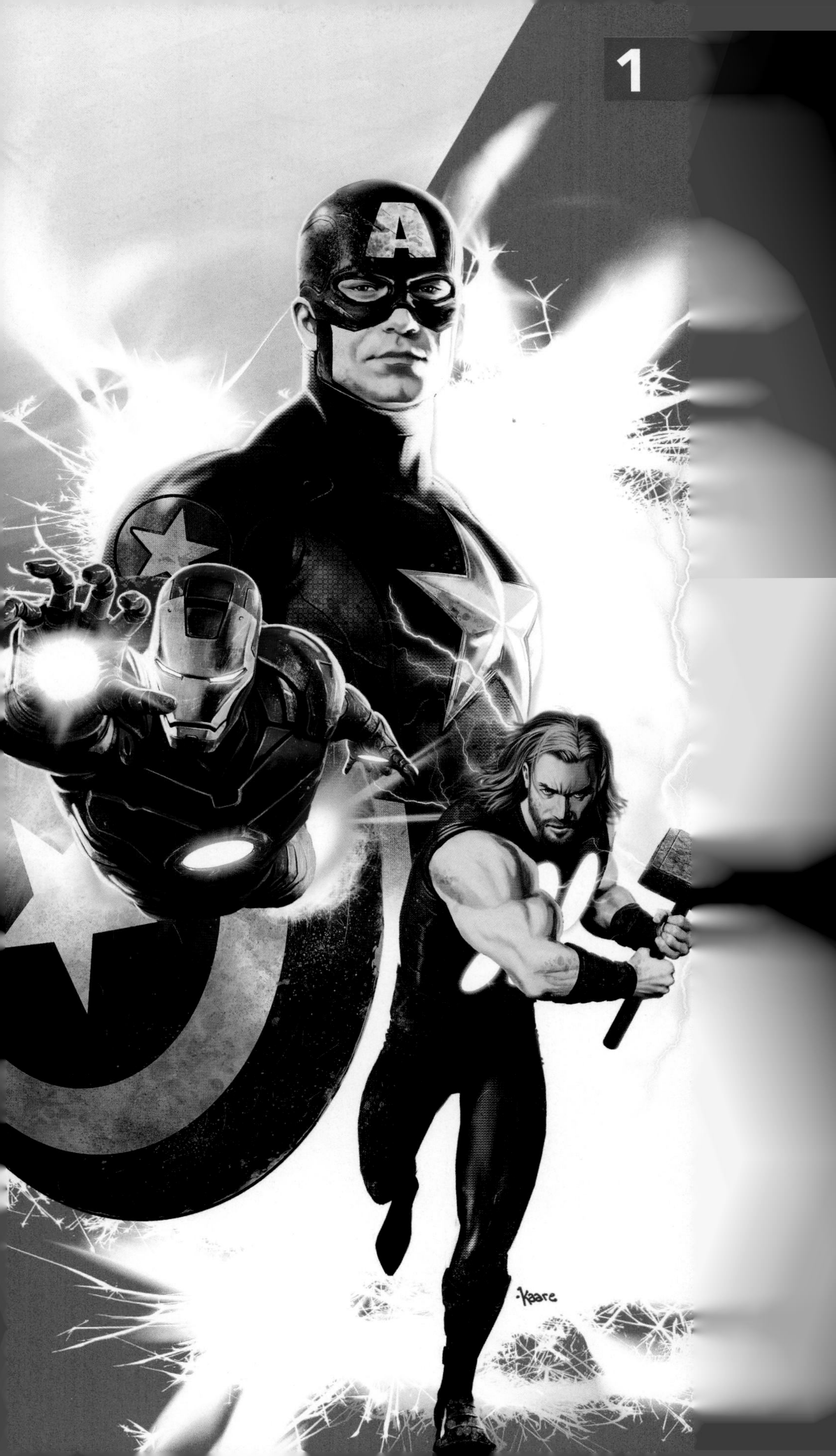
1
Kaare

#1 VARIANT
BY ESAD RIBIC

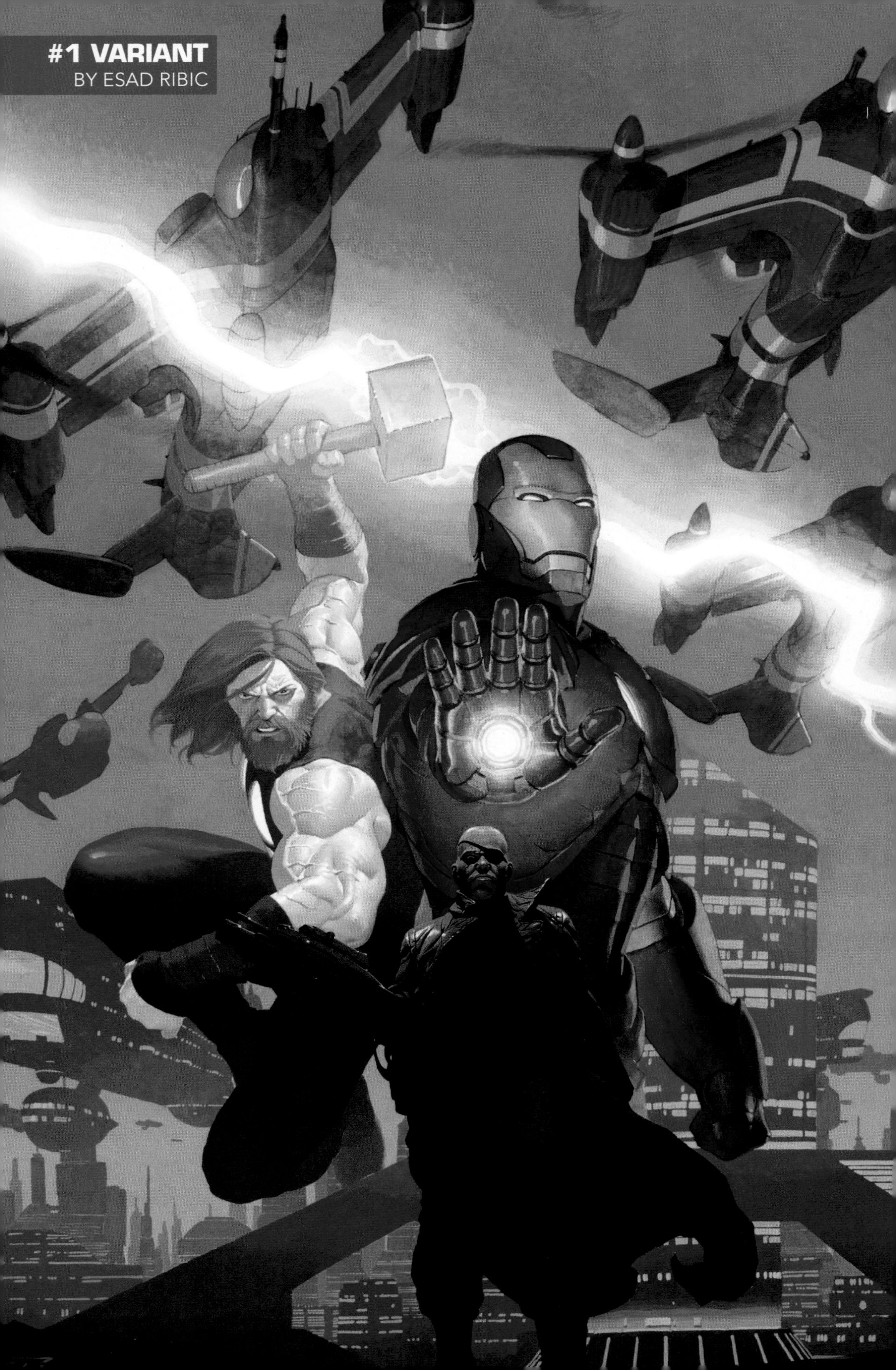

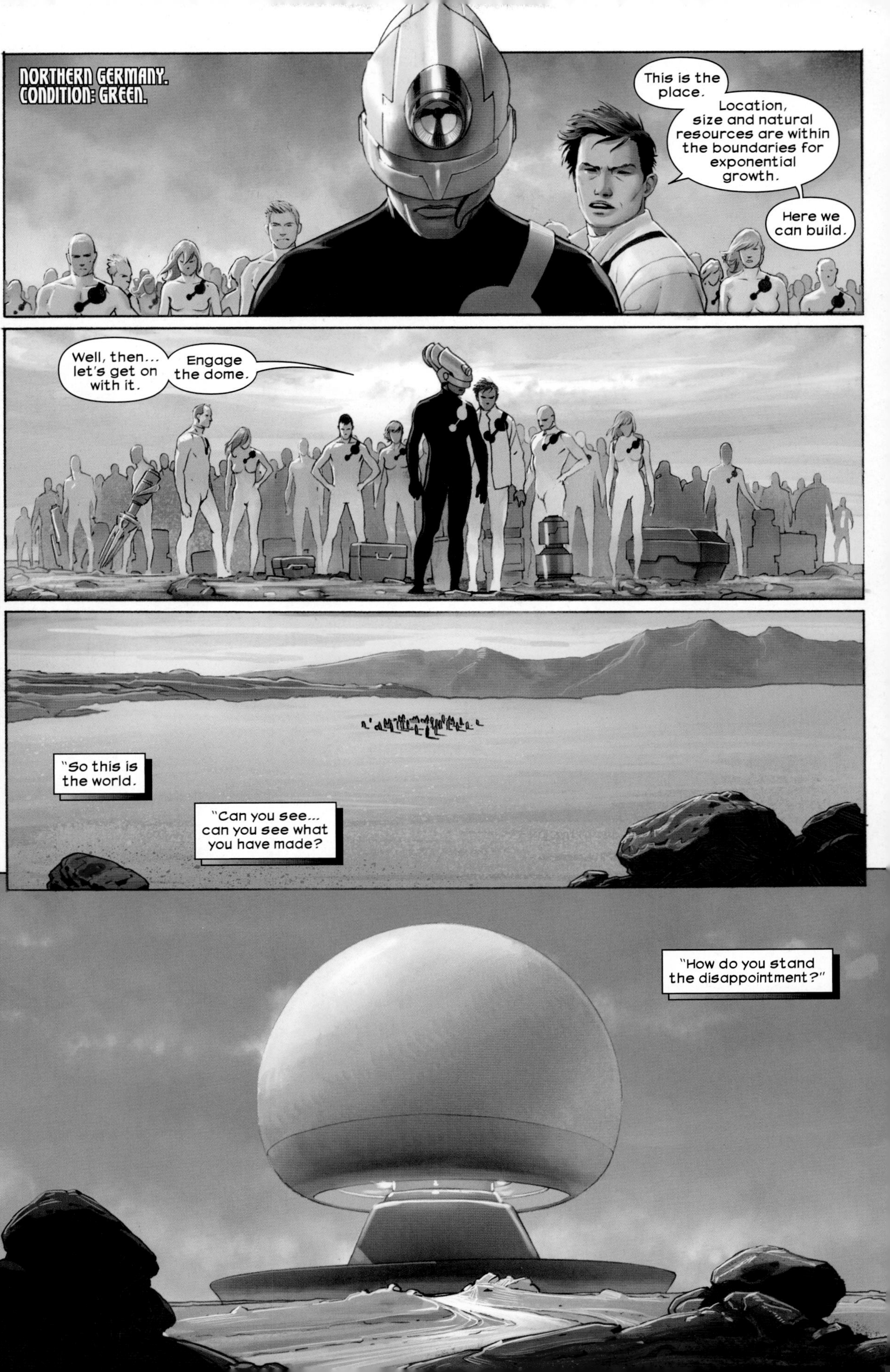
NORTHERN GERMANY.
CONDITION: GREEN.
This is the place.
Location, size and natural resources are within the boundaries for exponential growth.
Here we can build.
Well, then... let's get on with it.
Engage the dome.
"So this is the world.
"Can you see... can you see what you have made?
"How do you stand the disappointment?"

THE ULTIM

ATES

HICKMAN · RIBIC · WHITE

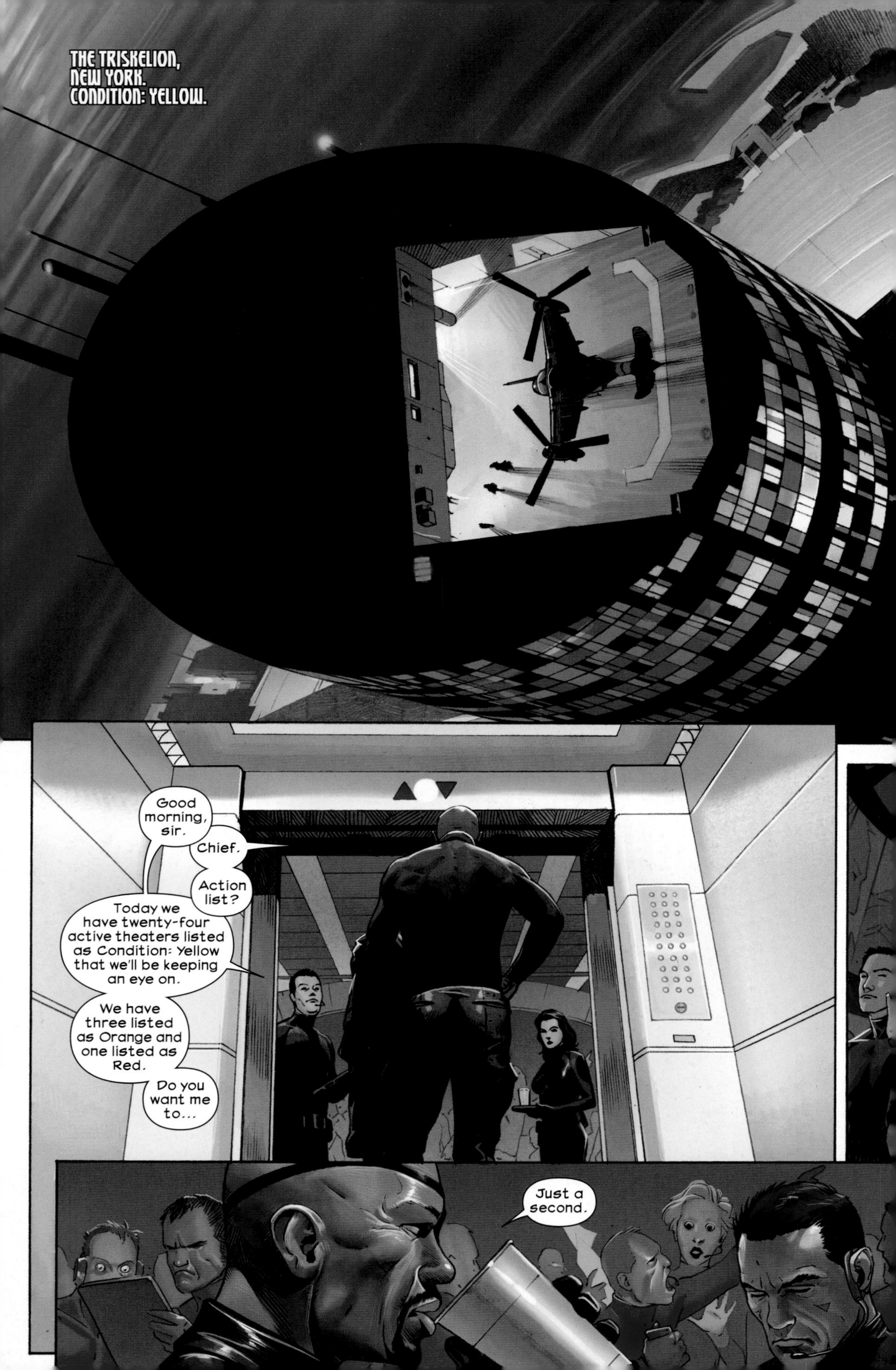
THE TRISKELION, NEW YORK. CONDITION: YELLOW.
Good morning, sir.
Chief.
Action list?
Today we have twenty-four active theaters listed as Condition: Yellow that we'll be keeping an eye on.
We have three listed as Orange and one listed as Red.
Do you want me to...
Just a second.

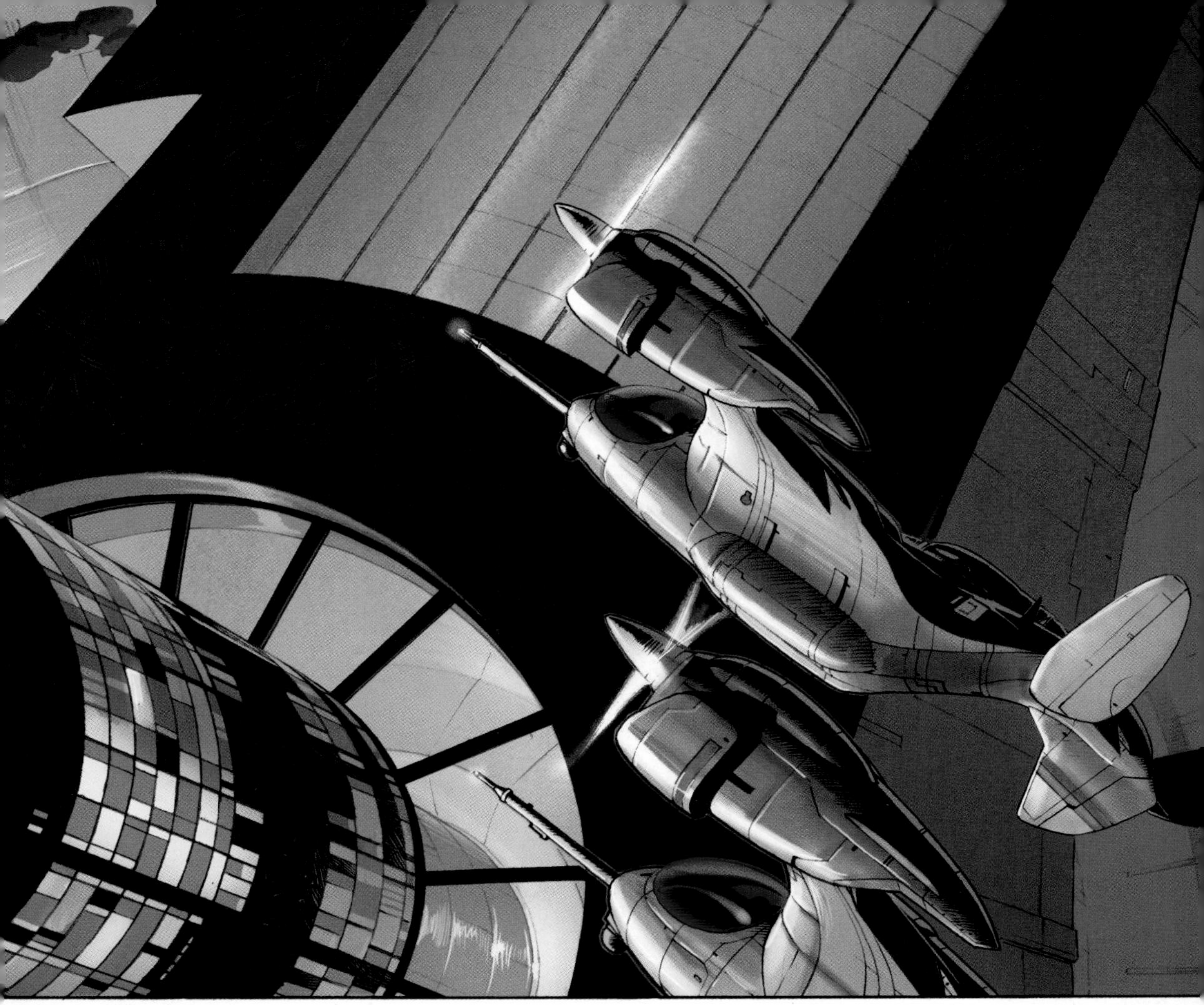

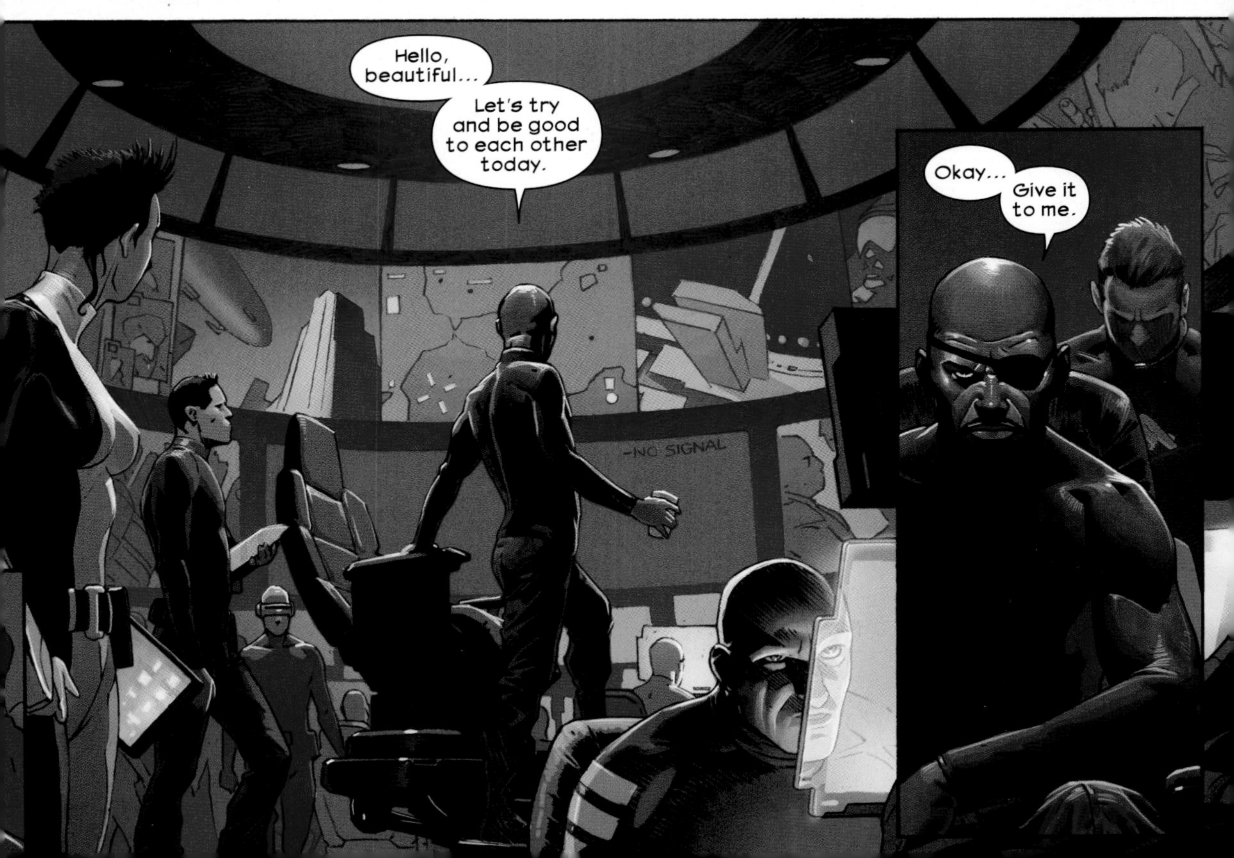
Hello, beautiful...
Let's try and be good to each other today.
Okay... Give it to me.
-NO SIGNAL

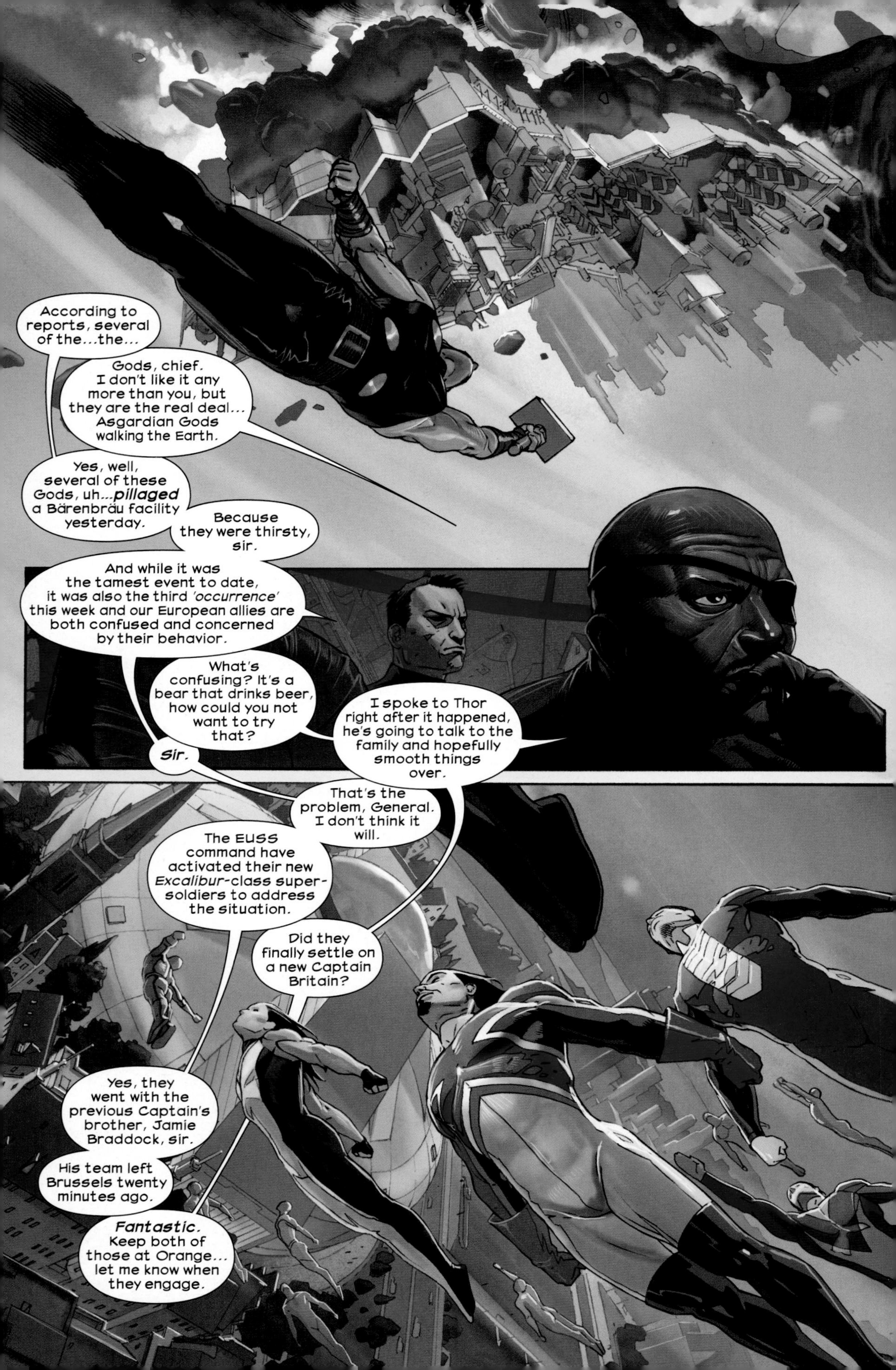
According to reports, several of the...the...
Gods, chief. I don't like it any more than you, but they are the real deal... Asgardian Gods walking the Earth.
Yes, well, several of these Gods, uh...*pillaged* a Bärenbräu facility yesterday.
Because they were thirsty, sir.
And while it was the tamest event to date, it was also the third *'occurrence'* this week and our European allies are both confused and concerned by their behavior.
What's confusing? It's a bear that drinks beer, how could you not want to try that?
Sir.
I spoke to Thor right after it happened, he's going to talk to the family and hopefully smooth things over.
That's the problem, General. I don't think it will.
The EUSS command have activated their new *Excalibur*-class super-soldiers to address the situation.
Did they finally settle on a new Captain Britain?
Yes, they went with the previous Captain's brother, Jamie Braddock, sir.
His team left Brussels twenty minutes ago.
Fantastic. Keep both of those at Orange... let me know when they engage.

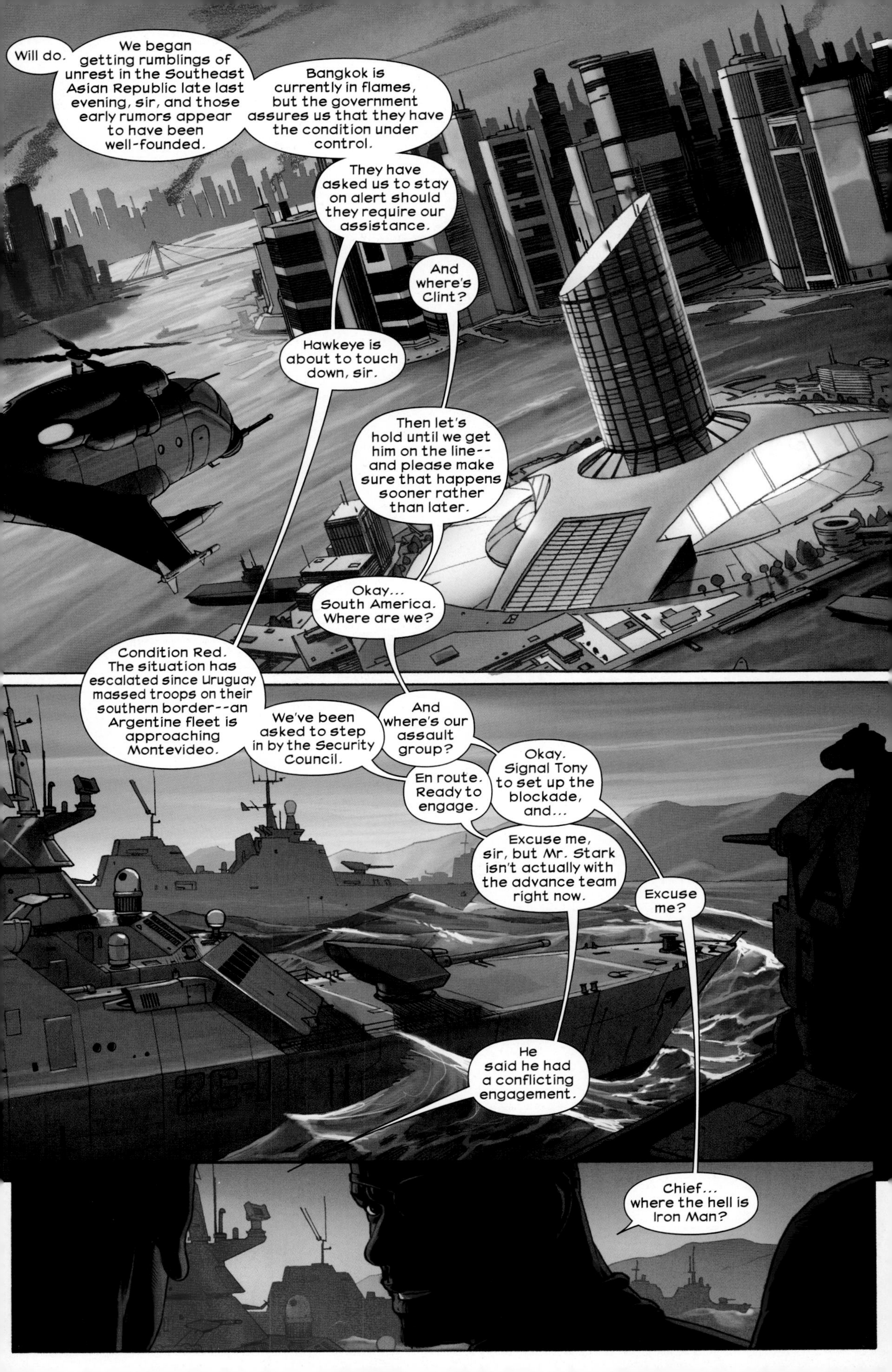
Will do.
We began getting rumblings of unrest in the Southeast Asian Republic late last evening, sir, and those early rumors appear to have been well-founded.
Bangkok is currently in flames, but the government assures us that they have the condition under control.
They have asked us to stay on alert should they require our assistance.
And where's Clint?
Hawkeye is about to touch down, sir.
Then let's hold until we get him on the line--and please make sure that happens sooner rather than later.
Okay... South America. Where are we?
Condition Red. The situation has escalated since Uruguay massed troops on their southern border--an Argentine fleet is approaching Montevideo.
We've been asked to step in by the Security Council.
And where's our assault group?
En route. Ready to engage.
Okay. Signal Tony to set up the blockade, and...
Excuse me, sir, but Mr. Stark isn't actually with the advance team right now.
Excuse me?
He said he had a conflicting engagement.
Chief... where the hell is Iron Man?

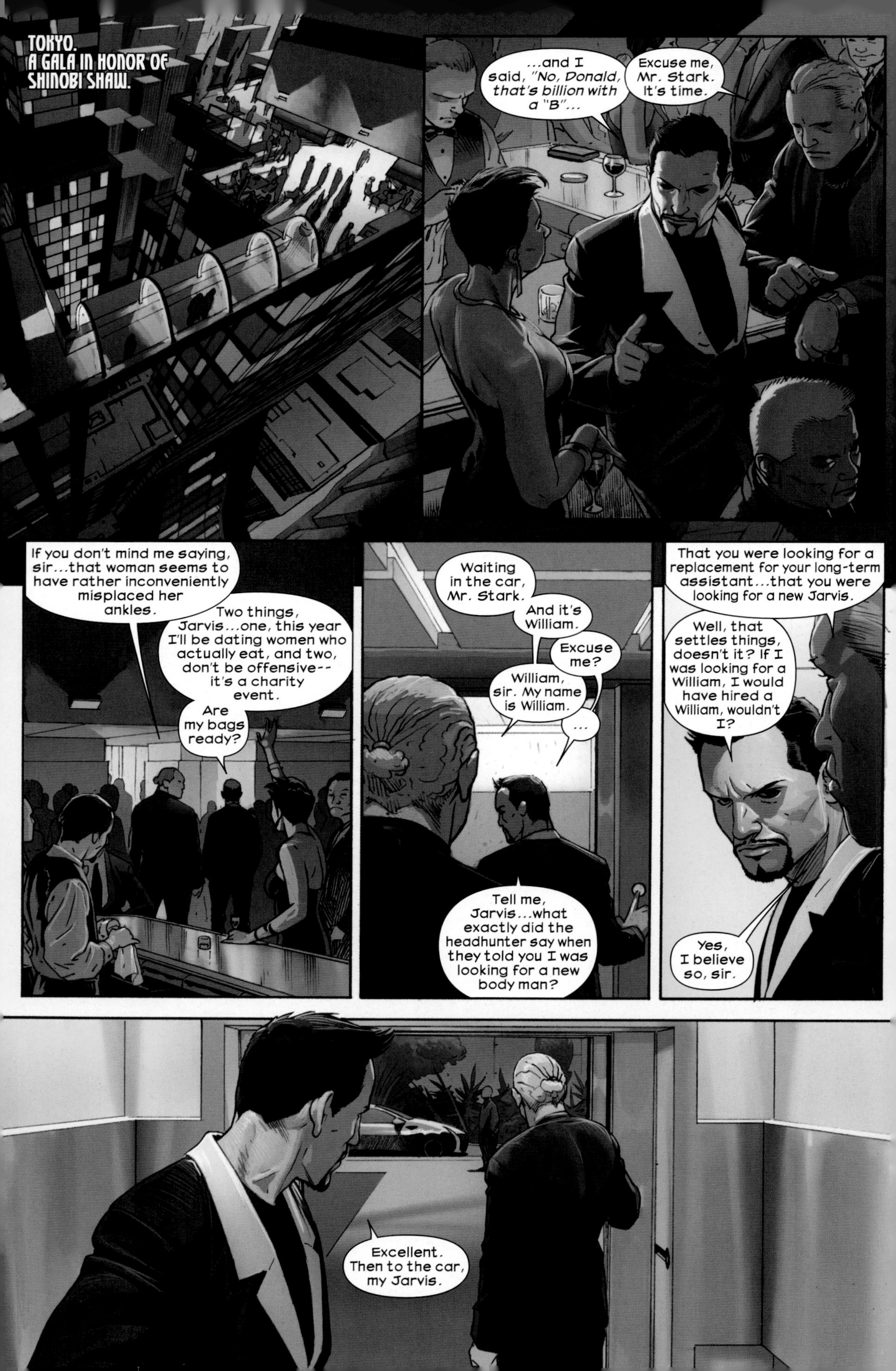
TOKYO.
A GALA IN HONOR OF SHINOBI SHAW.
...and I said, "No, Donald, that's billion with a "B"...
Excuse me, Mr. Stark. It's time.
If you don't mind me saying, sir...that woman seems to have rather inconveniently misplaced her ankles.
Two things, Jarvis...one, this year I'll be dating women who actually eat, and two, don't be offensive--it's a charity event.
Are my bags ready?
Waiting in the car, Mr. Stark.
And it's William.
Excuse me?
William, sir. My name is William.
...
Tell me, Jarvis...what exactly did the headhunter say when they told you I was looking for a new body man?
That you were looking for a replacement for your long-term assistant...that you were looking for a new Jarvis.
Well, that settles things, doesn't it? If I was looking for a William, I would have hired a William, wouldn't I?
Yes, I believe so, sir.
Excellent. Then to the car, my Jarvis.

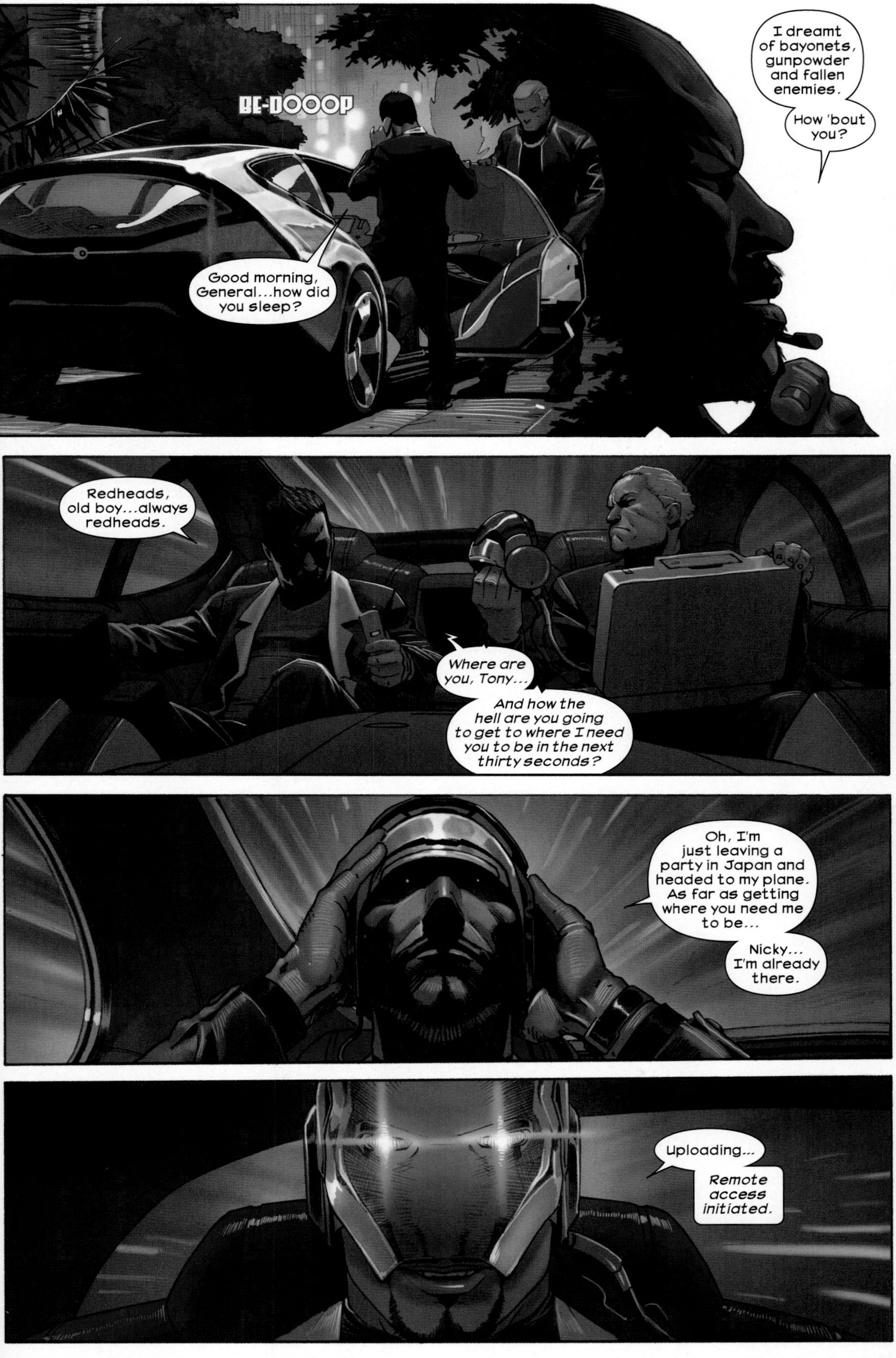
BE-DOOOP
Good morning, General...how did you sleep?
I dreamt of bayonets, gunpowder and fallen enemies.
How 'bout you?
Redheads, old boy...always redheads.
Where are you, Tony...
And how the hell are you going to get to where I need you to be in the next thirty seconds?
Oh, I'm just leaving a party in Japan and headed to my plane. As far as getting where you need me to be...
Nicky... I'm already there.
Uploading...
Remote access initiated.

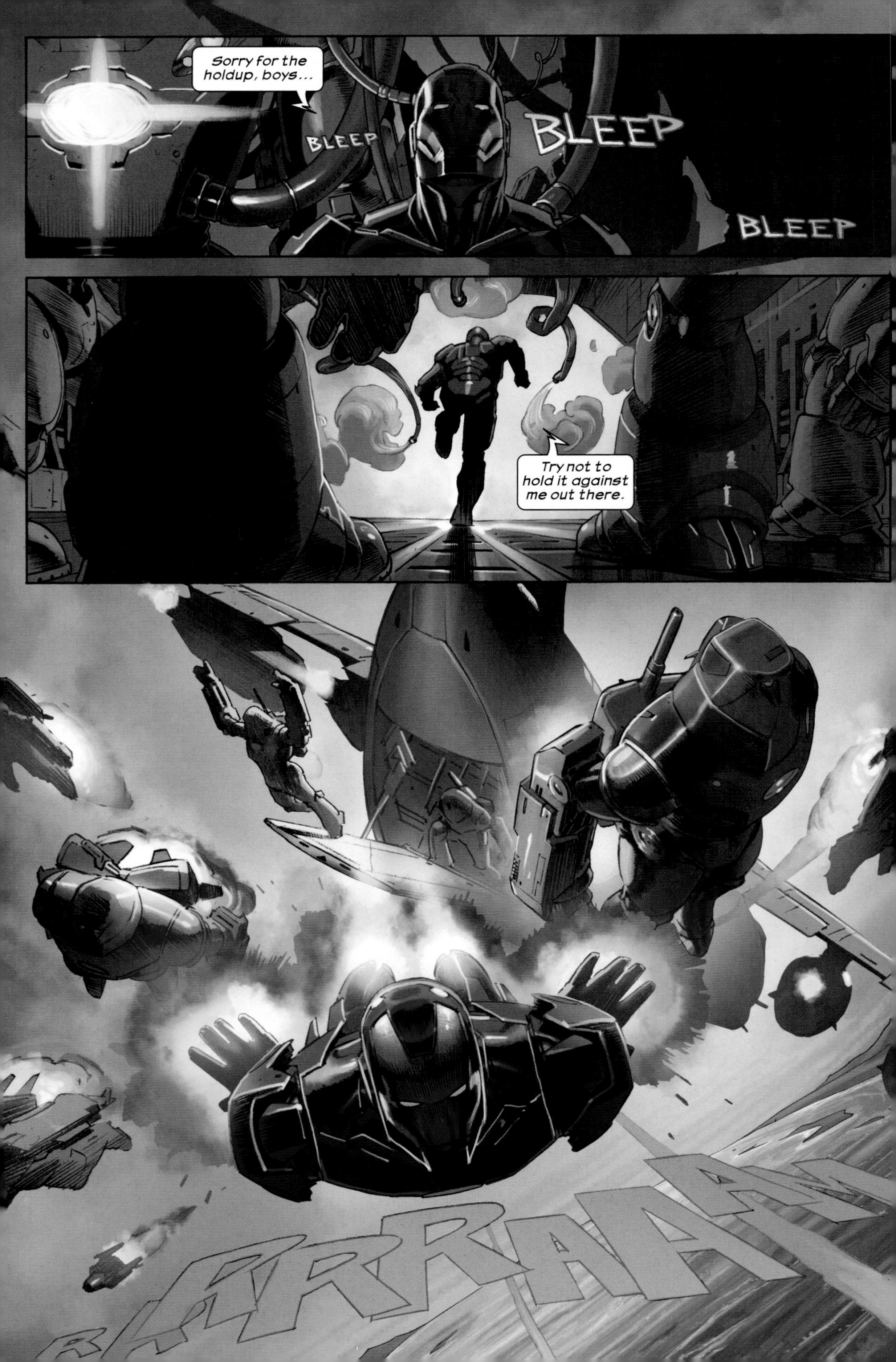
Sorry for the holdup, boys...
BLEEP
BLEEP
BLEEP
Try not to hold it against me out there.
BRRRAAAM

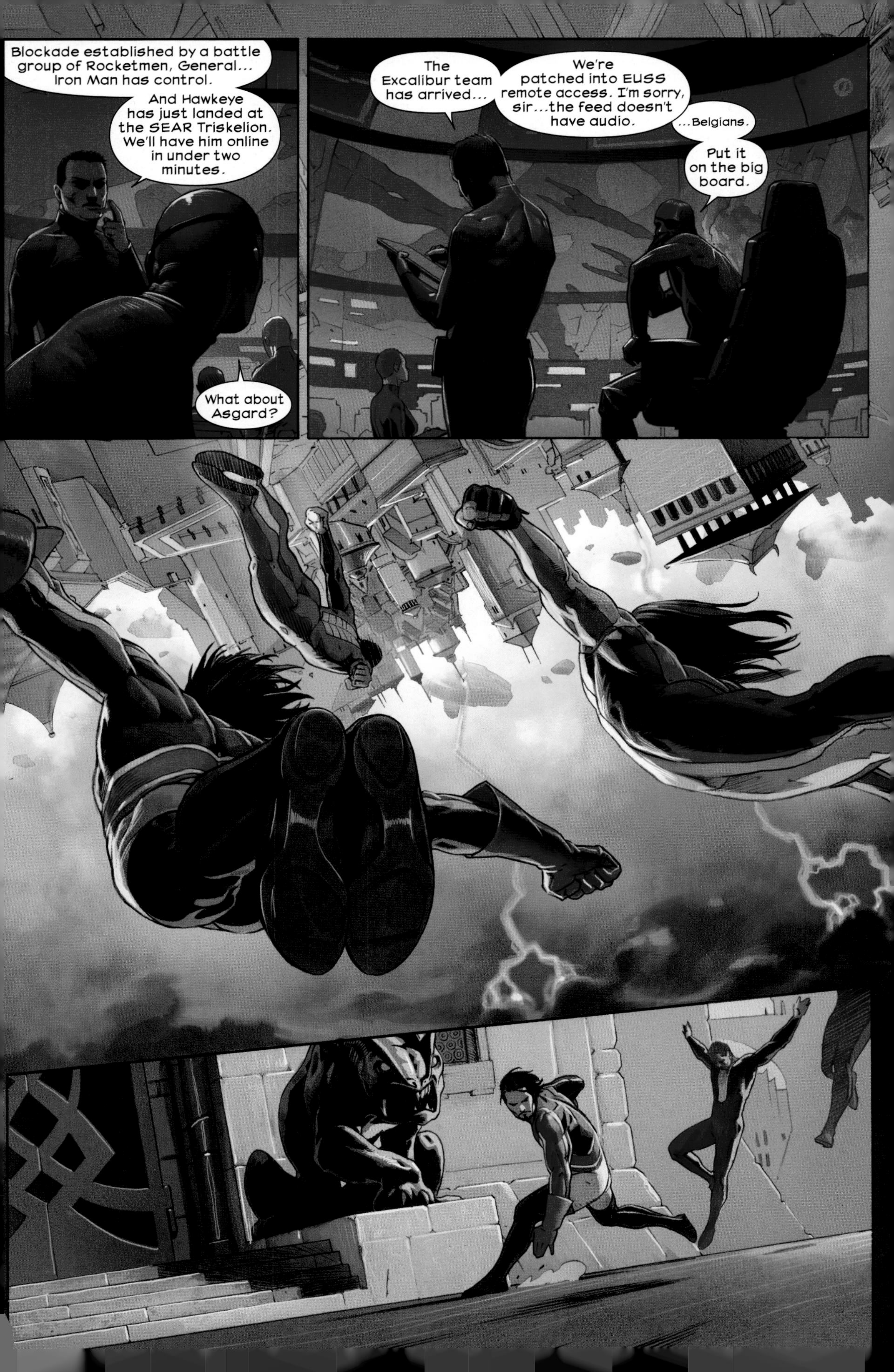
Blockade established by a battle group of Rocketmen, General... Iron Man has control.
And Hawkeye has just landed at the SEAR Triskelion. We'll have him online in under two minutes.
What about Asgard?
The Excalibur team has arrived...
We're patched into EUSS remote access. I'm sorry, sir...the feed doesn't have audio.
...Belgians.
Put it on the big board.

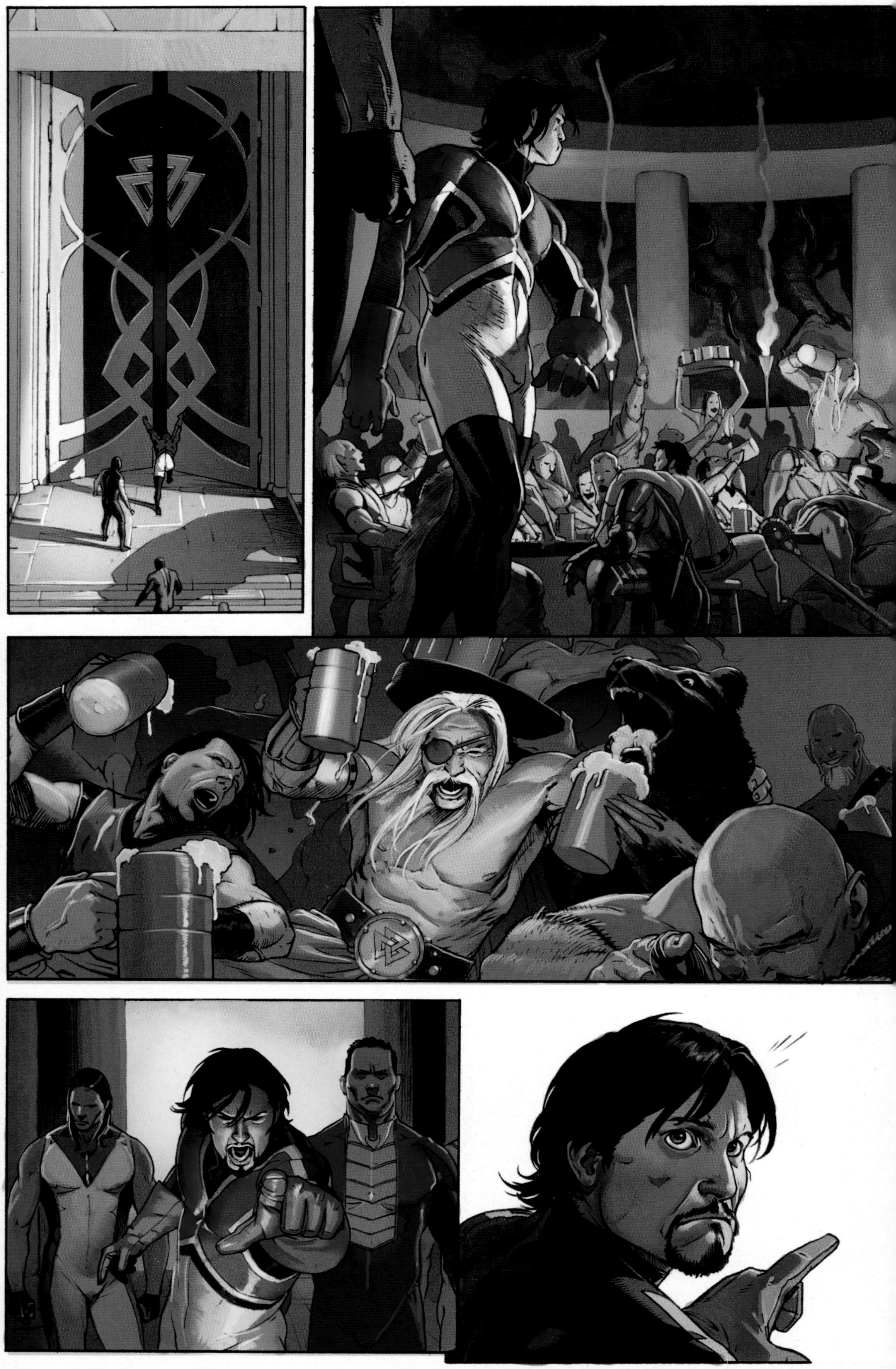

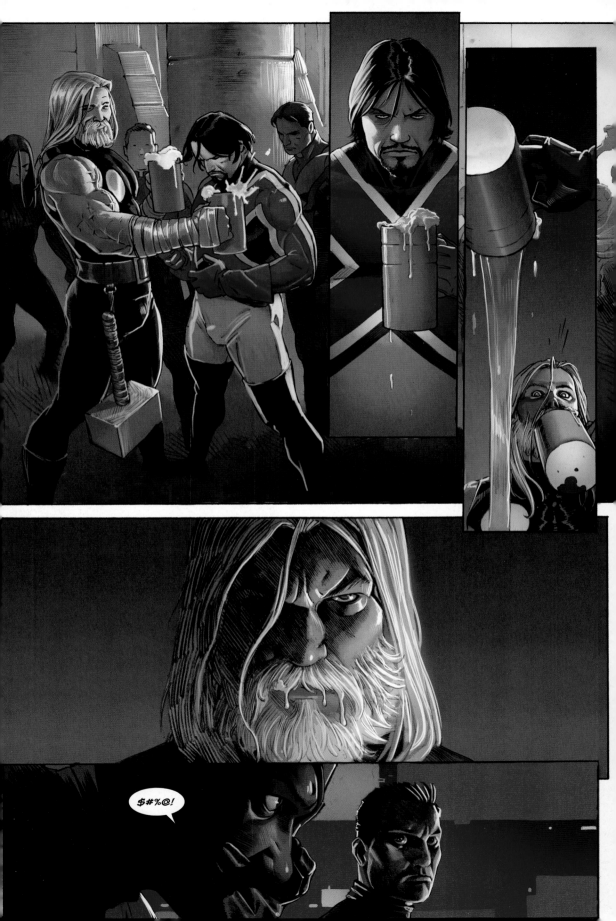

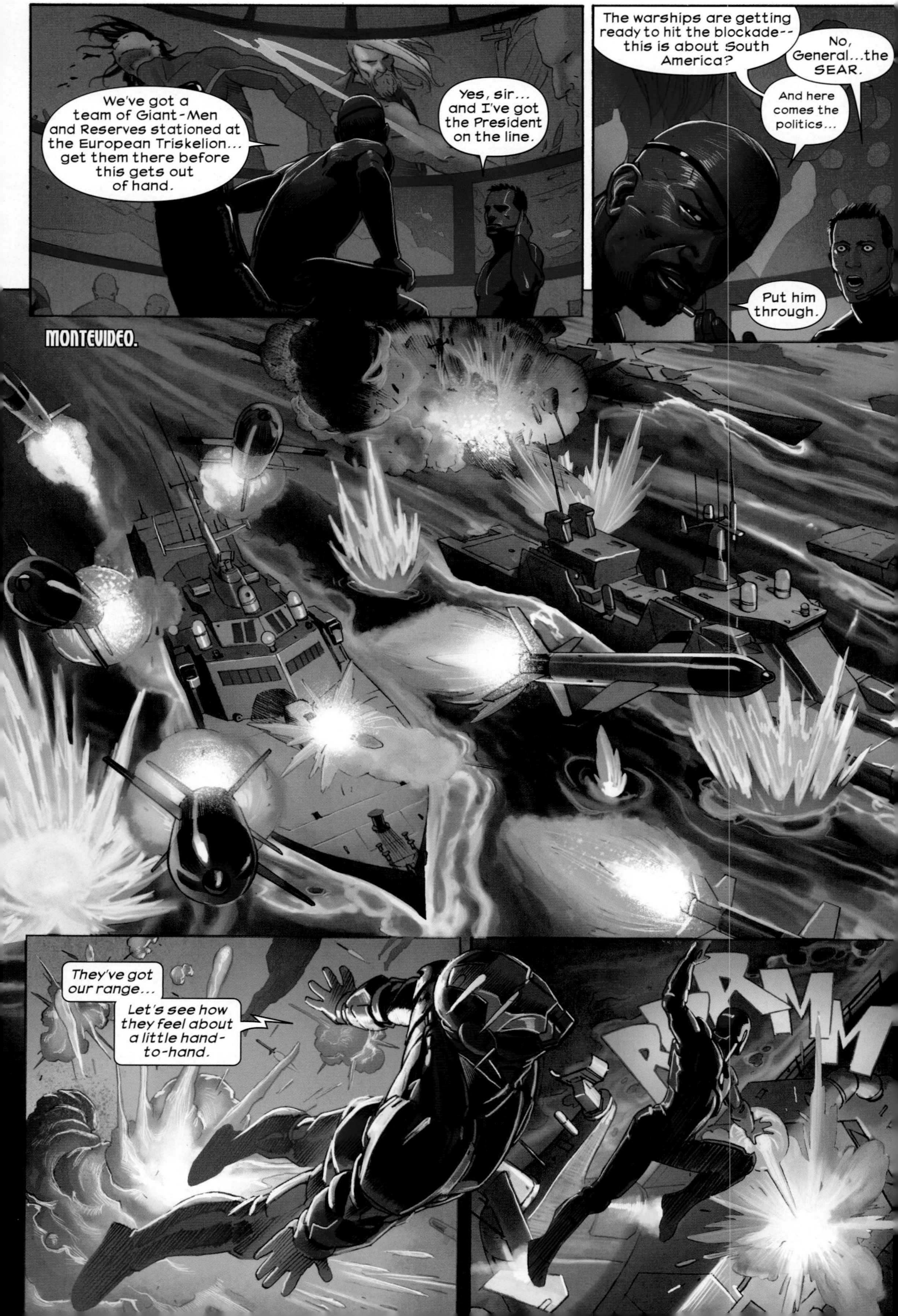
We've got a team of Giant-Men and Reserves stationed at the European Triskelion... get them there before this gets out of hand.
Yes, sir... and I've got the President on the line.
The warships are getting ready to hit the blockade-- this is about South America?
No, General...the SEAR.
And here comes the politics...
Put him through.
MONTEVIDEO.
They've got our range...
Let's see how they feel about a little hand-to-hand.
BRRMMM

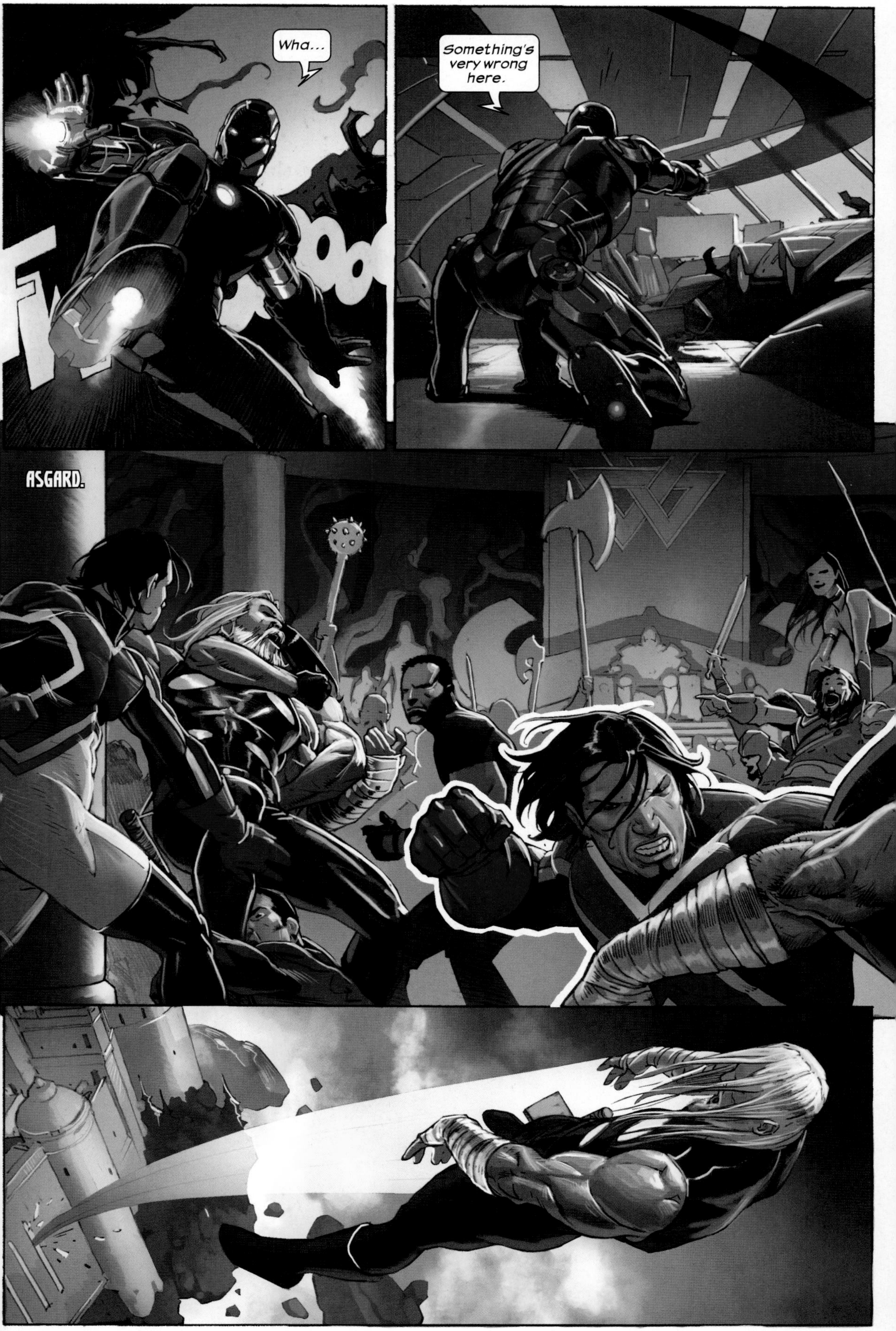
Wha...
Something's very wrong here.
ASGARD.

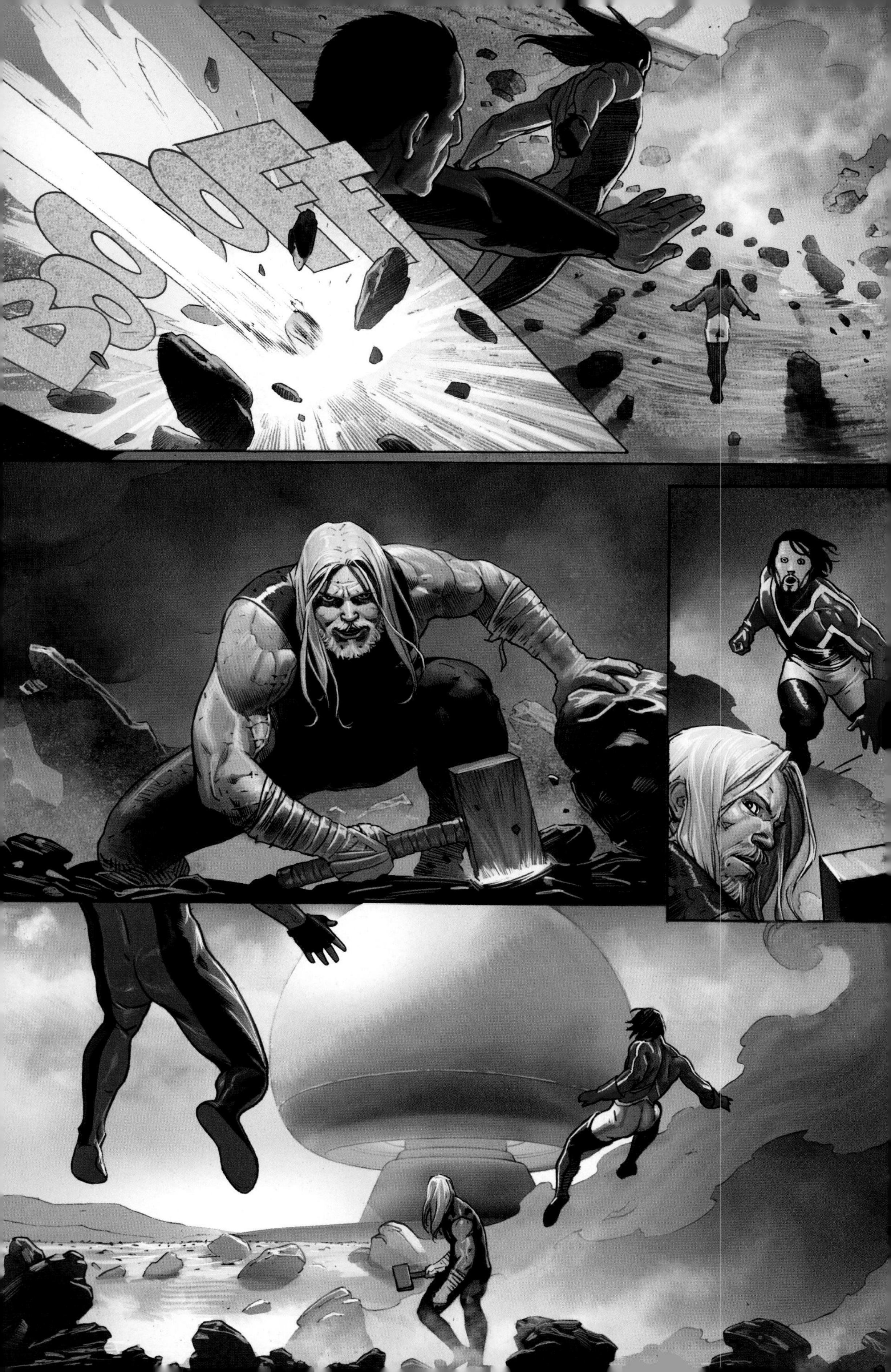
BOOOFF

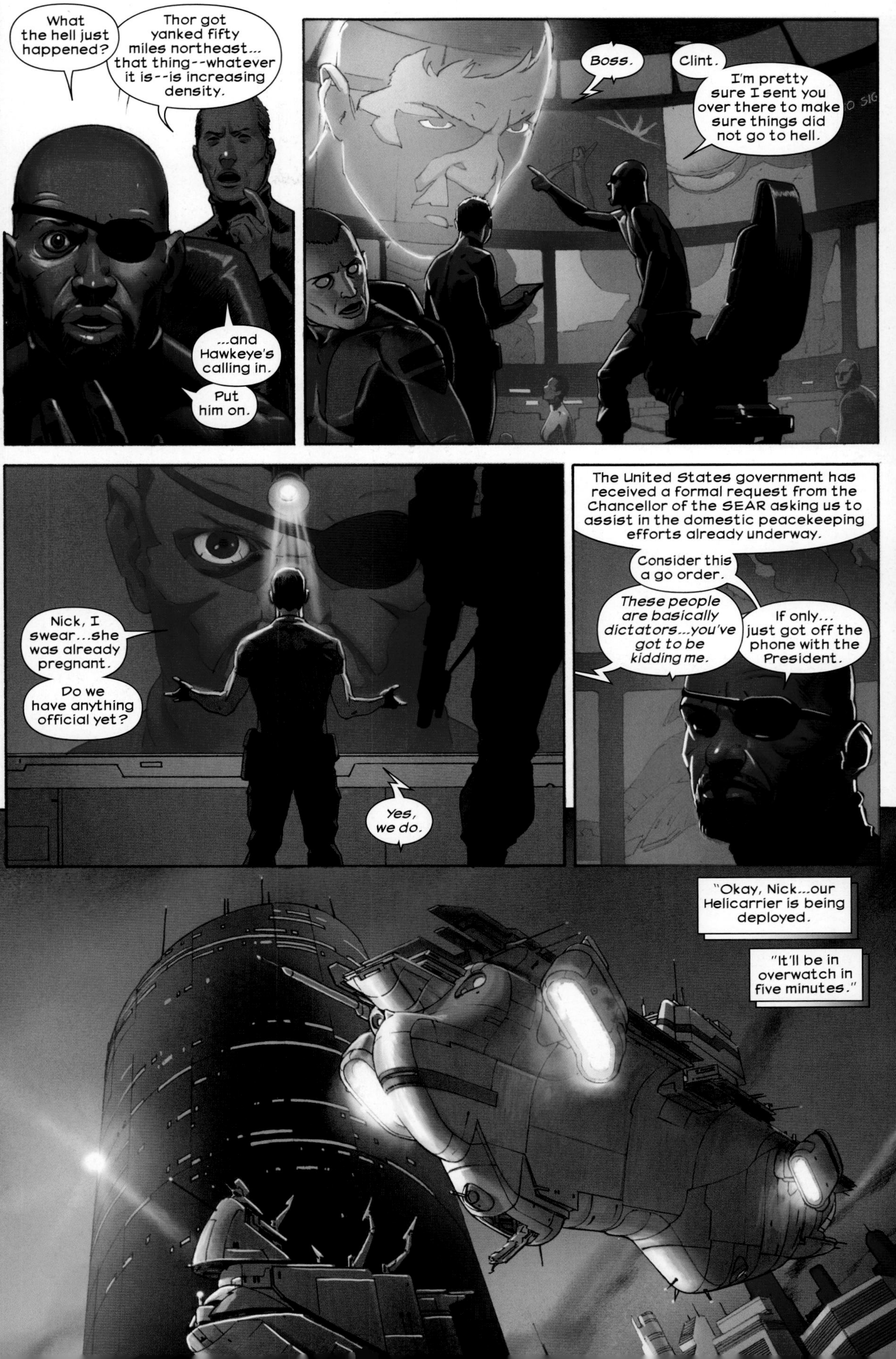
What the hell just happened?
Thor got yanked fifty miles northeast... that thing--whatever it is--is increasing density.
...and Hawkeye's calling in.
Put him on.
Boss.
Clint.
I'm pretty sure I sent you over there to make sure things did not go to hell.
Nick, I swear...she was already pregnant.
Do we have anything official yet?
Yes, we do.
The United States government has received a formal request from the Chancellor of the SEAR asking us to assist in the domestic peacekeeping efforts already underway.
Consider this a go order.
These people are basically dictators...you've got to be kidding me.
If only... just got off the phone with the President.
"Okay, Nick...our Helicarrier is being deployed.
"It'll be in overwatch in five minutes."

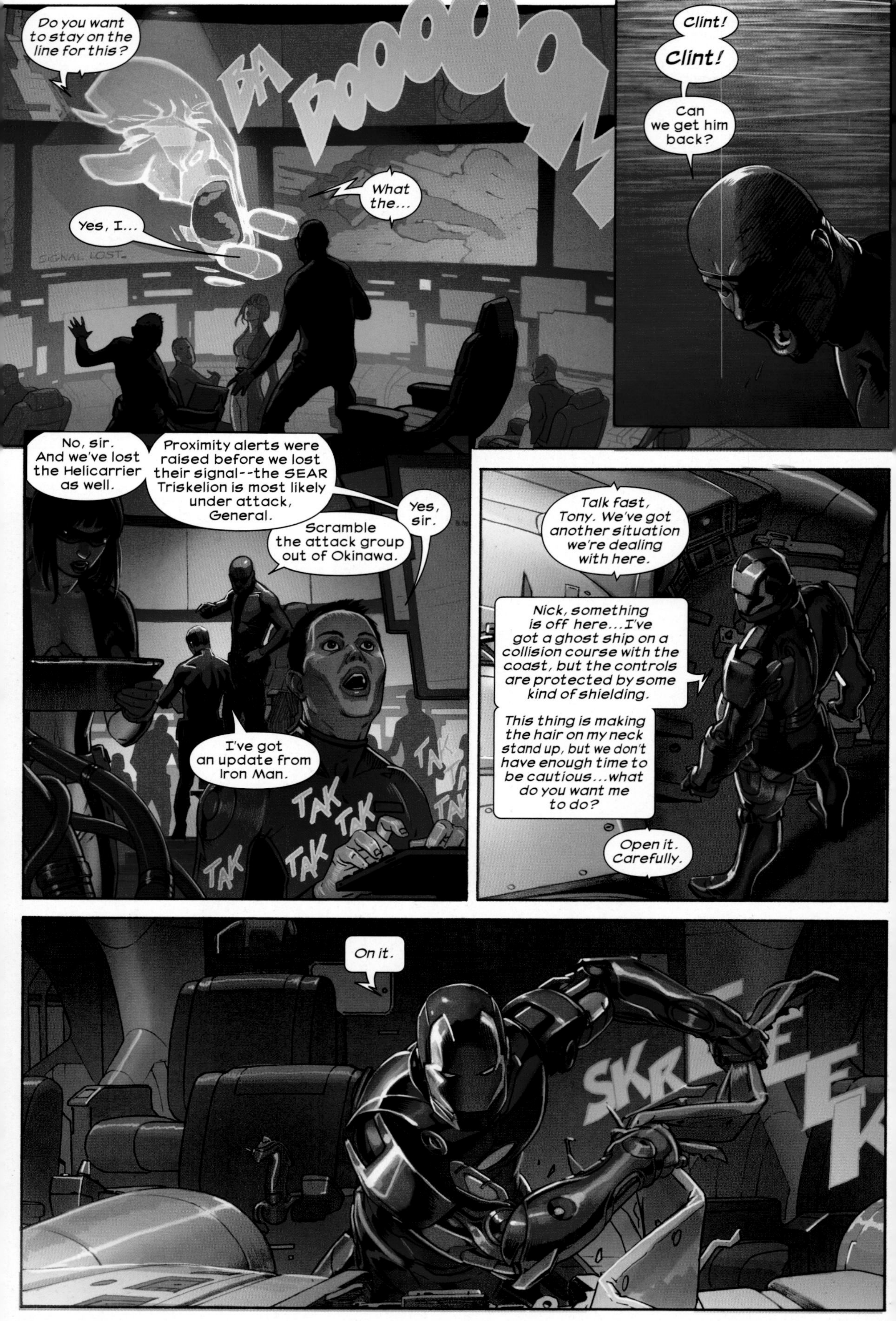
Do you want to stay on the line for this?
BA BOOOOOOM
What the...
Yes, I...
SIGNAL LOST
Clint!
Clint!
Can we get him back?
No, sir. And we've lost the Helicarrier as well.
Proximity alerts were raised before we lost their signal--the SEAR Triskelion is most likely under attack, General.
Scramble the attack group out of Okinawa.
Yes, sir.
I've got an update from Iron Man.
TAK TAK TAK TAK TAK
Talk fast, Tony. We've got another situation we're dealing with here.
Nick, something is off here...I've got a ghost ship on a collision course with the coast, but the controls are protected by some kind of shielding.
This thing is making the hair on my neck stand up, but we don't have enough time to be cautious...what do you want me to do?
Open it. Carefully.
On it.
SKREEEK

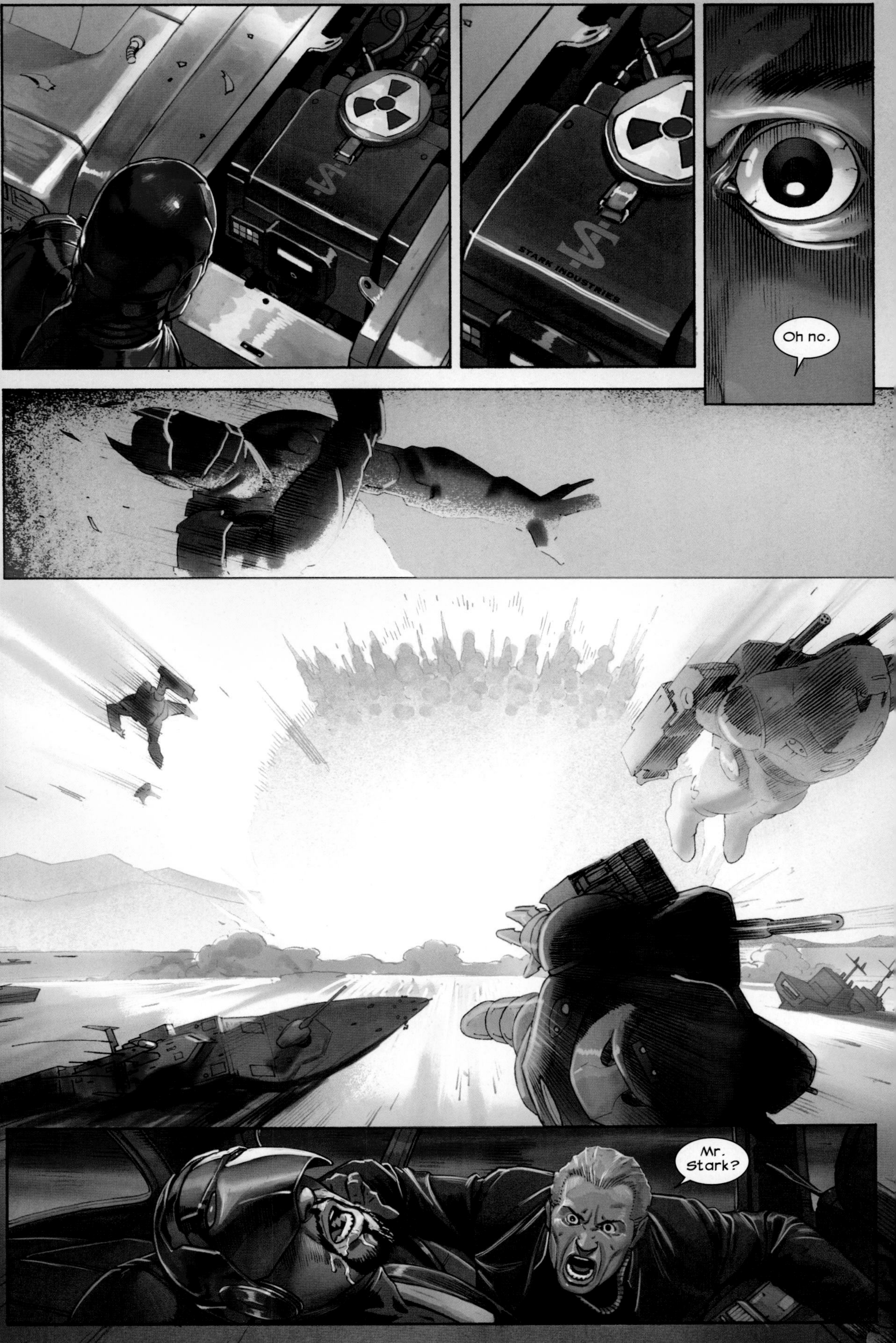
STARK INDUSTRIES
Oh no.
Mr. Stark?

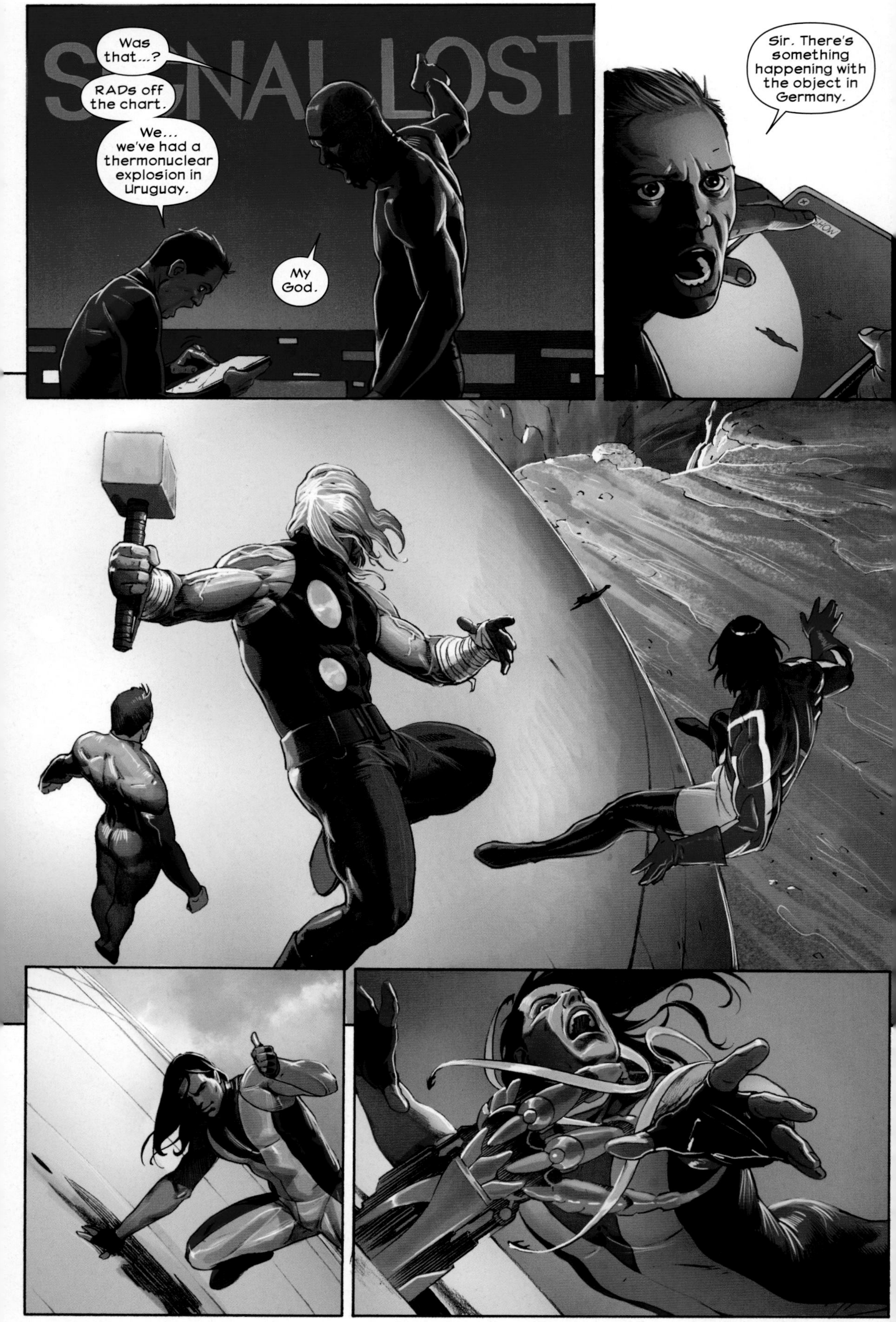
SIGNAL LOST
Was that...?
RADs off the chart.
We... we've had a thermonuclear explosion in Uruguay.
My God.
Sir. There's something happening with the object in Germany.

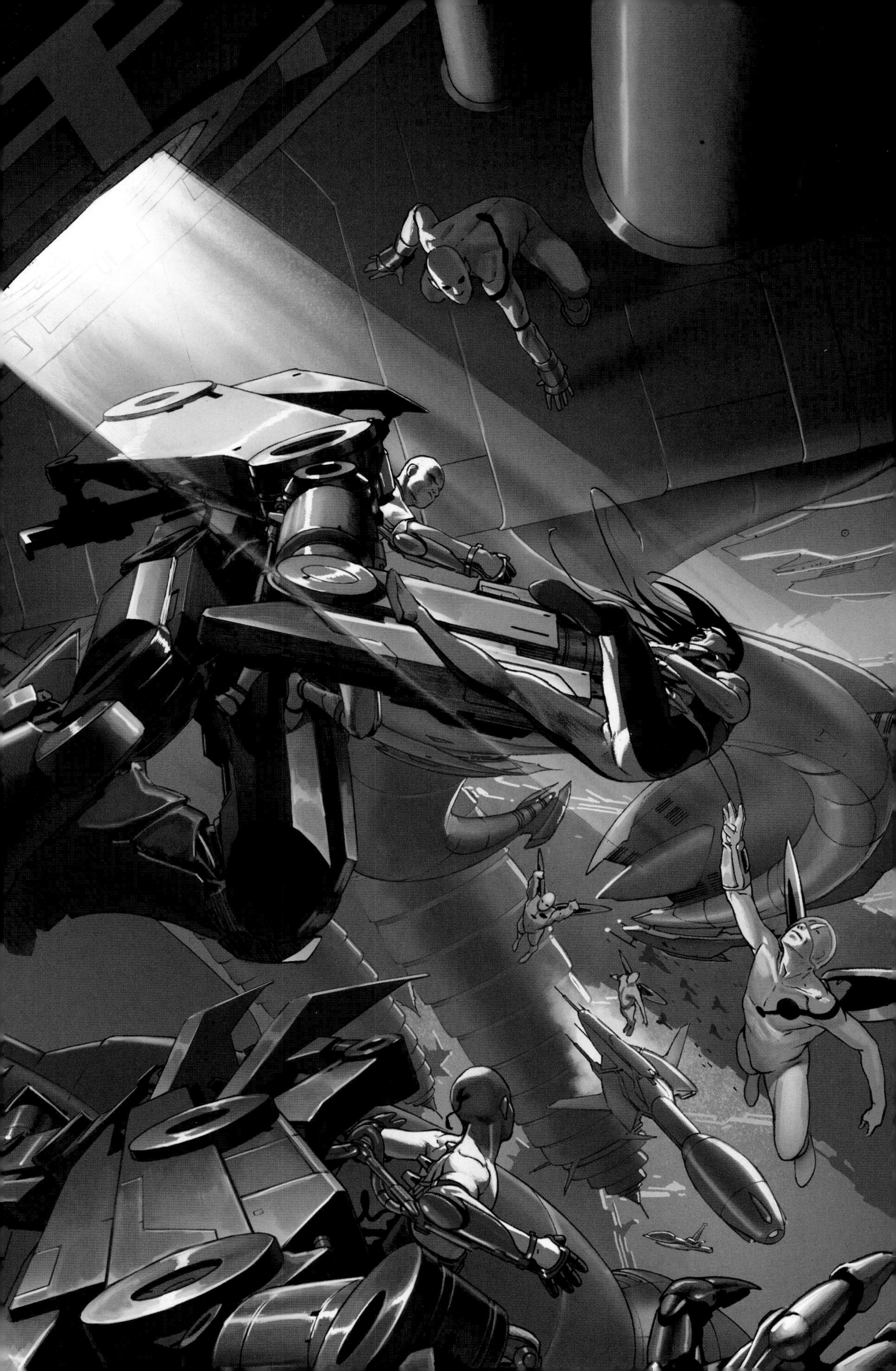

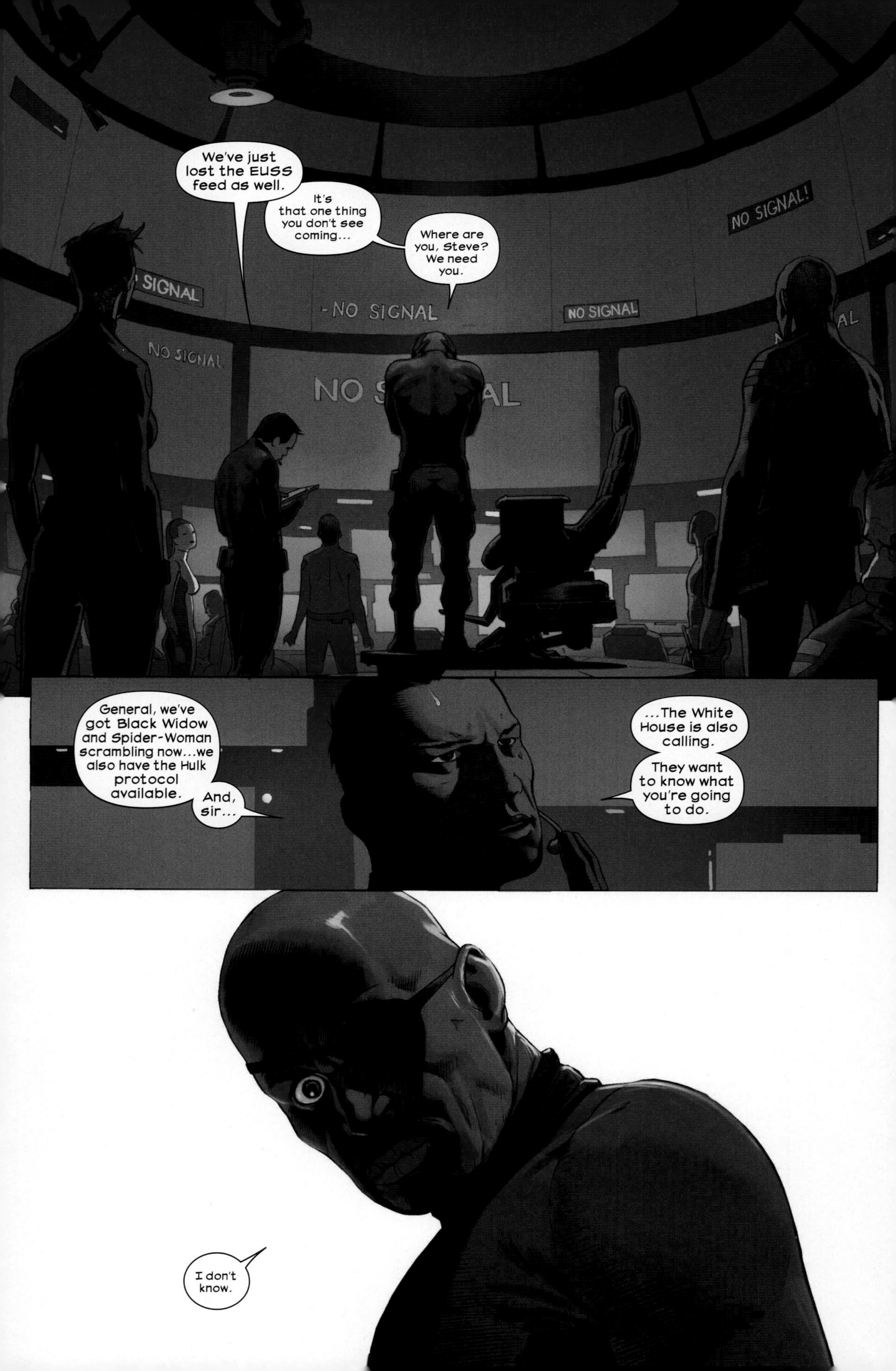

We've just lost the EUSS feed as well.
It's that one thing you don't see coming...
Where are you, Steve? We need you.
NO SIGNAL!
SIGNAL
-NO SIGNAL
NO SIGNAL
NO SIGNAL
NO S AL
General, we've got Black Widow and Spider-Woman scrambling now...we also have the Hulk protocol available.
And, sir...
...The White House is also calling.
They want to know what you're going to do.
I don't know.

THE REPUBLIC IS BURNING

2

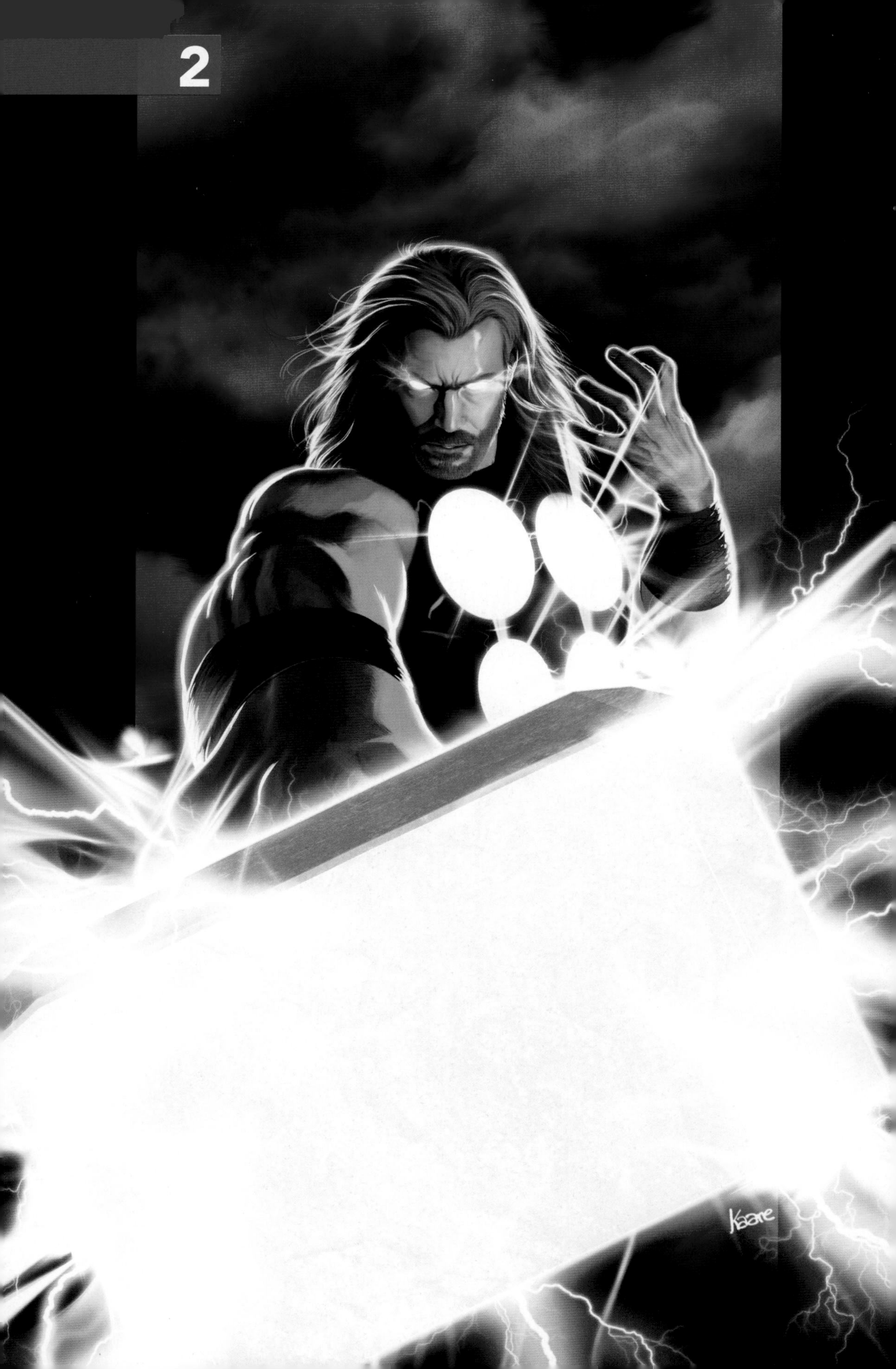

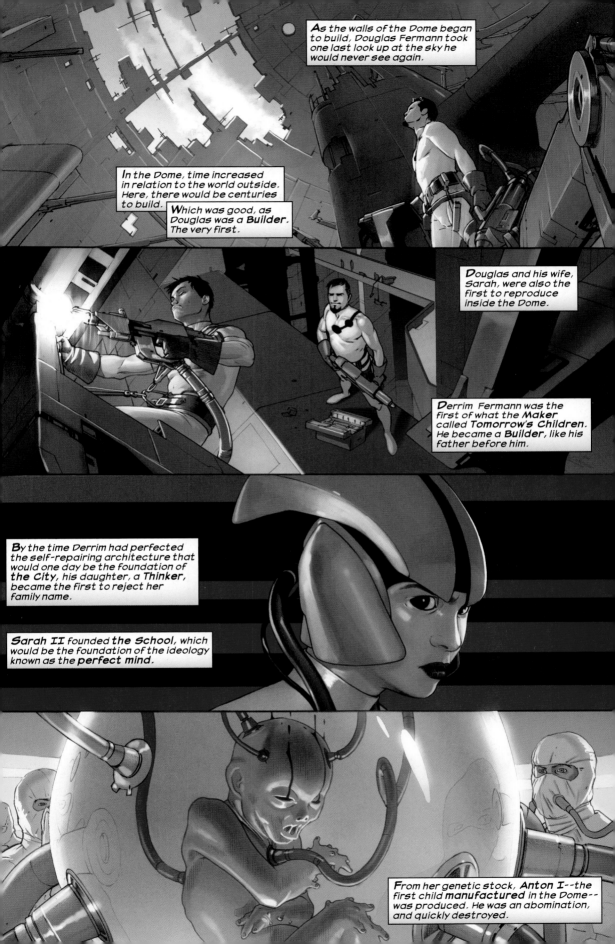

As the walls of the Dome began to build, Douglas Fermann took one last look up at the sky he would never see again.

In the Dome, time increased in relation to the world outside. Here, there would be centuries to build. Which was good, as Douglas was a **Builder**. The very first.

Douglas and his wife, Sarah, were also the first to reproduce inside the Dome.

Derrim Fermann was the first of what the **Maker** called **Tomorrow's Children**. He became a **Builder**, like his father before him.

By the time Derrim had perfected the self-repairing architecture that would one day be the foundation of **the City**, his daughter, a **Thinker**, became the first to reject her family name.

Sarah II founded **the School**, which would be the foundation of the ideology known as the **perfect mind**.

From her genetic stock, **Anton I**--the first child **manufactured** in the Dome-- was produced. He was an abomination, and quickly destroyed.

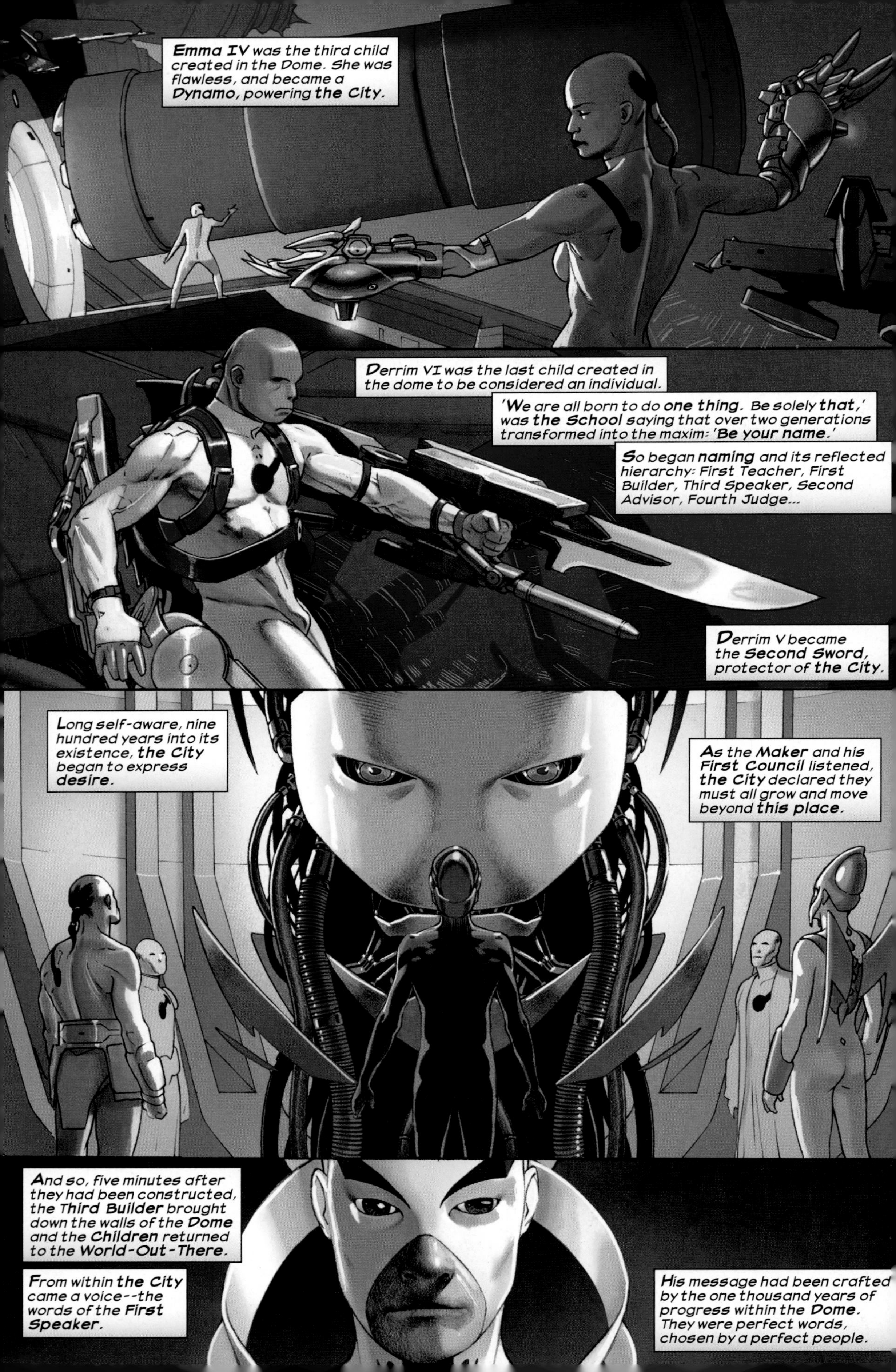
Emma IV was the third child created in the Dome. She was flawless, and became a Dynamo, powering the City.
Derrim VI was the last child created in the dome to be considered an individual.
'We are all born to do one thing. Be solely that,' was the School saying that over two generations transformed into the maxim: 'Be your name.'
So began naming and its reflected hierarchy: First Teacher, First Builder, Third Speaker, Second Advisor, Fourth Judge...
Derrim V became the Second Sword, protector of the City.
Long self-aware, nine hundred years into its existence, the City began to express desire.
As the Maker and his First Council listened, the City declared they must all grow and move beyond this place.
And so, five minutes after they had been constructed, the Third Builder brought down the walls of the Dome and the Children returned to the World-Out-There.
From within the City came a voice--the words of the First Speaker.
His message had been crafted by the one thousand years of progress within the Dome. They were perfect words, chosen by a perfect people.

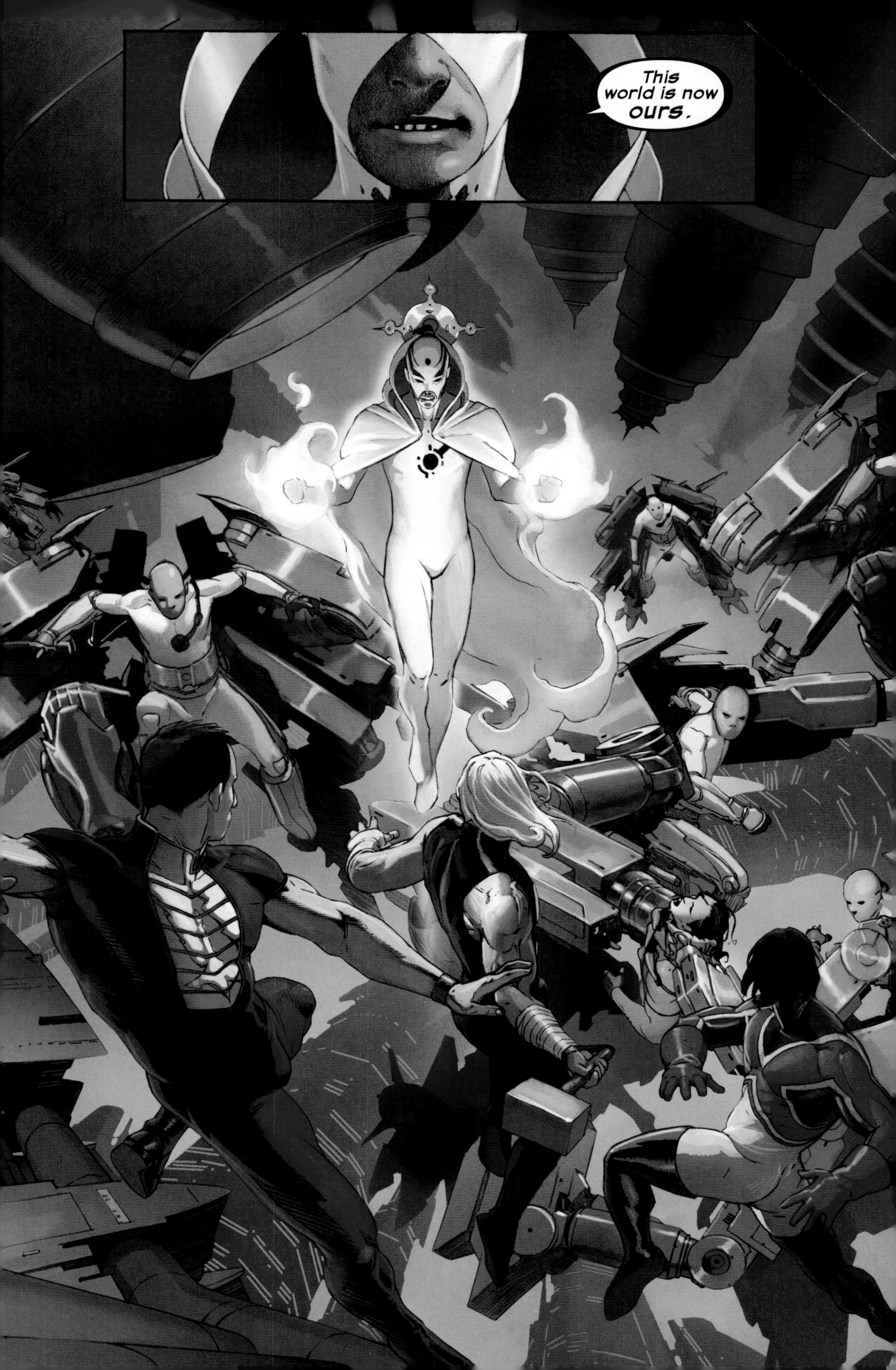
This world is now ours.

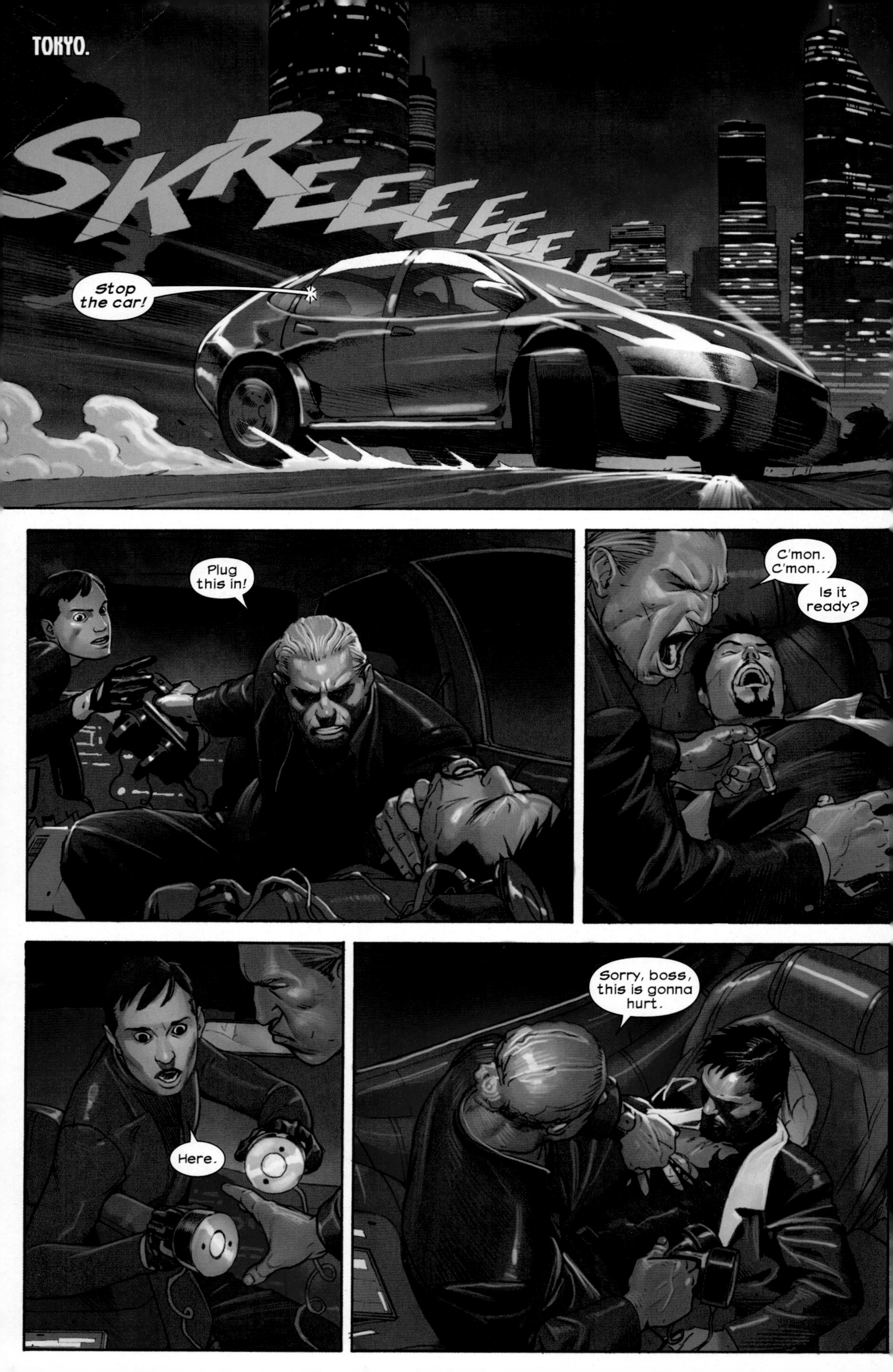
TOKYO.
SKREEEEEEE
Stop the car!
Plug this in!
C'mon. C'mon...
Is it ready?
Here.
Sorry, boss, this is gonna hurt.

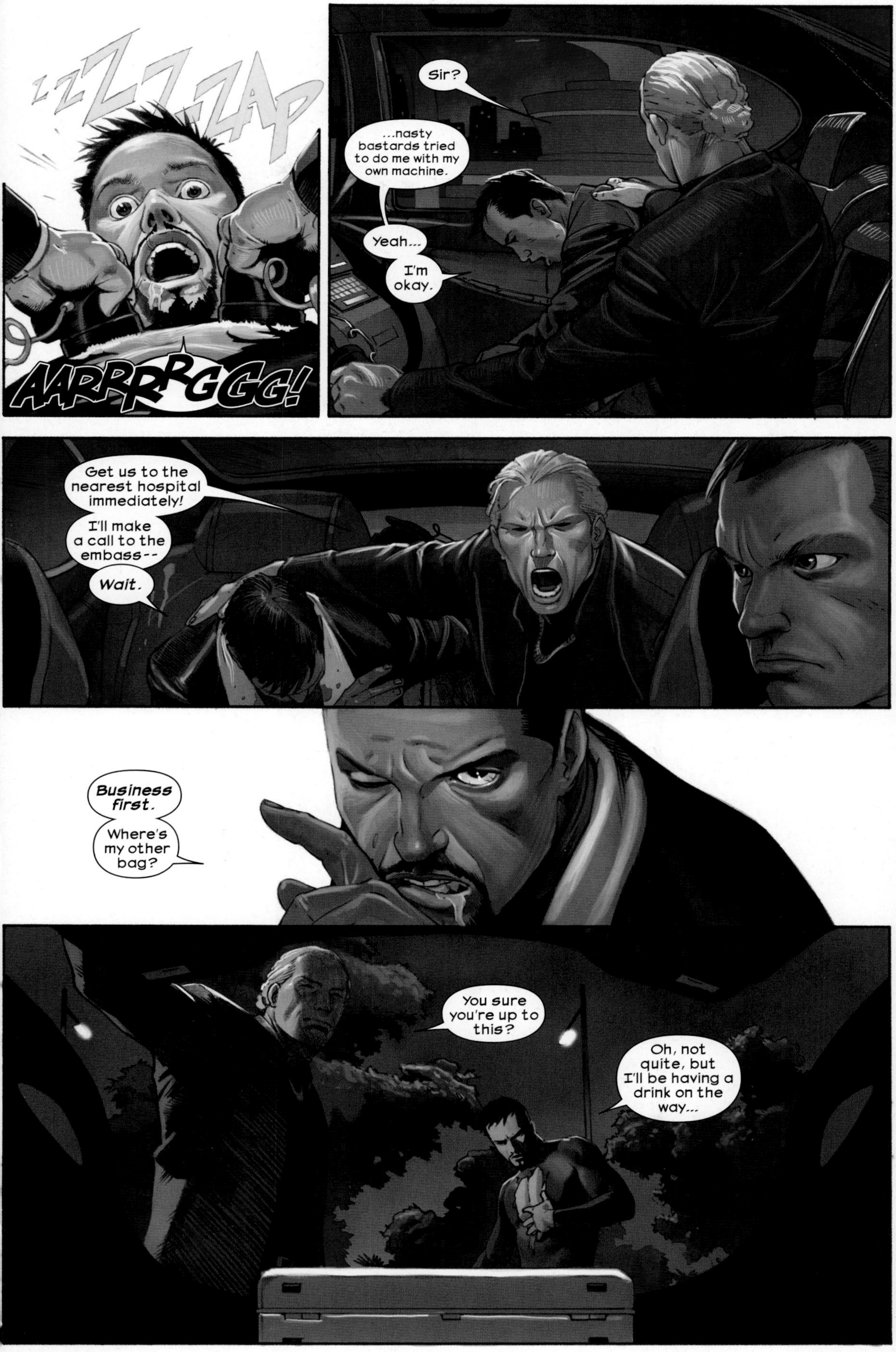

ZZZZZZAP
AARRRRGGG!
Sir?
...nasty bastards tried to do me with my own machine.
Yeah...
I'm okay.
Get us to the nearest hospital immediately!
I'll make a call to the embass--
Wait.
Business first.
Where's my other bag?
You sure you're up to this?
Oh, not quite, but I'll be having a drink on the way...

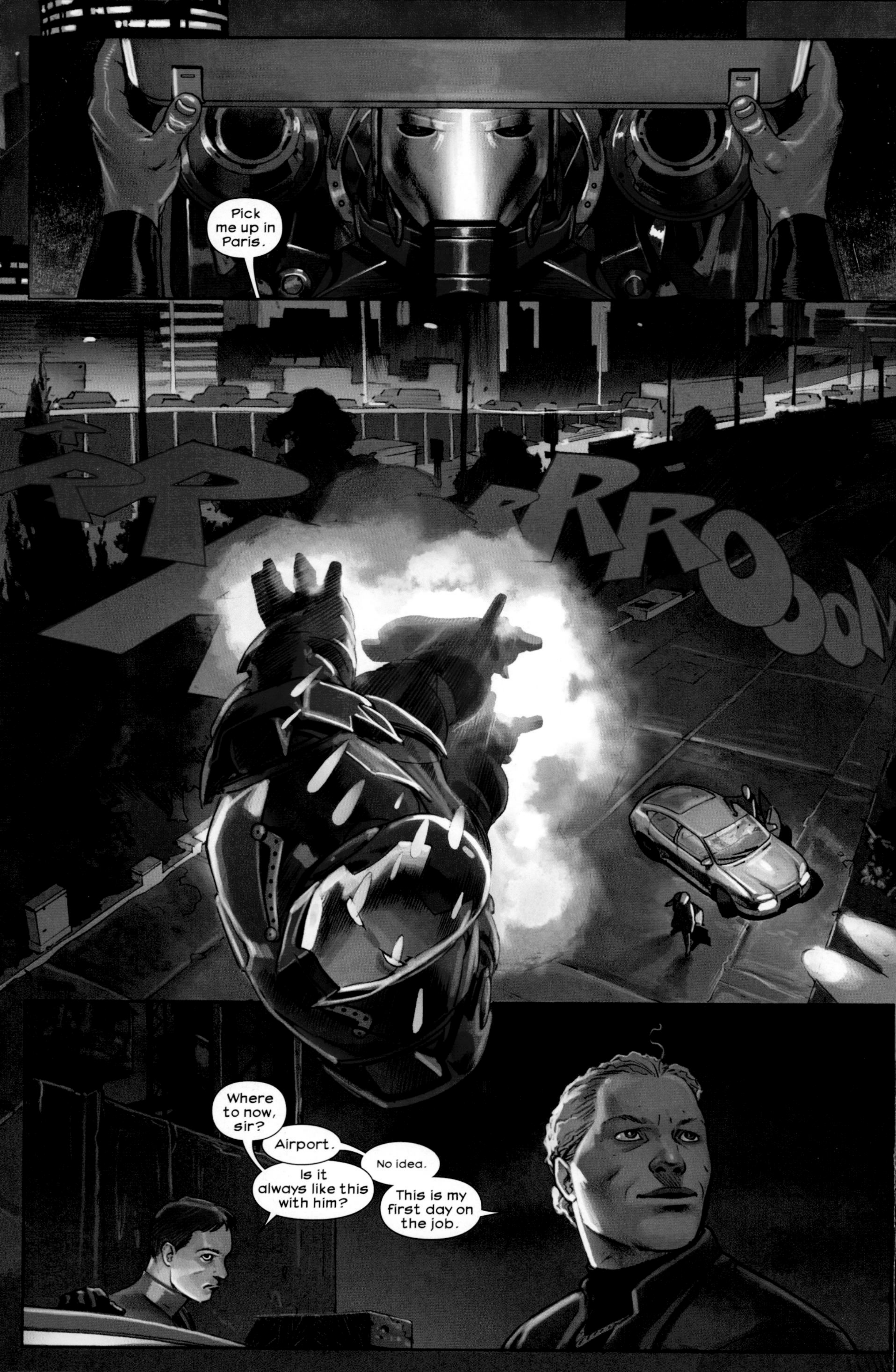
Pick me up in Paris.
Where to now, sir?
Airport.
Is it always like this with him?
No idea.
This is my first day on the job.

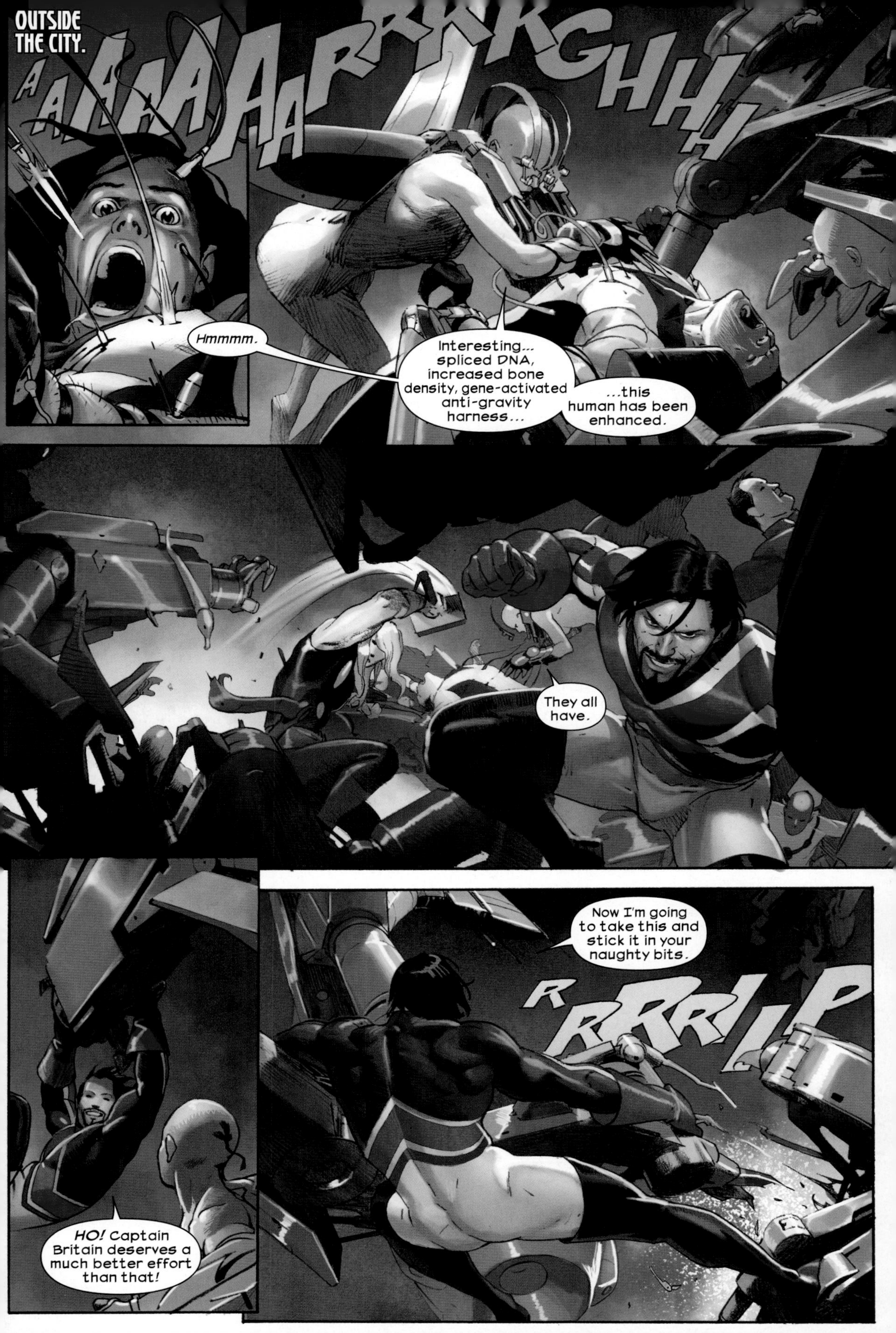
OUTSIDE THE CITY.
AAAAAAAARRRKKGHHH
Hmmmm.
Interesting... spliced DNA, increased bone density, gene-activated anti-gravity harness...
...this human has been enhanced.
They all have.
HO! Captain Britain deserves a much better effort than that!
Now I'm going to take this and stick it in your naughty bits.
RRRRIIP

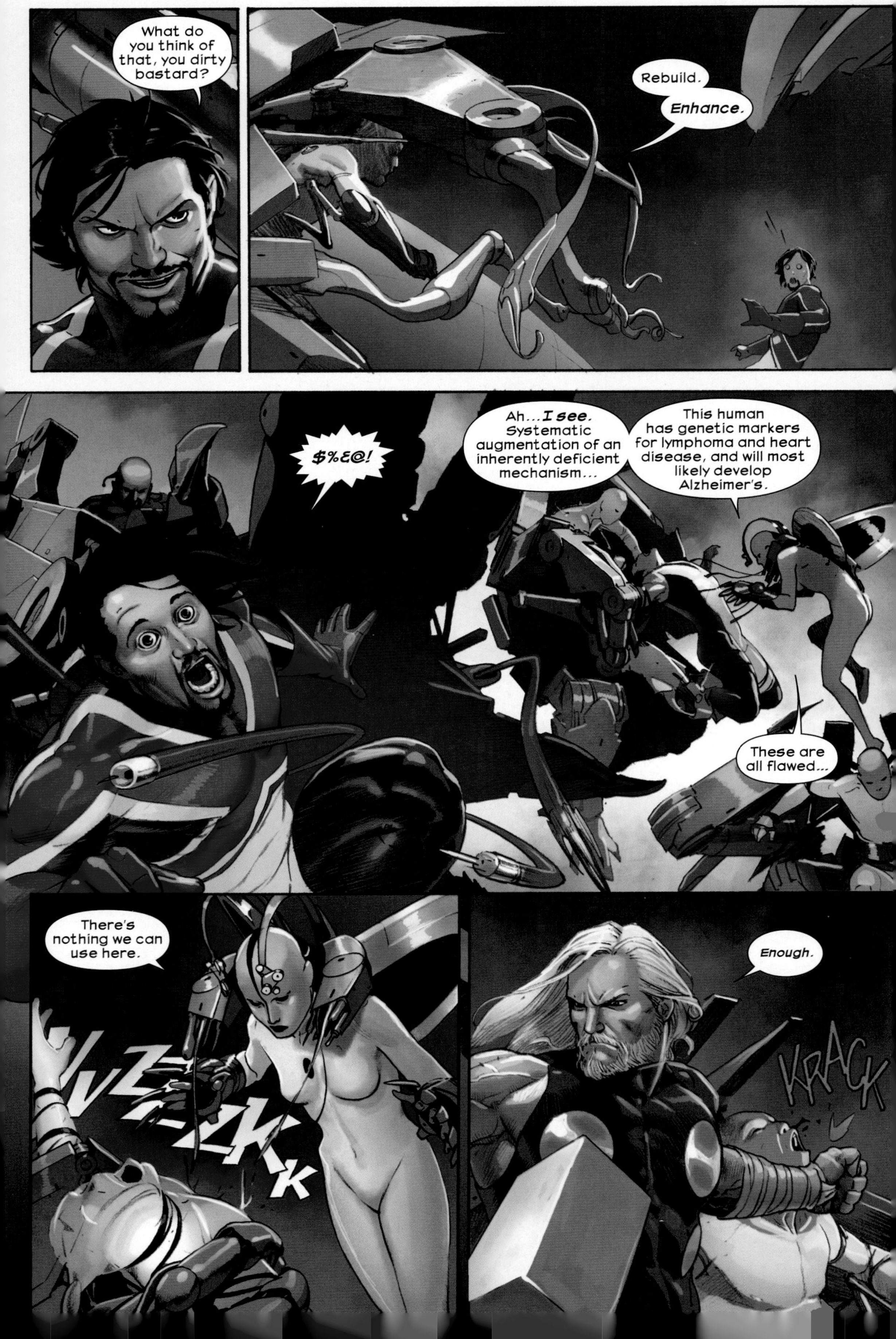
What do you think of that, you dirty bastard?
Rebuild.
Enhance.
$%£@!
Ah... I see. Systematic augmentation of an inherently deficient mechanism...
This human has genetic markers for lymphoma and heart disease, and will most likely develop Alzheimer's.
These are all flawed...
There's nothing we can use here.
VVZZZKKK
Enough.
KRACK

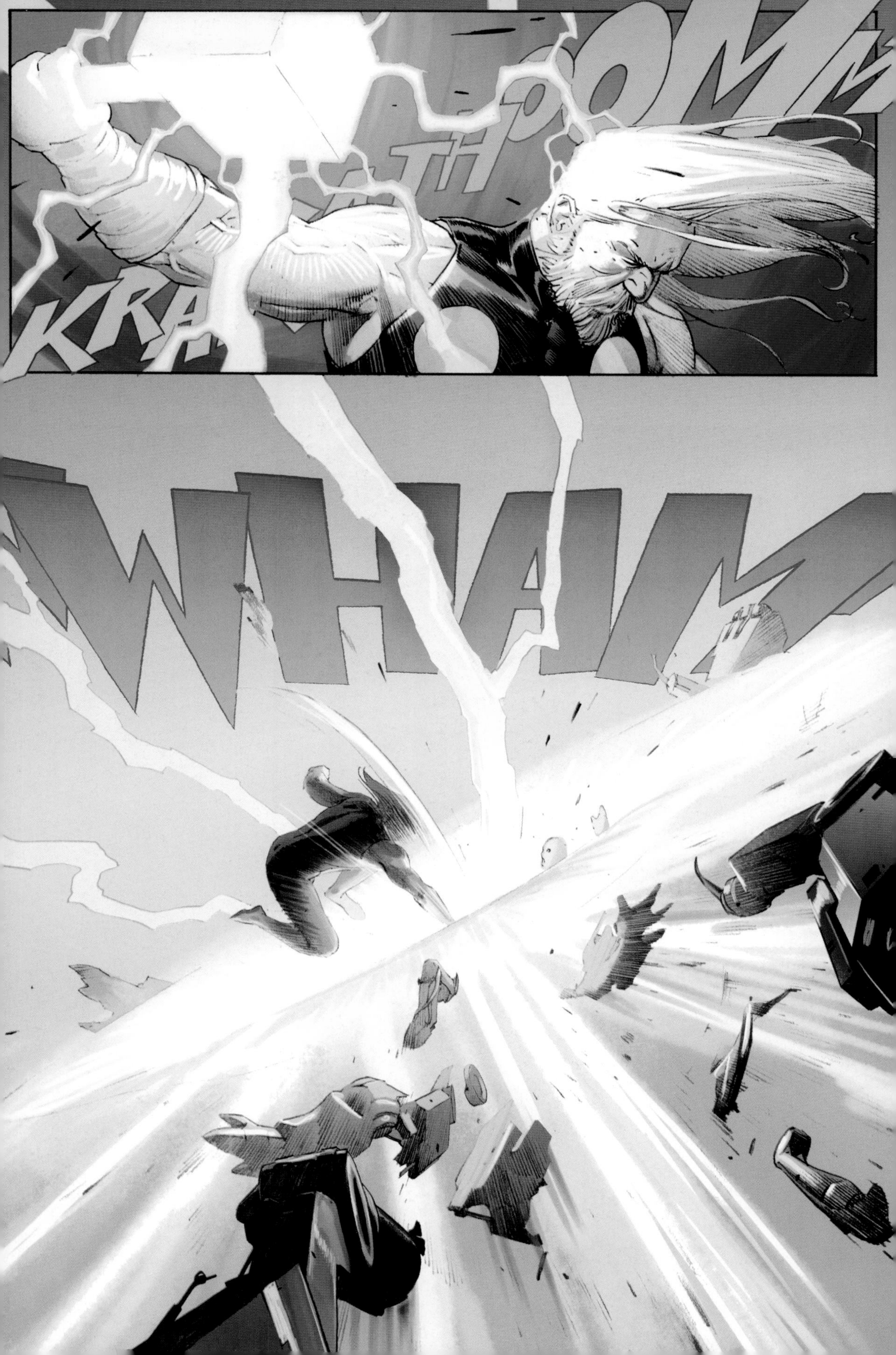
KRA
THOOM
WHAM

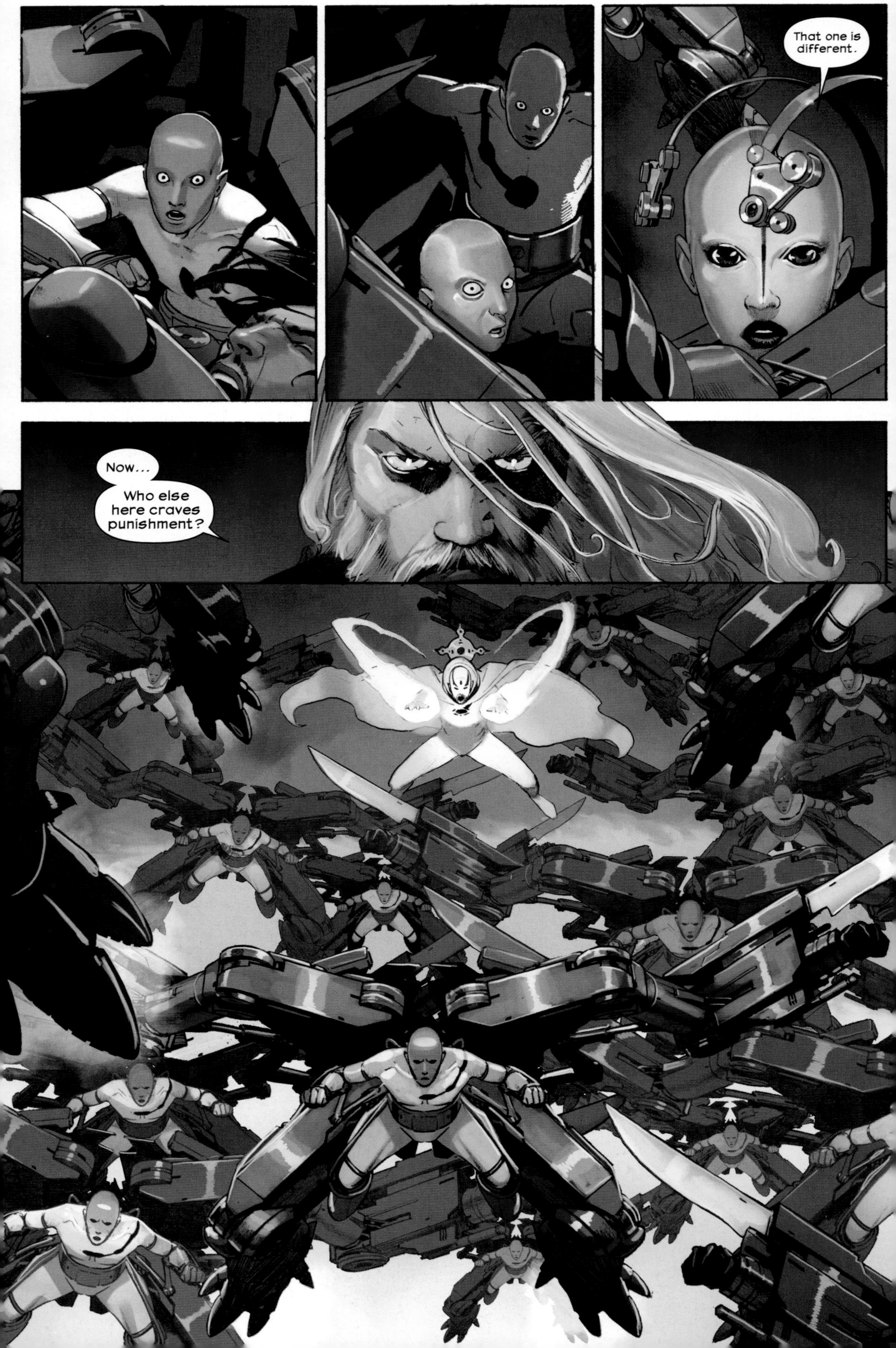
That one is different.
Now...
Who else here craves punishment?

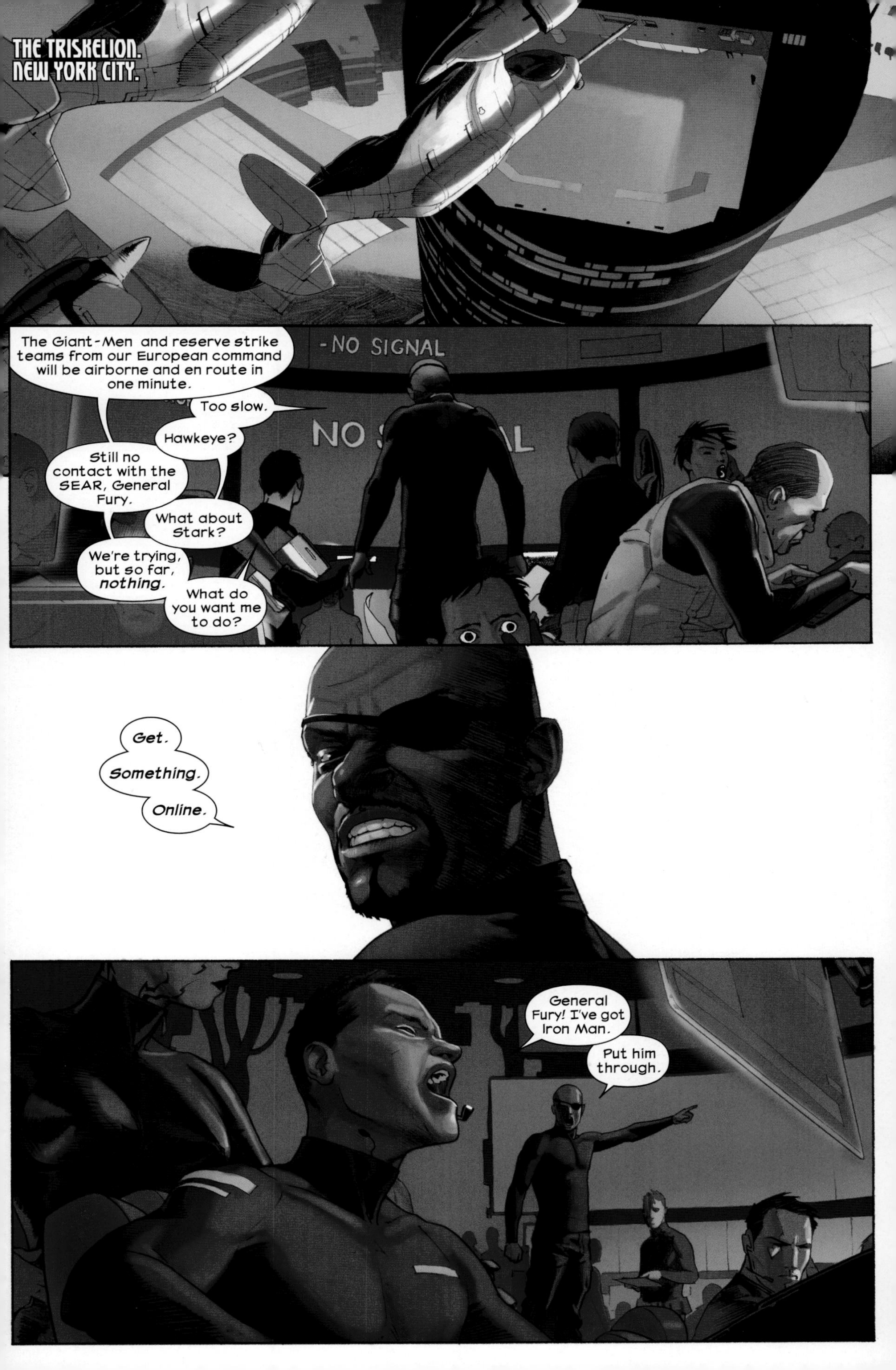
THE TRISKELION. NEW YORK CITY.
The Giant-Men and reserve strike teams from our European command will be airborne and en route in one minute.
Too slow.
Hawkeye?
Still no contact with the SEAR, General Fury.
What about Stark?
We're trying, but so far, *nothing.*
What do you want me to do?
-NO SIGNAL
Get.
Something.
Online.
General Fury! I've got Iron Man.
Put him through.

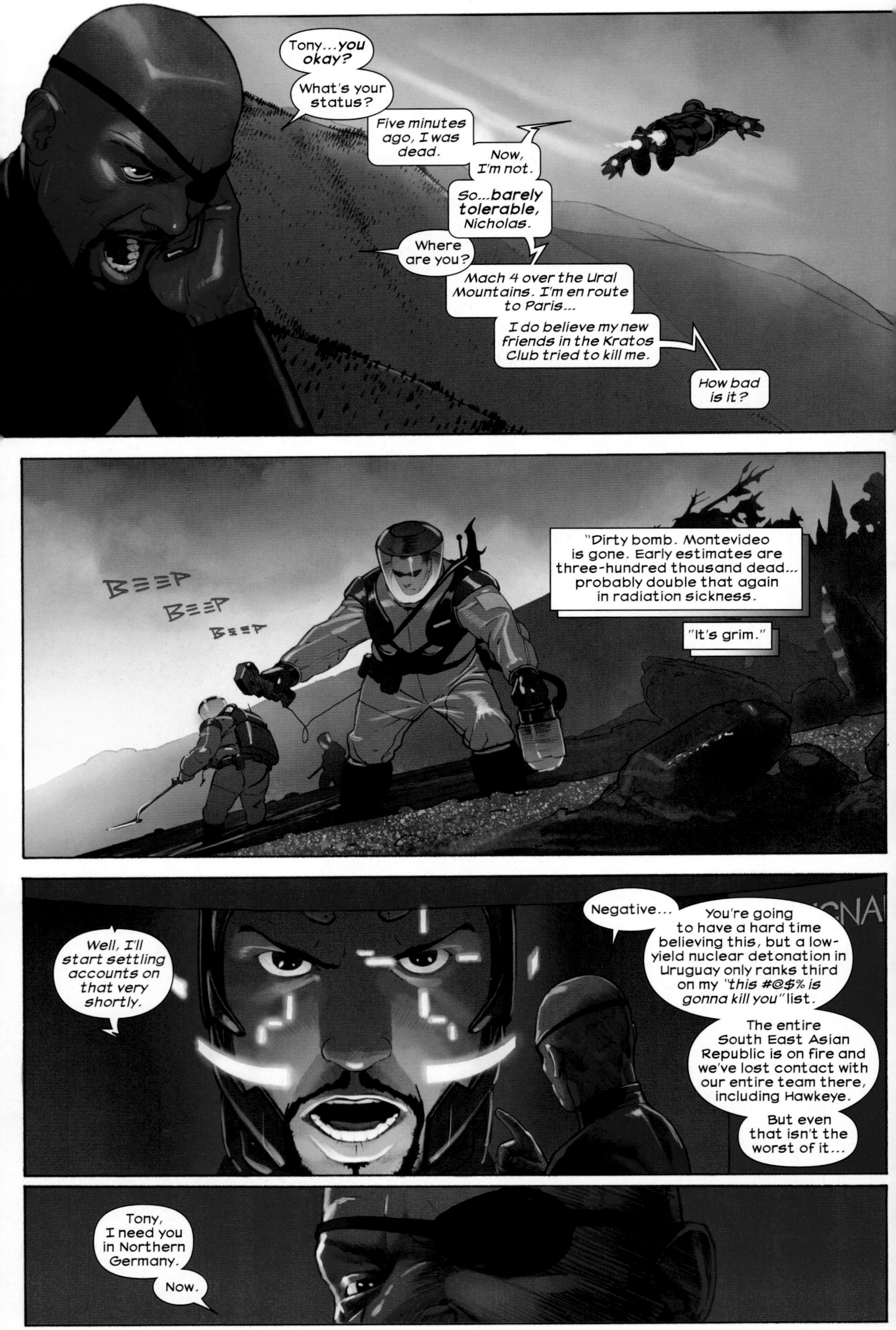

Tony...you okay?
What's your status?
Five minutes ago, I was dead.
Now, I'm not.
So...barely tolerable, Nicholas.
Where are you?
Mach 4 over the Ural Mountains. I'm en route to Paris...
I do believe my new friends in the Kratos Club tried to kill me.
How bad is it?
BEEP
BEEP
BEEP
"Dirty bomb. Montevideo is gone. Early estimates are three-hundred thousand dead... probably double that again in radiation sickness.
"It's grim."
Well, I'll start settling accounts on that very shortly.
Negative...
You're going to have a hard time believing this, but a low-yield nuclear detonation in Uruguay only ranks third on my "this #@$% is gonna kill you" list.
The entire South East Asian Republic is on fire and we've lost contact with our entire team there, including Hawkeye.
But even that isn't the worst of it...
Tony, I need you in Northern Germany.
Now.

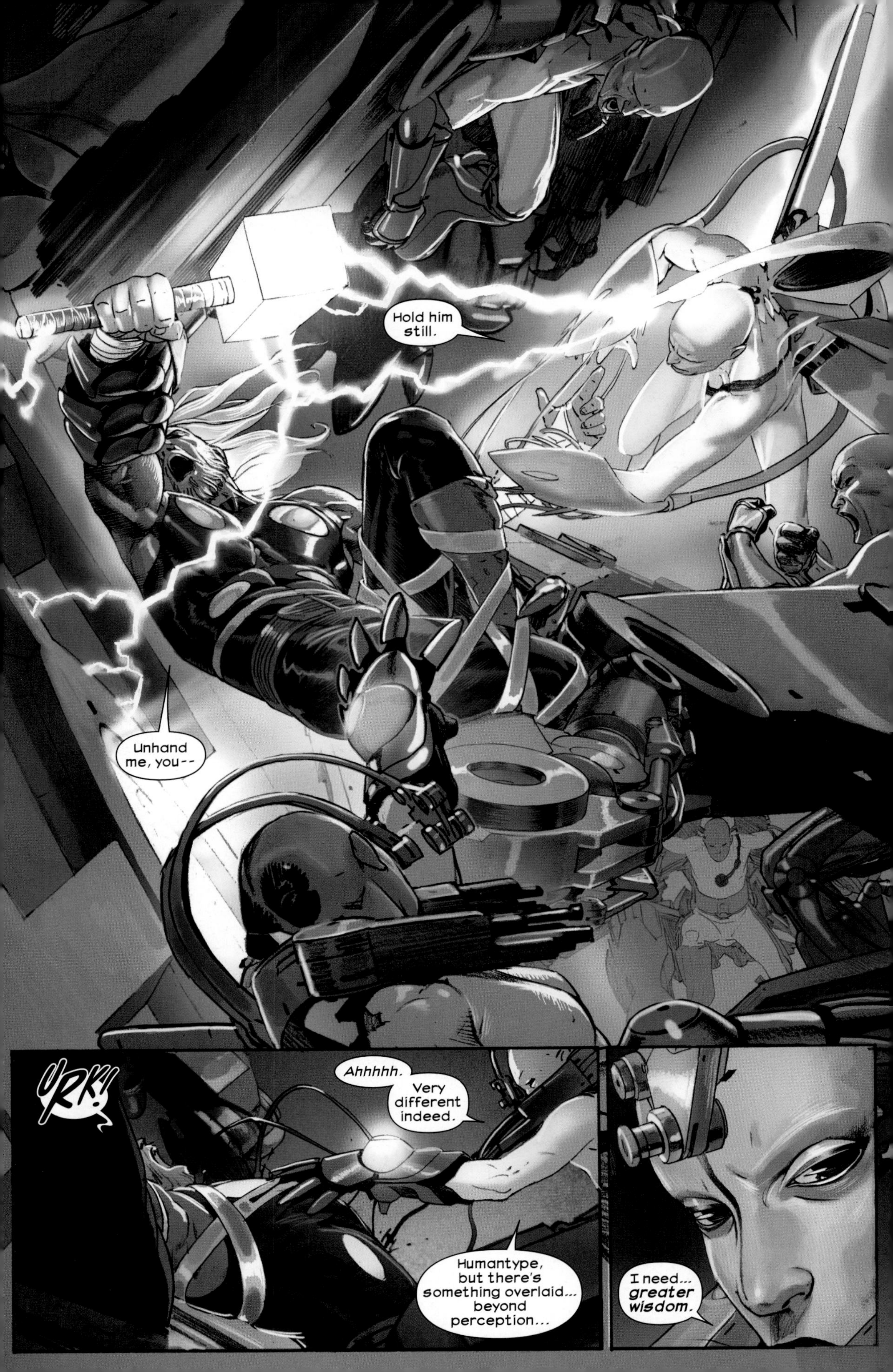
Hold him still.
Unhand me, you--
URK!
Ahhhhh. Very different indeed.
Humantype, but there's something overlaid... beyond perception...
I need... greater wisdom.

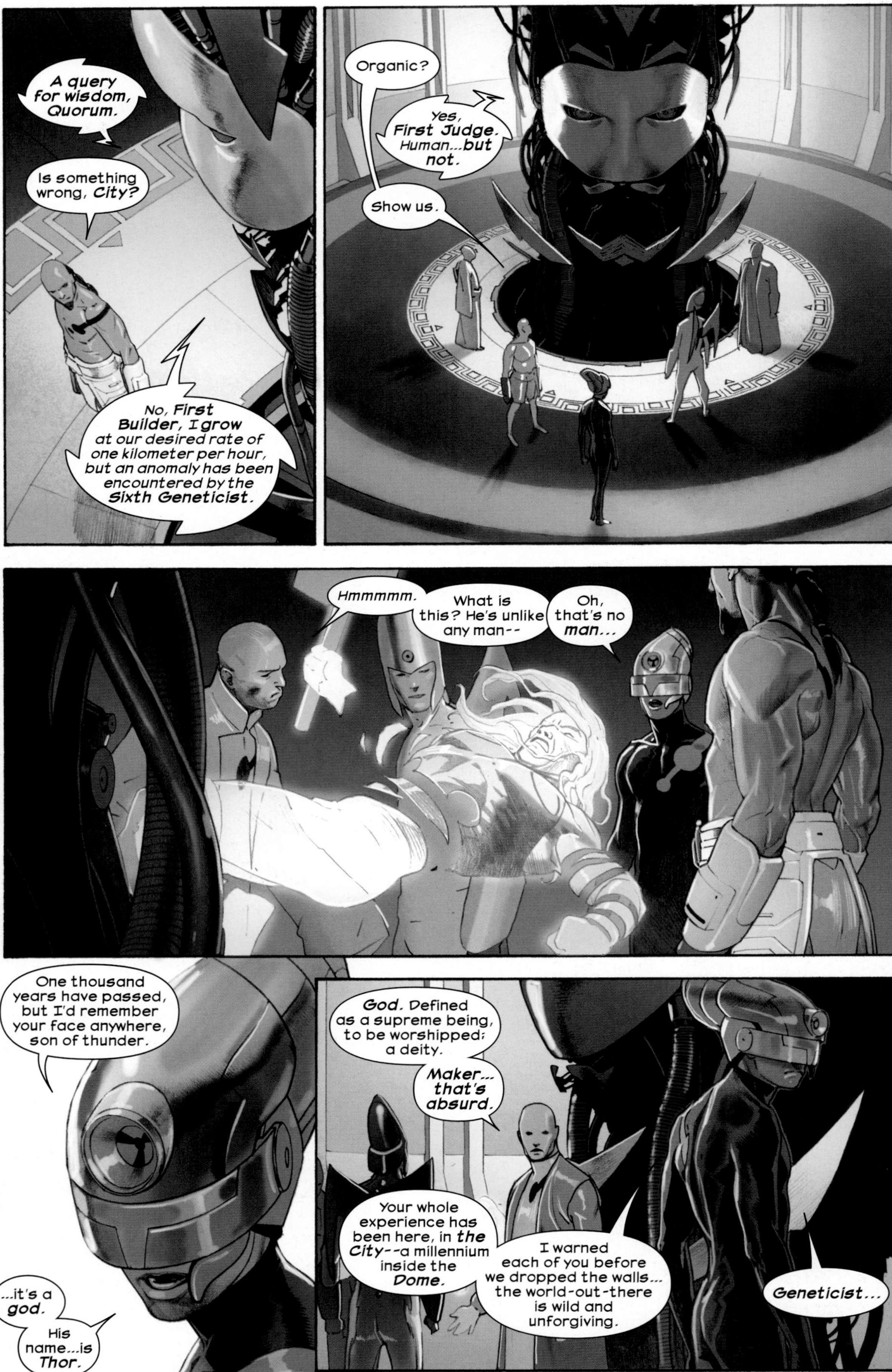
A query for wisdom, Quorum.
Is something wrong, City?
No, First Builder, I grow at our desired rate of one kilometer per hour, but an anomaly has been encountered by the Sixth Geneticist.
Organic?
Yes, First Judge. Human...but not.
Show us.
Hmmmmm.
What is this? He's unlike any man--
Oh, that's no man...
One thousand years have passed, but I'd remember your face anywhere, son of thunder.
...it's a god.
His name...is Thor.
God. Defined as a supreme being, to be worshipped; a deity.
Maker... that's absurd.
Your whole experience has been here, in the City--a millennium inside the Dome.
I warned each of you before we dropped the walls... the world-out-there is wild and unforgiving.
Geneticist...

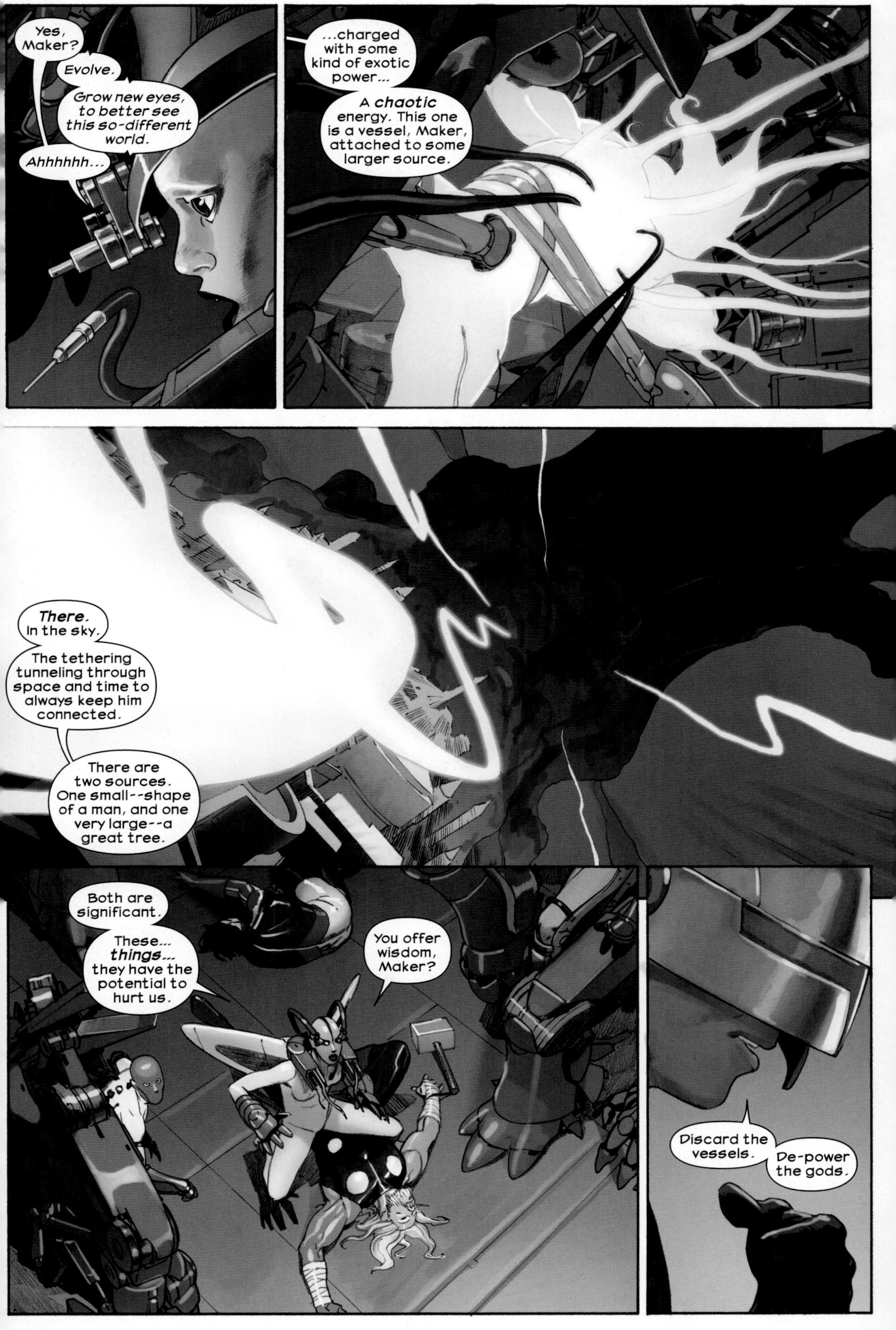
Yes, Maker?
Evolve.
Grow new eyes, to better see this so-different world.
Ahhhhhh...
...charged with some kind of exotic power...
A chaotic energy. This one is a vessel, Maker, attached to some larger source.
There. In the sky.
The tethering tunneling through space and time to always keep him connected.
There are two sources. One small--shape of a man, and one very large--a great tree.
Both are significant.
These... things... they have the potential to hurt us.
You offer wisdom, Maker?
Discard the vessels.
De-power the gods.

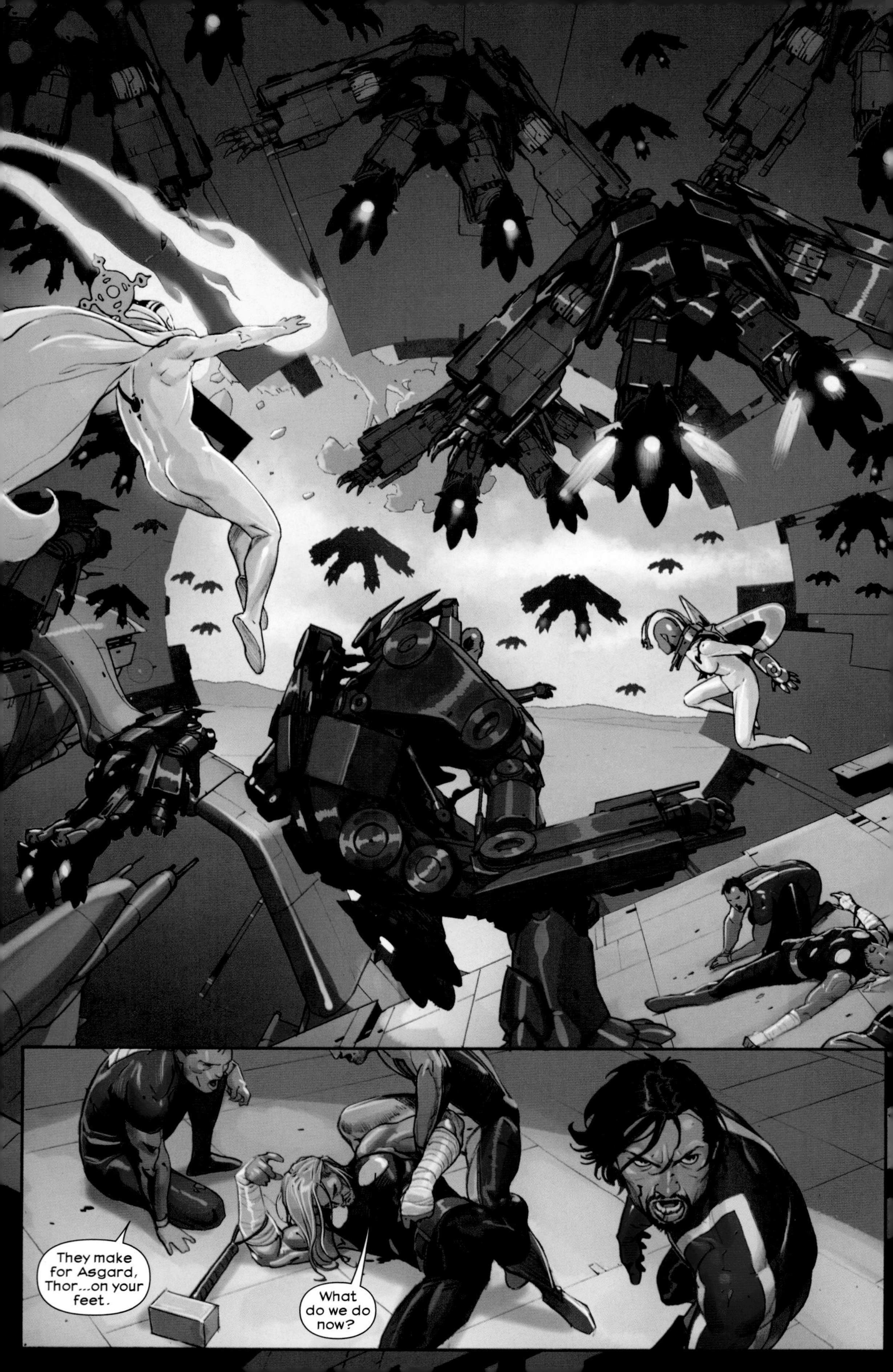
They make for Asgard, Thor...on your feet.
What do we do now?

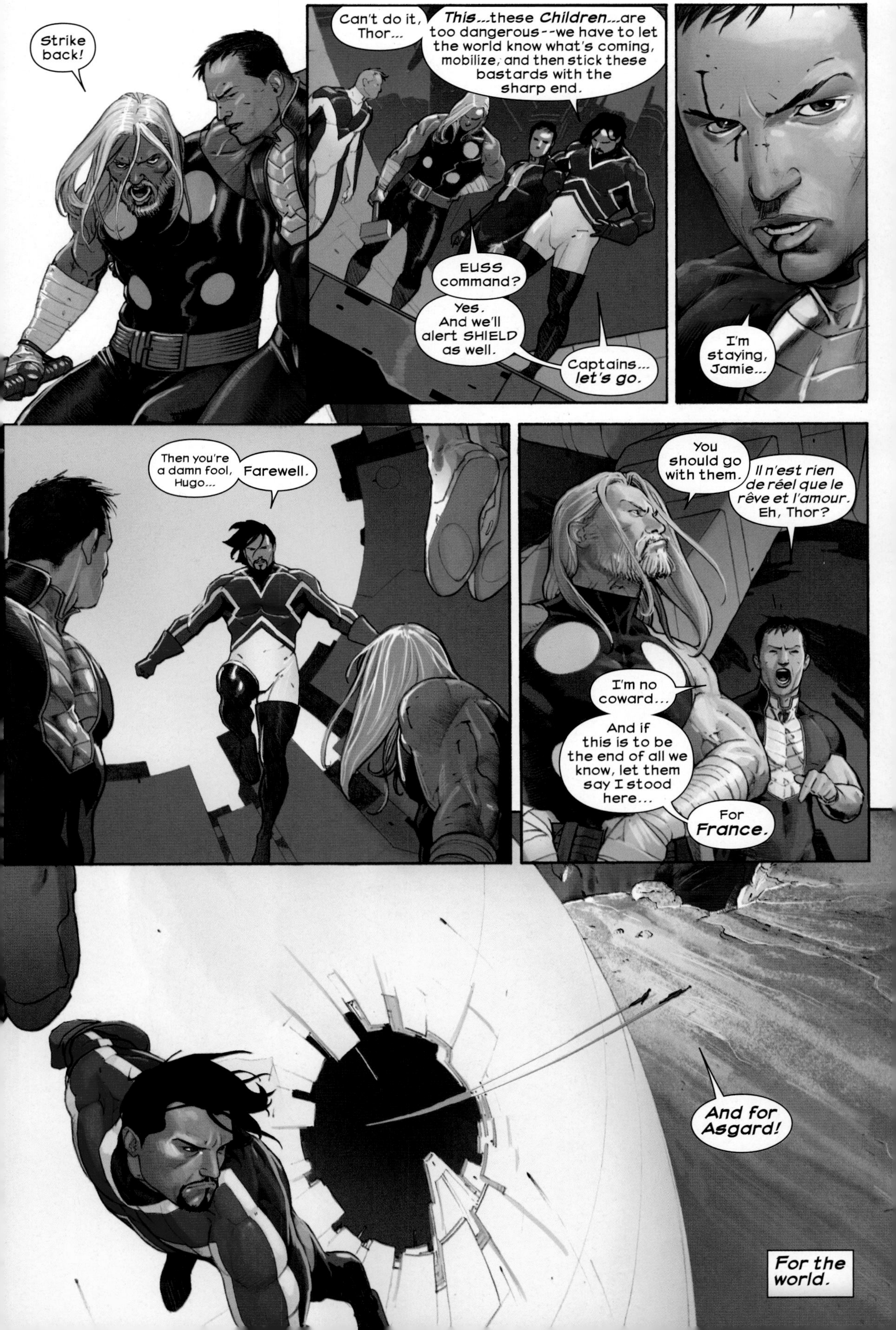
Strike back!
Can't do it, Thor...
This...these Children...are too dangerous--we have to let the world know what's coming, mobilize, and then stick these bastards with the sharp end.
EUSS command?
Yes. And we'll alert SHIELD as well.
Captains... let's go.
I'm staying, Jamie...
Then you're a damn fool, Hugo...
Farewell.
You should go with them.
Il n'est rien de réel que le rêve et l'amour. Eh, Thor?
I'm no coward...
And if this is to be the end of all we know, let them say I stood here...
For France.
And for Asgard!
For the world.

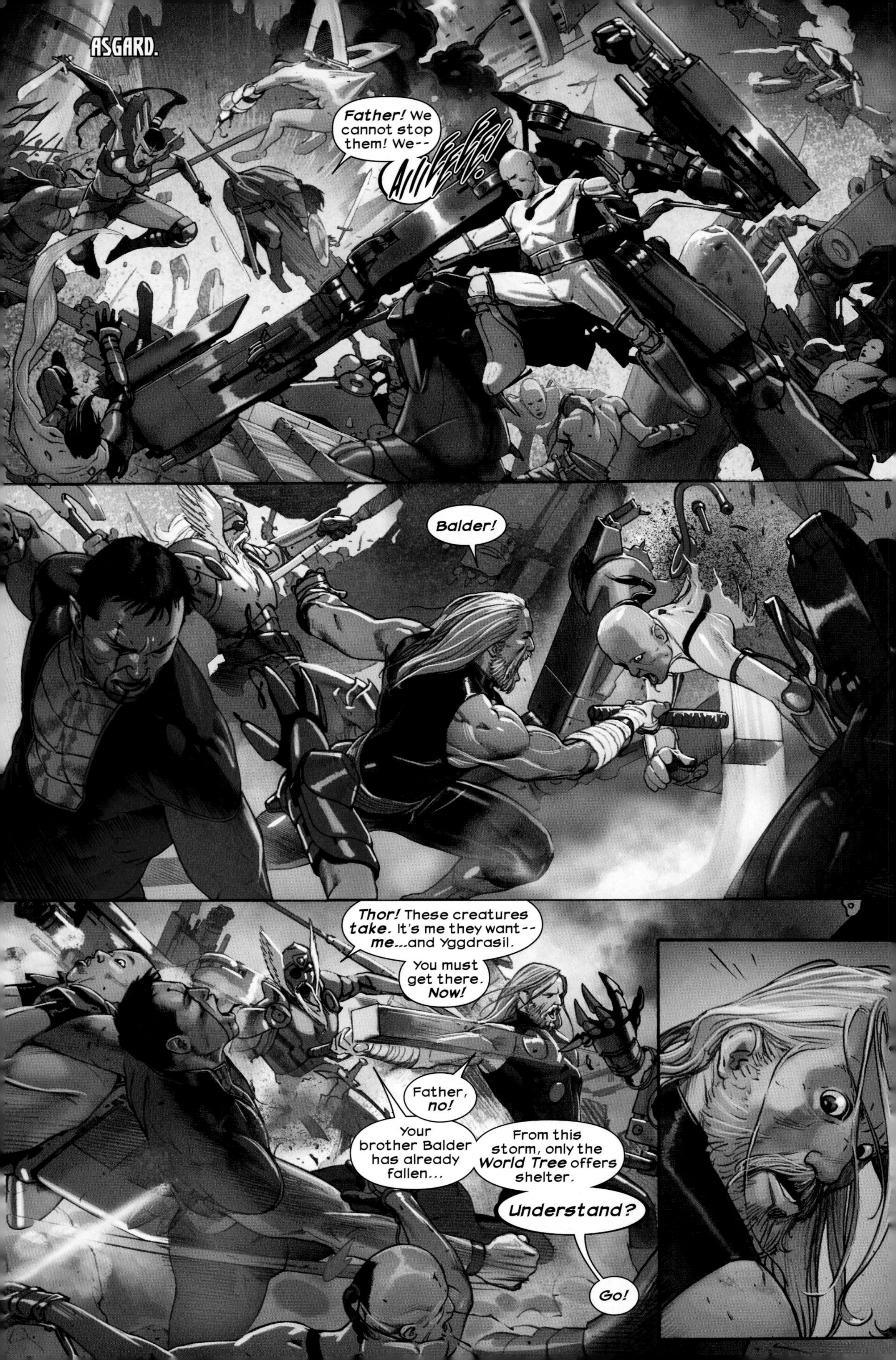
ASGARD.
Father! We cannot stop them! We--
AIIIEEEEE!
Balder!
Thor! These creatures take. It's me they want-- me...and Yggdrasil.
You must get there. Now!
Father, no!
Your brother Balder has already fallen...
From this storm, only the World Tree offers shelter.
Understand?
Go!

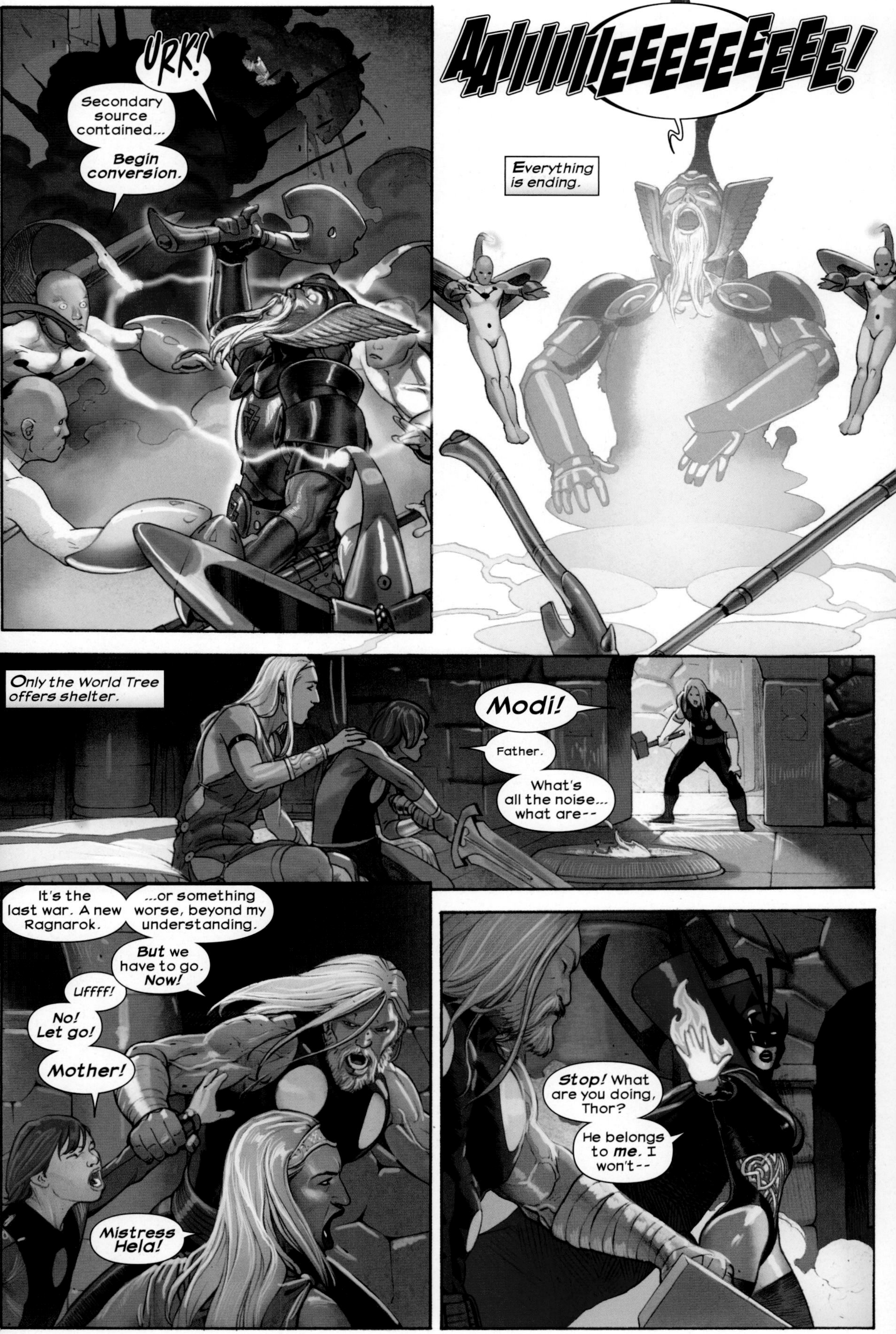
URK!
Secondary source contained...
Begin conversion.
AAIIIIIIIEEEEEEEEEE!
Everything is ending.
Only the World Tree offers shelter.
Modi!
Father.
What's all the noise... what are--
It's the last war. A new Ragnarok.
...or something worse, beyond my understanding.
But we have to go. Now!
Uffff!
No! Let go!
Mother!
Mistress Hela!
Stop! What are you doing, Thor?
He belongs to me. I won't--

I have no time for this, woman...

"I must get to the World Tree...I must get to Salvation."

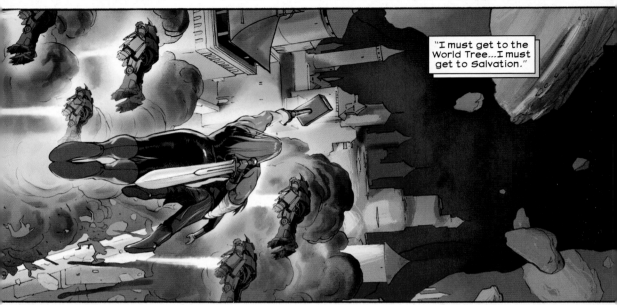

My father showed me this once. A *room* with *no doors*.

Father, *WHAT?*

Forgive me.

A way out, son... For when you are *worthy*.

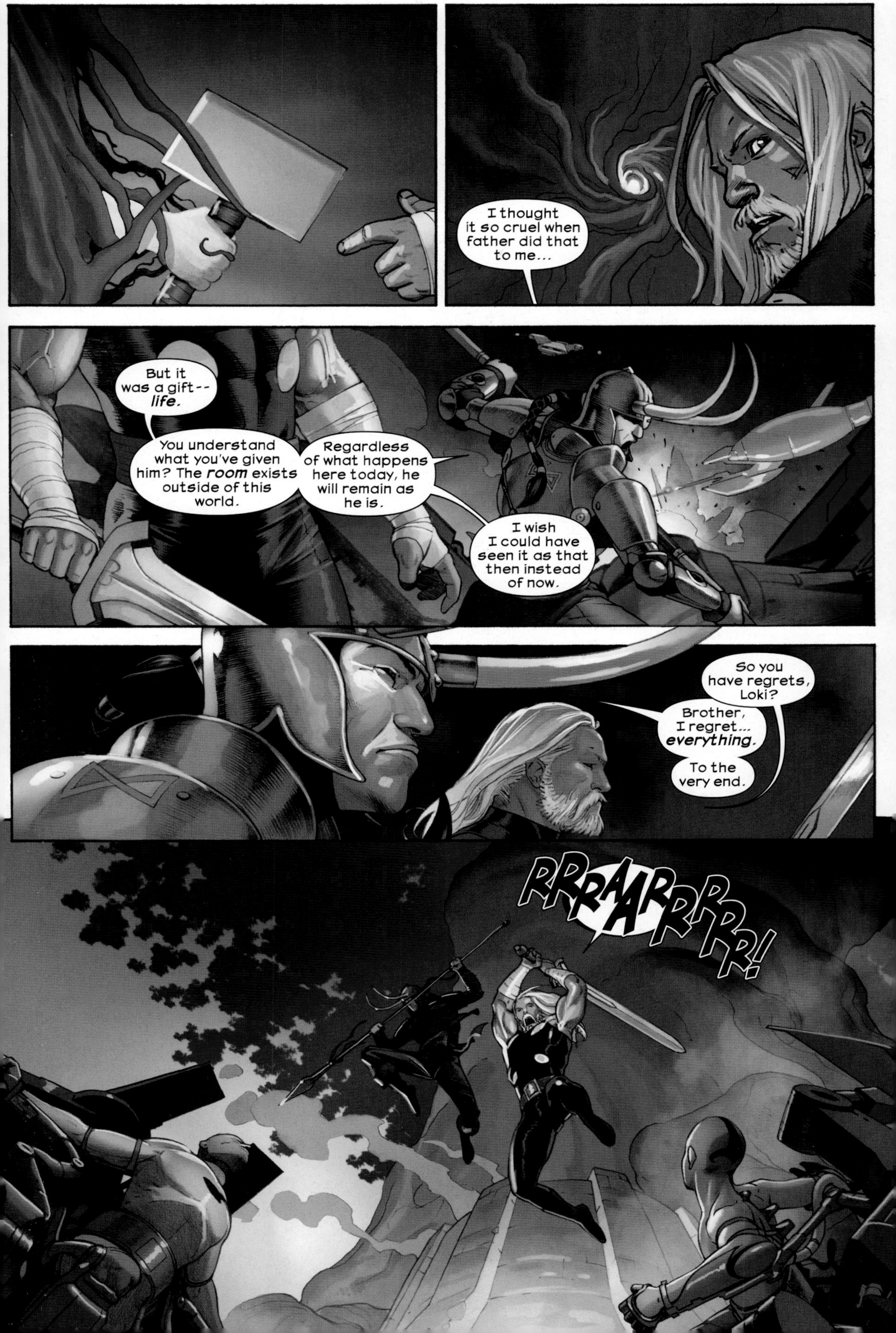
I thought it so cruel when father did that to me...
But it was a gift-- *life.*
You understand what you've given him? The *room* exists outside of this world.
Regardless of what happens here today, he will remain as he is.
I wish I could have seen it as that then instead of now.
So you have regrets, Loki?
Brother, I regret... *everything.*
To the very end.
RRRAARRRRR!

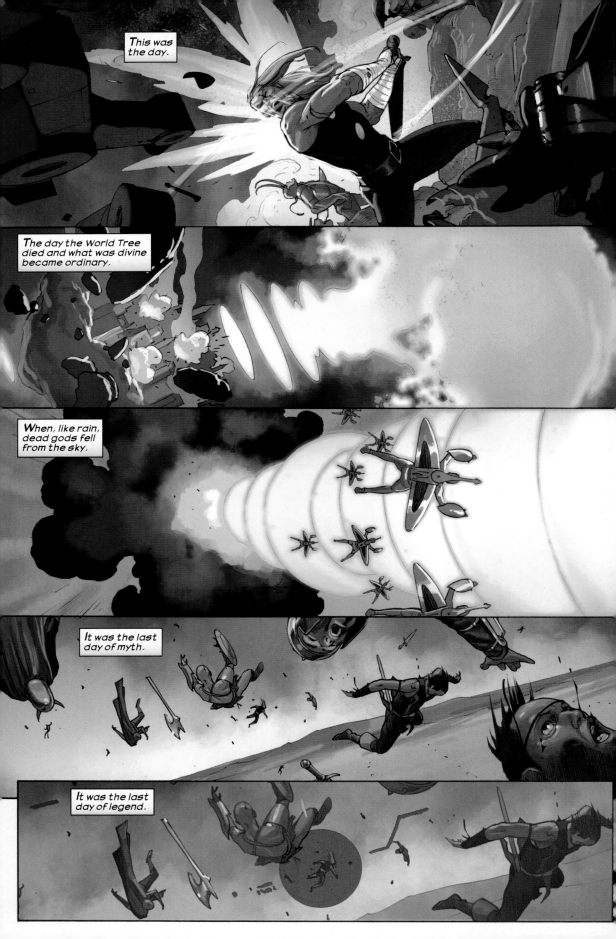

This was the day.

The day the World Tree died and what was divine became ordinary.

When, like rain, dead gods fell from the sky.

It was the last day of myth.

It was the last day of legend.

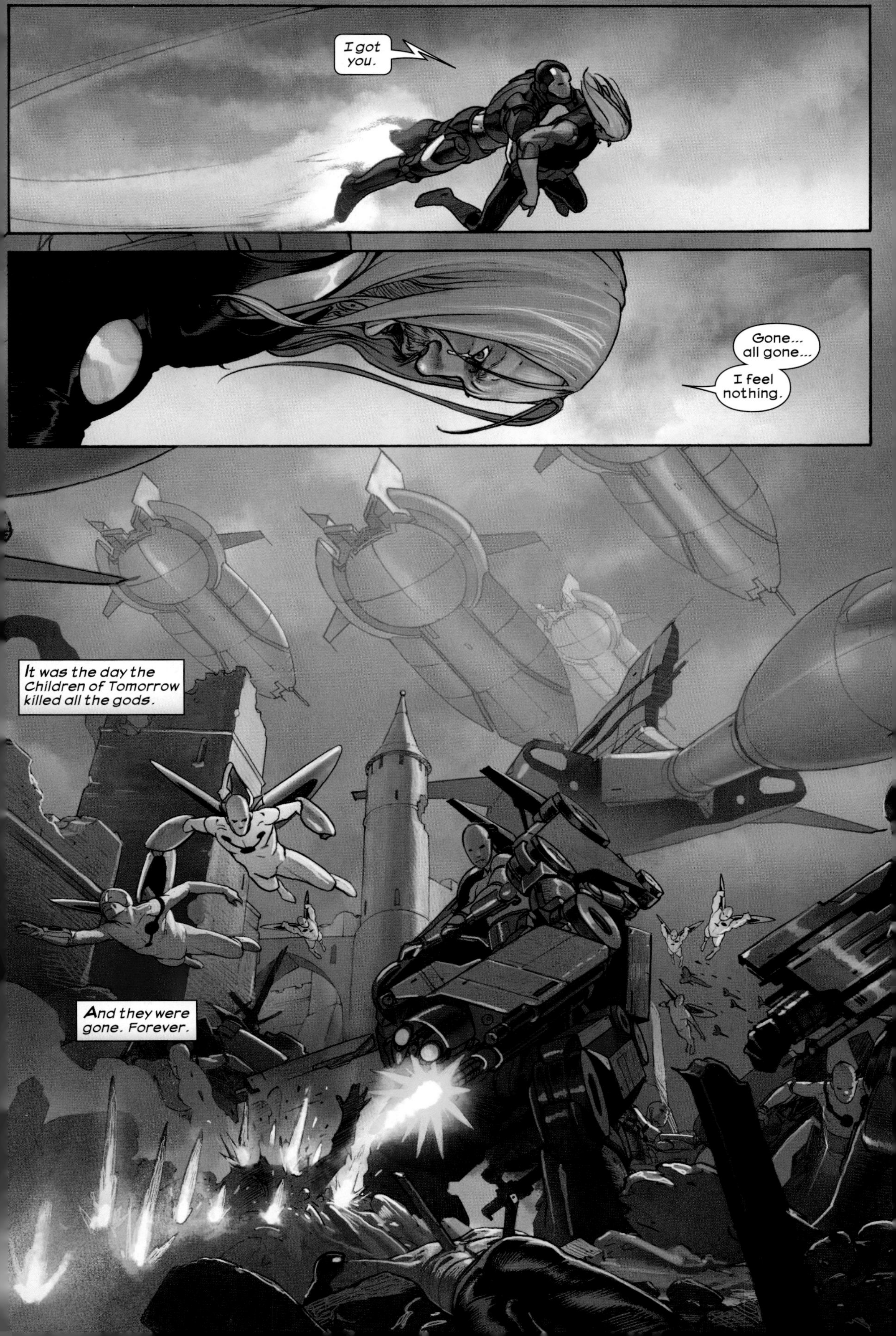

I got you.
Gone... all gone...
I feel nothing.
It was the day the Children of Tomorrow killed all the gods.
And they were gone. Forever.

3

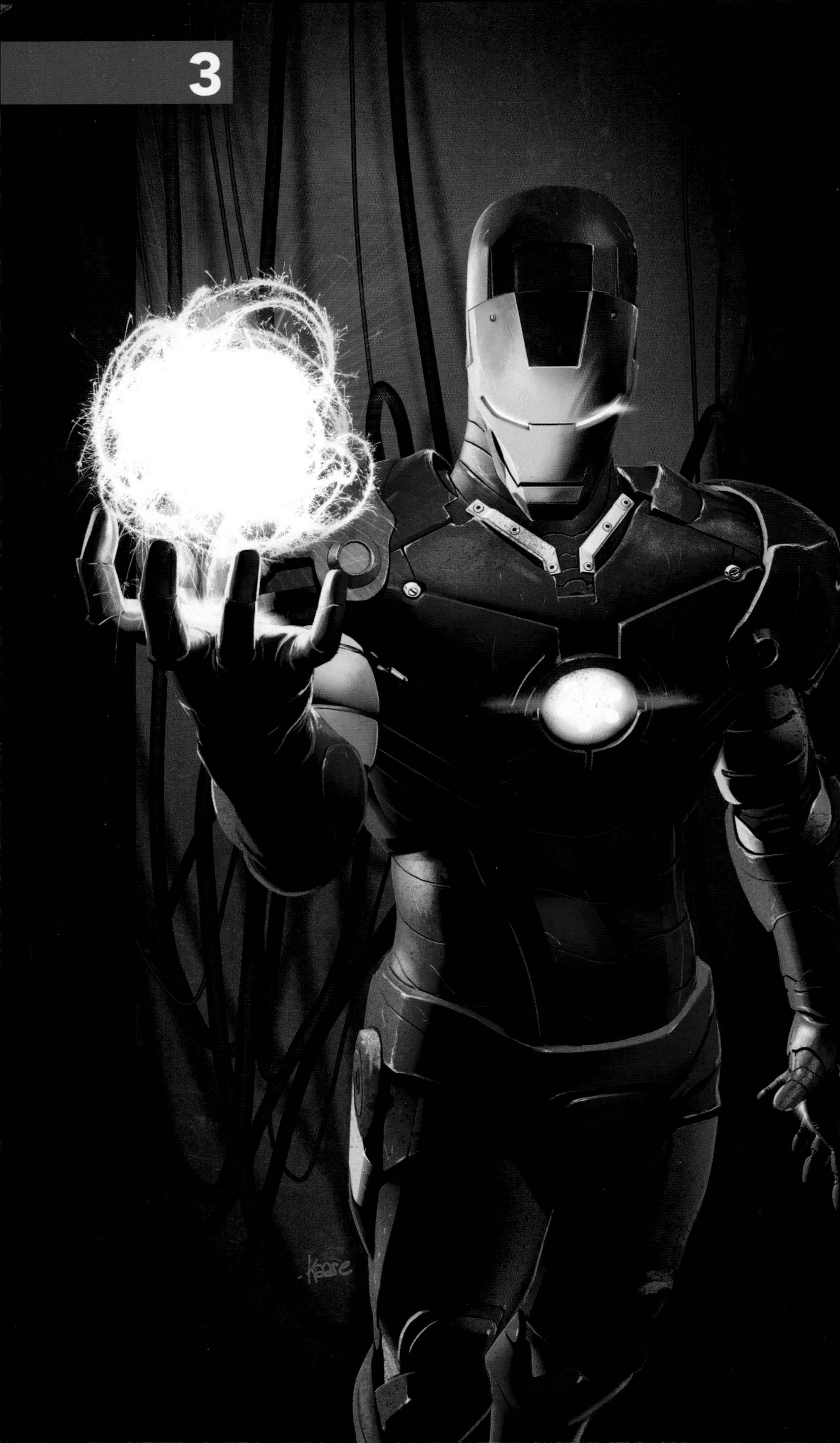

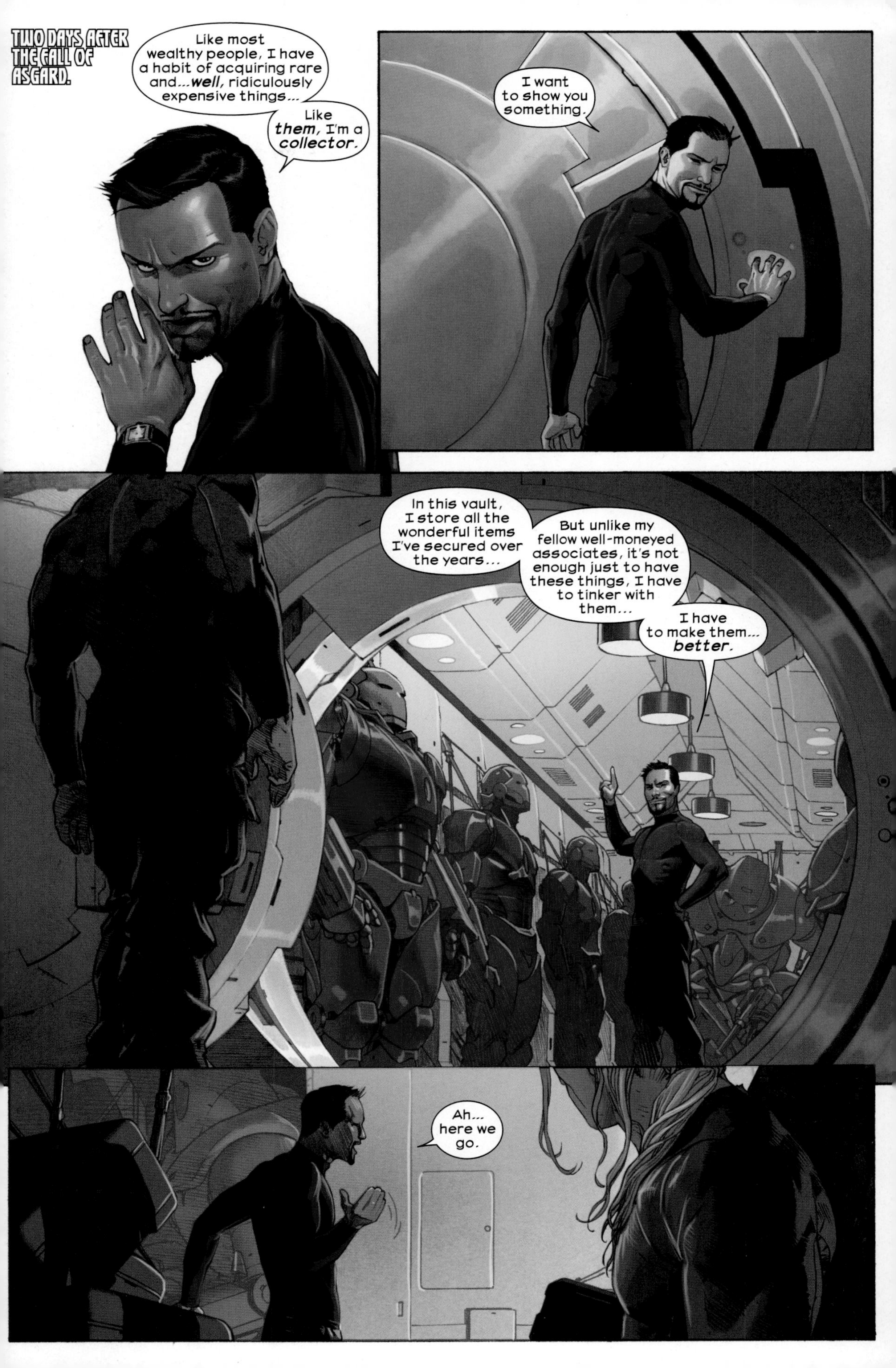
TWO DAYS AFTER THE FALL OF ASGARD.
Like most wealthy people, I have a habit of acquiring rare and... *well,* ridiculously expensive things...
Like *them,* I'm a *collector.*
I want to show you something.
In this vault, I store all the wonderful items I've secured over the years...
But unlike my fellow well-moneyed associates, it's not enough just to have these things, I have to tinker with them...
I have to make them... *better.*
Ah... here we go.

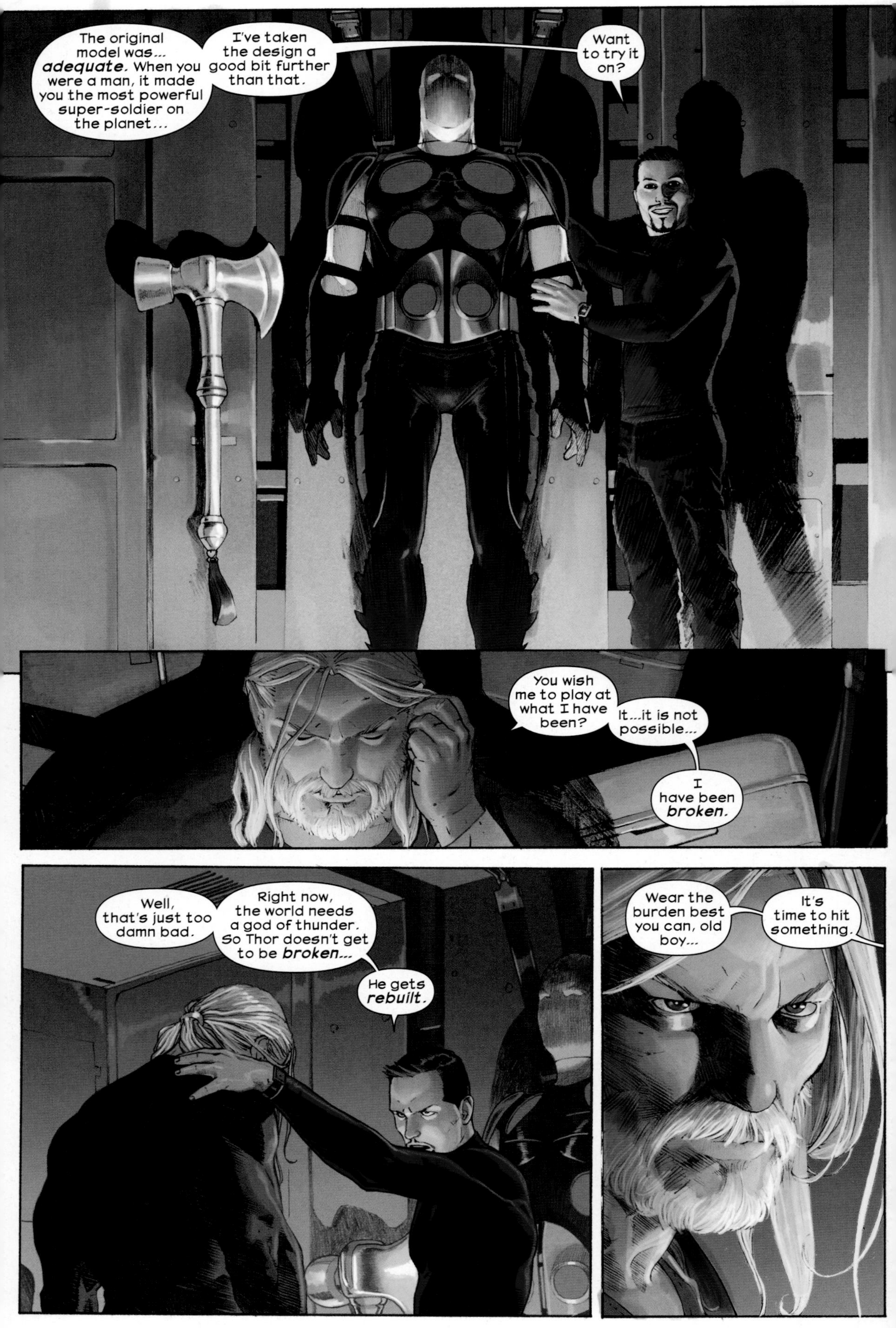
The original model was... *adequate.* When you were a man, it made you the most powerful super-soldier on the planet...
I've taken the design a good bit further than that.
Want to try it on?
You wish me to play at what I have been?
It...it is not possible...
I have been *broken.*
Well, that's just too damn bad.
Right now, the world needs a god of thunder. So Thor doesn't get to be *broken...*
He gets *rebuilt.*
Wear the burden best you can, old boy...
It's time to hit something.

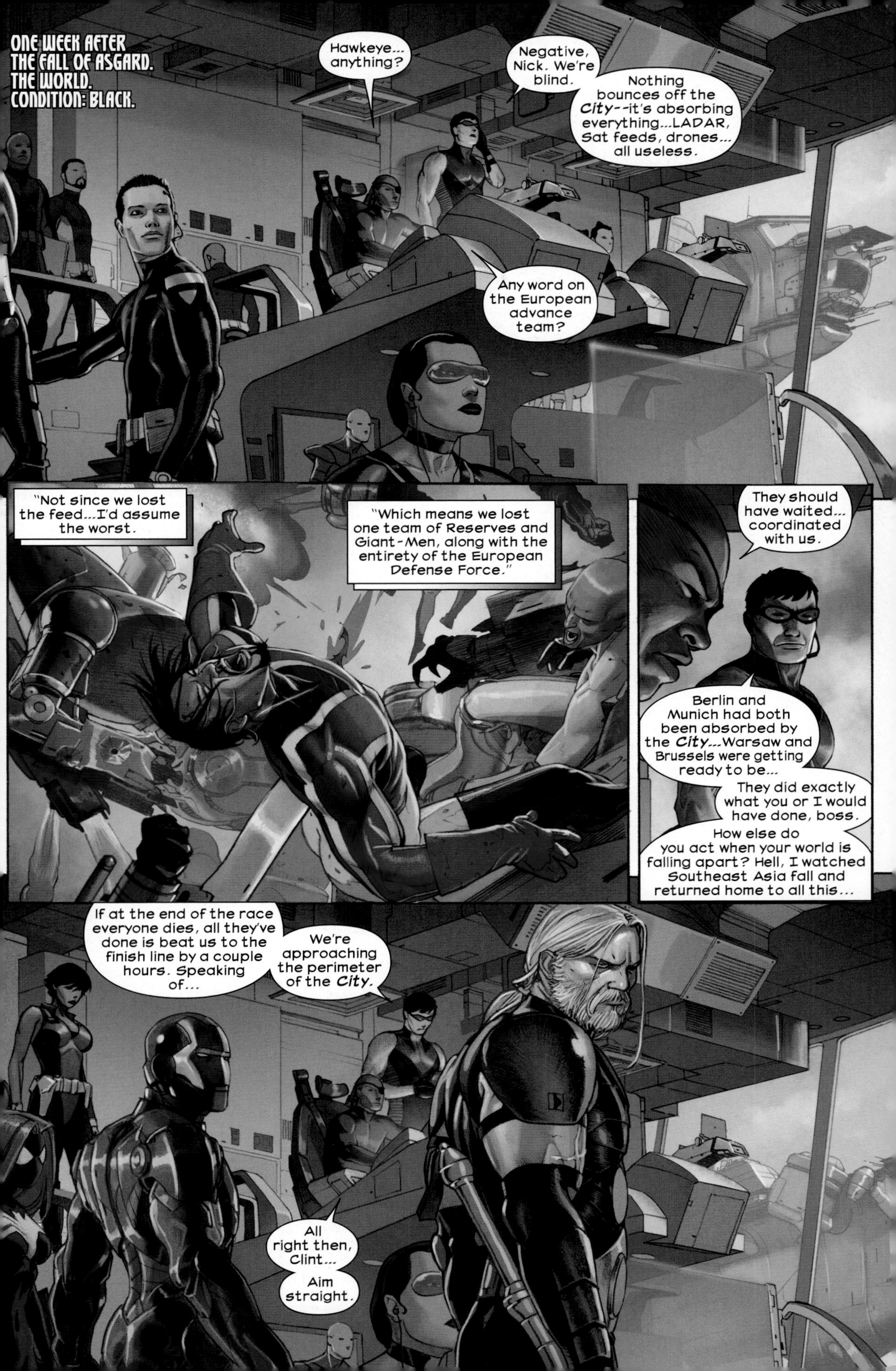
ONE WEEK AFTER THE FALL OF ASGARD. THE WORLD. CONDITION: BLACK.
Hawkeye... anything?
Negative, Nick. We're blind.
Nothing bounces off the City--it's absorbing everything...LADAR, Sat feeds, drones... all useless.
Any word on the European advance team?
"Not since we lost the feed...I'd assume the worst.
"Which means we lost one team of Reserves and Giant-Men, along with the entirety of the European Defense Force."
They should have waited... coordinated with us.
Berlin and Munich had both been absorbed by the City...Warsaw and Brussels were getting ready to be...
They did exactly what you or I would have done, boss.
How else do you act when your world is falling apart? Hell, I watched Southeast Asia fall and returned home to all this...
If at the end of the race everyone dies, all they've done is beat us to the finish line by a couple hours. Speaking of...
We're approaching the perimeter of the City.
All right then, Clint...
Aim straight.

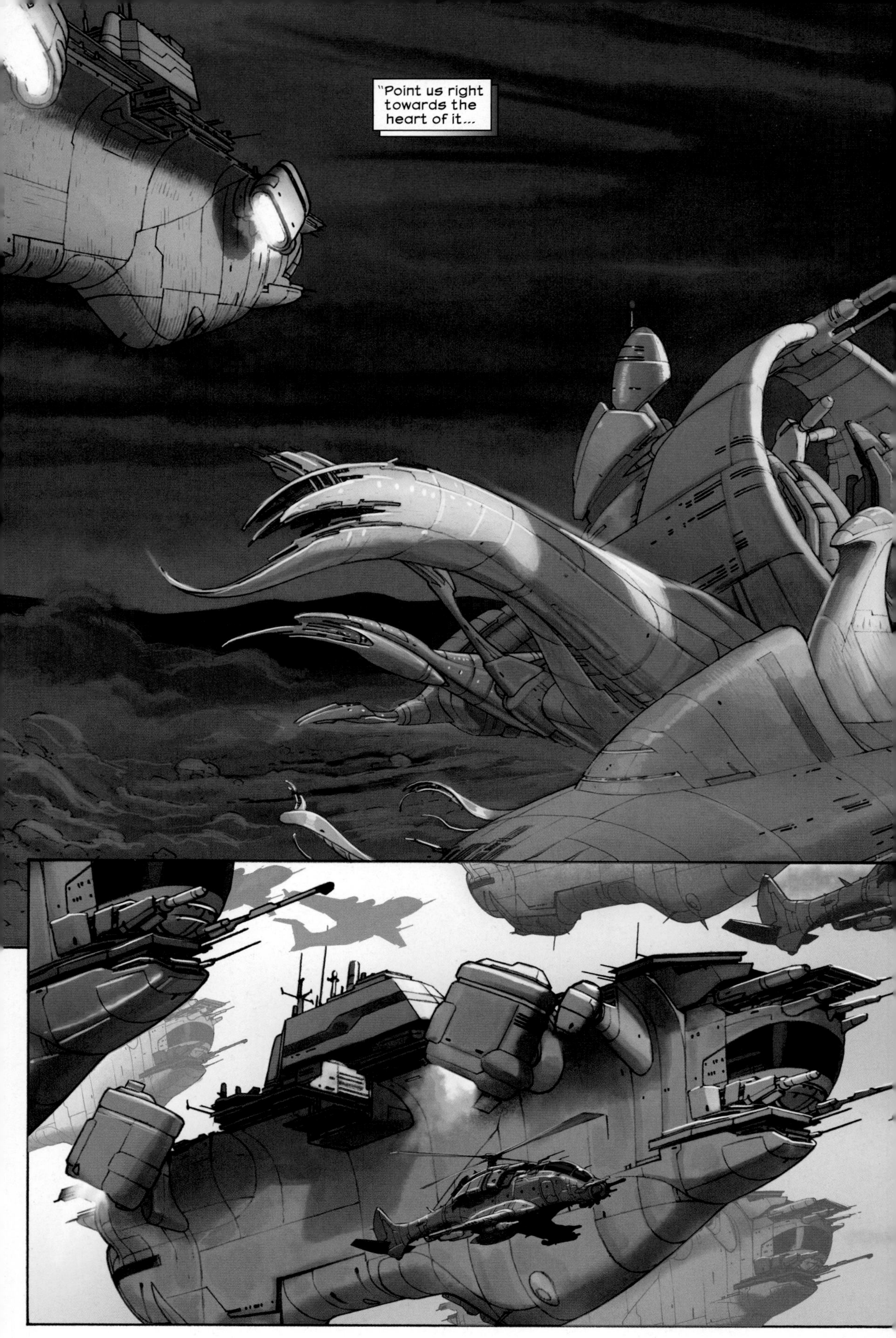
"Point us right towards the heart of it...

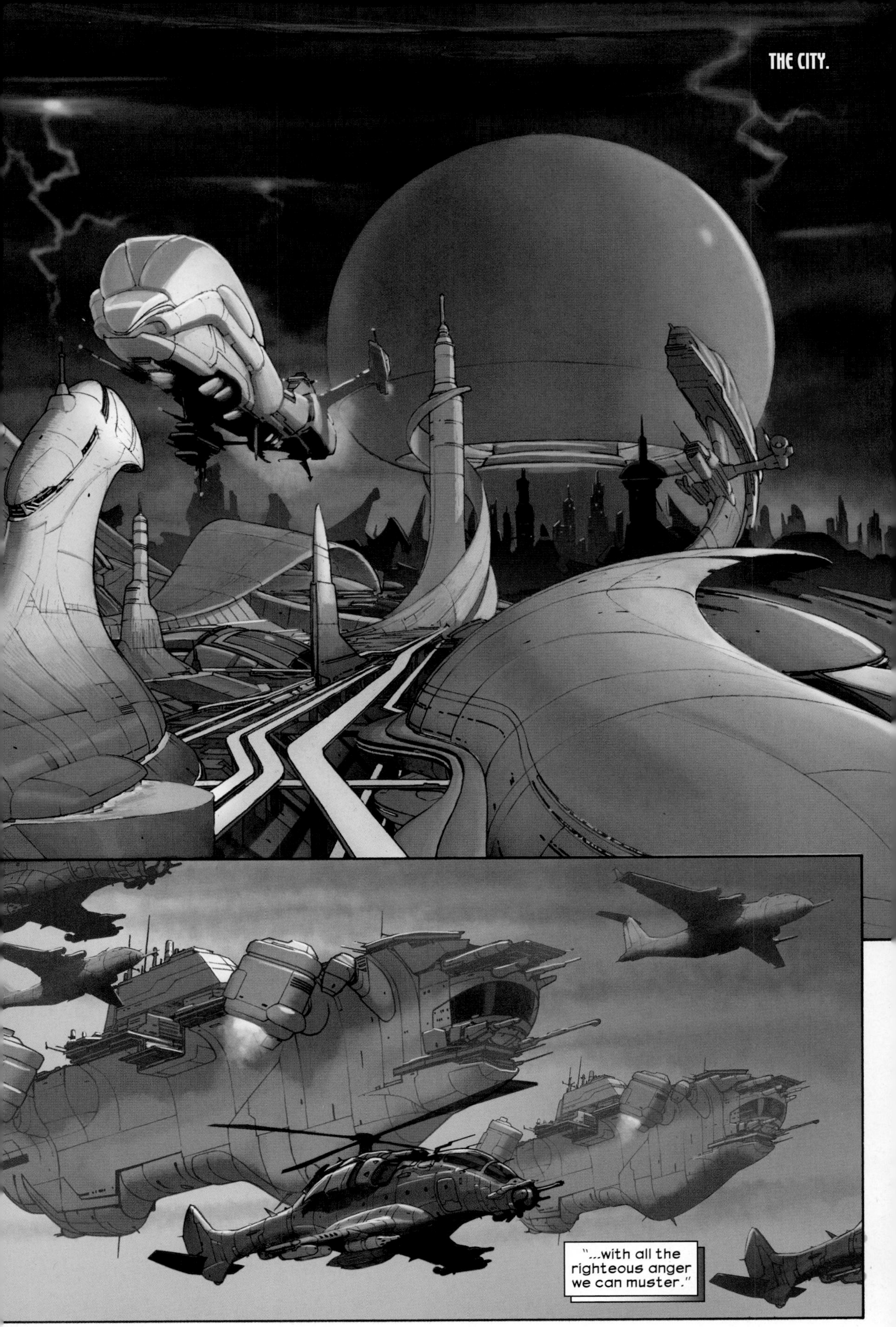
THE CITY.
"...with all the righteous anger we can muster."

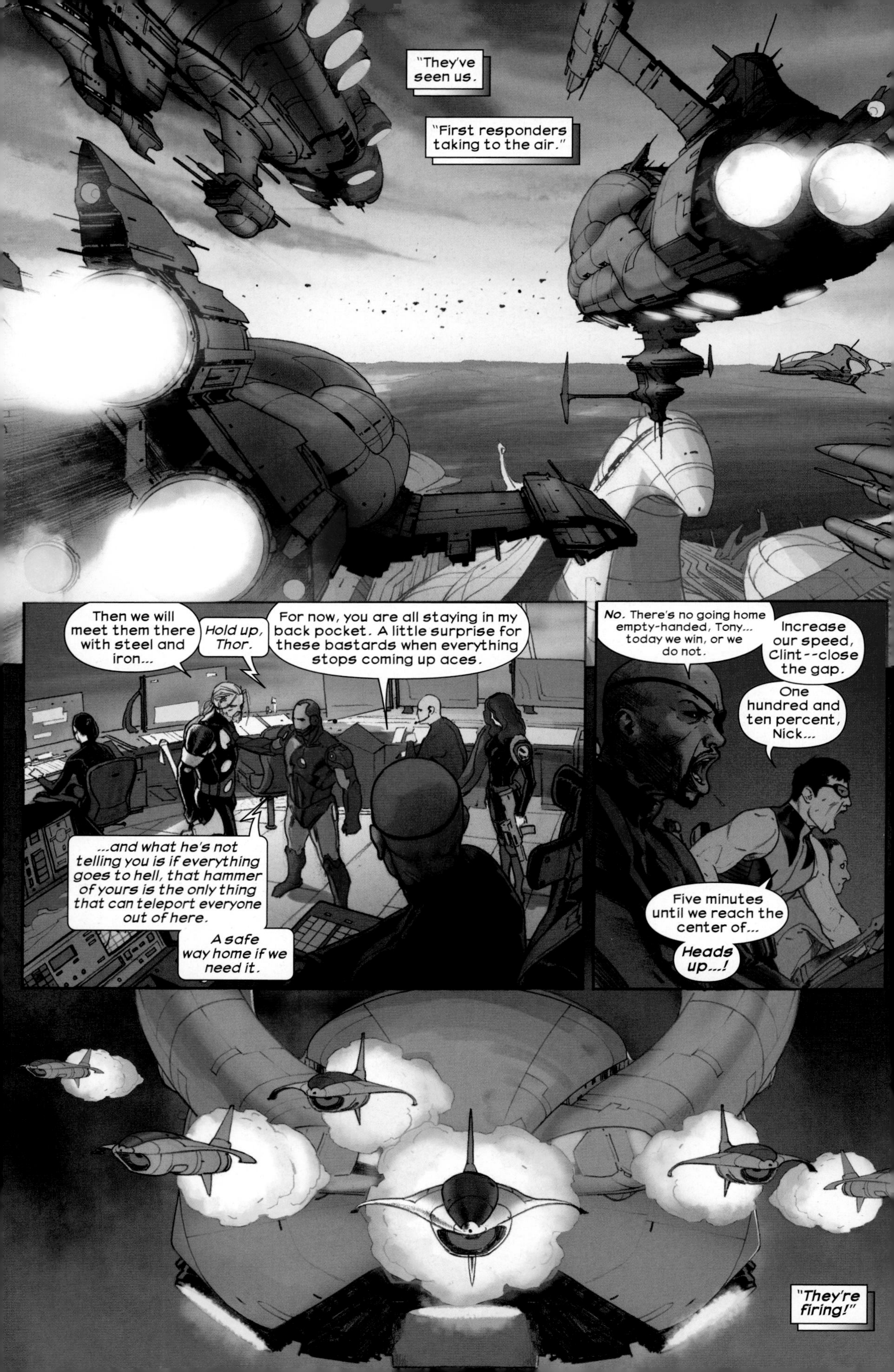
"They've seen us.
"First responders taking to the air."
Then we will meet them there with steel and iron...
Hold up, Thor.
For now, you are all staying in my back pocket. A little surprise for these bastards when everything stops coming up aces.
...and what he's not telling you is if everything goes to hell, that hammer of yours is the only thing that can teleport everyone out of here.
A safe way home if we need it.
No. There's no going home empty-handed, Tony... today we win, or we do not.
Increase our speed, Clint--close the gap.
One hundred and ten percent, Nick...
Five minutes until we reach the center of...
Heads up...!
"They're firing!"

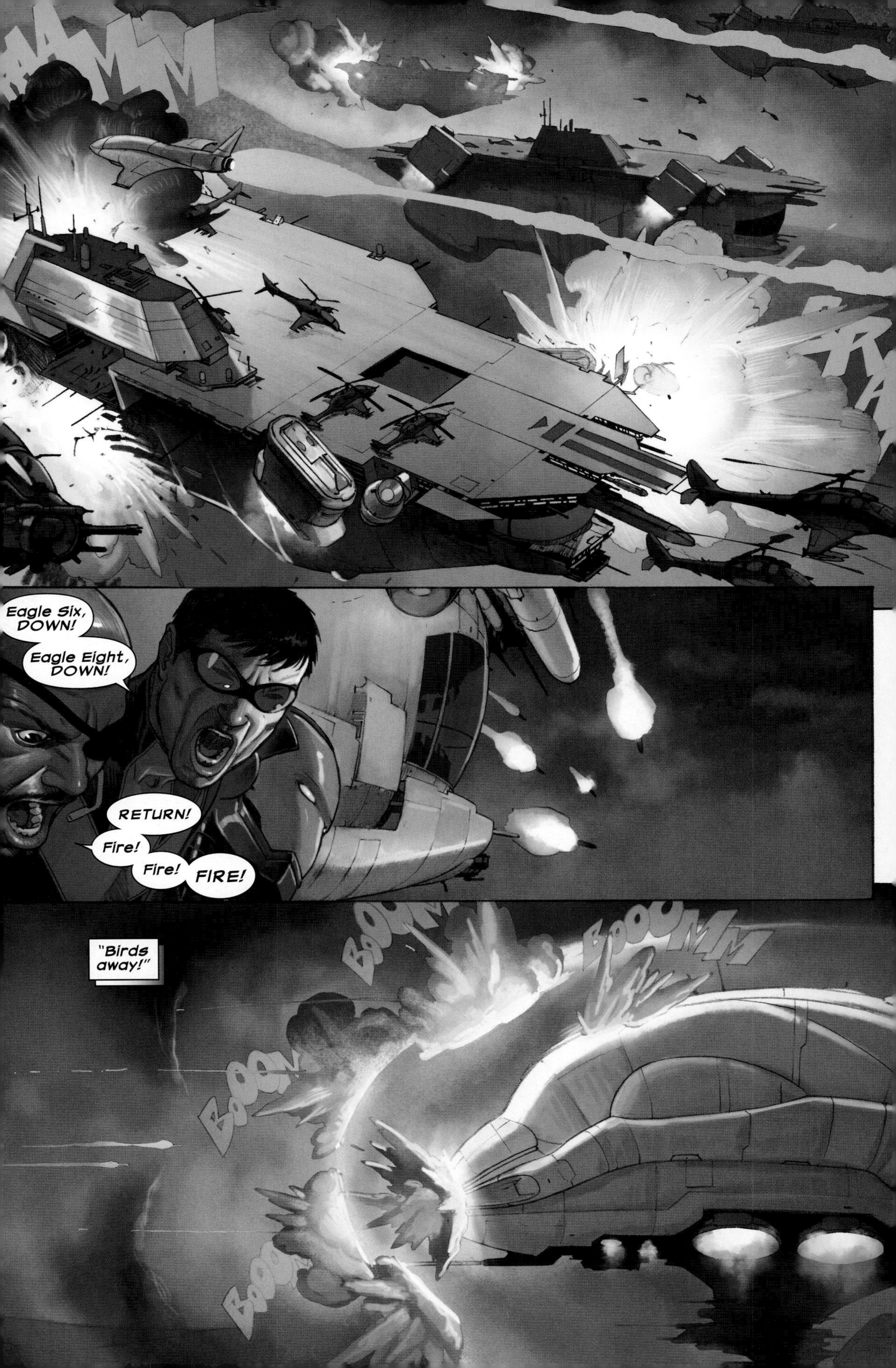

Eagle Six, DOWN!
Eagle Eight, DOWN!
RETURN!
Fire!
Fire!
FIRE!
"Birds away!"

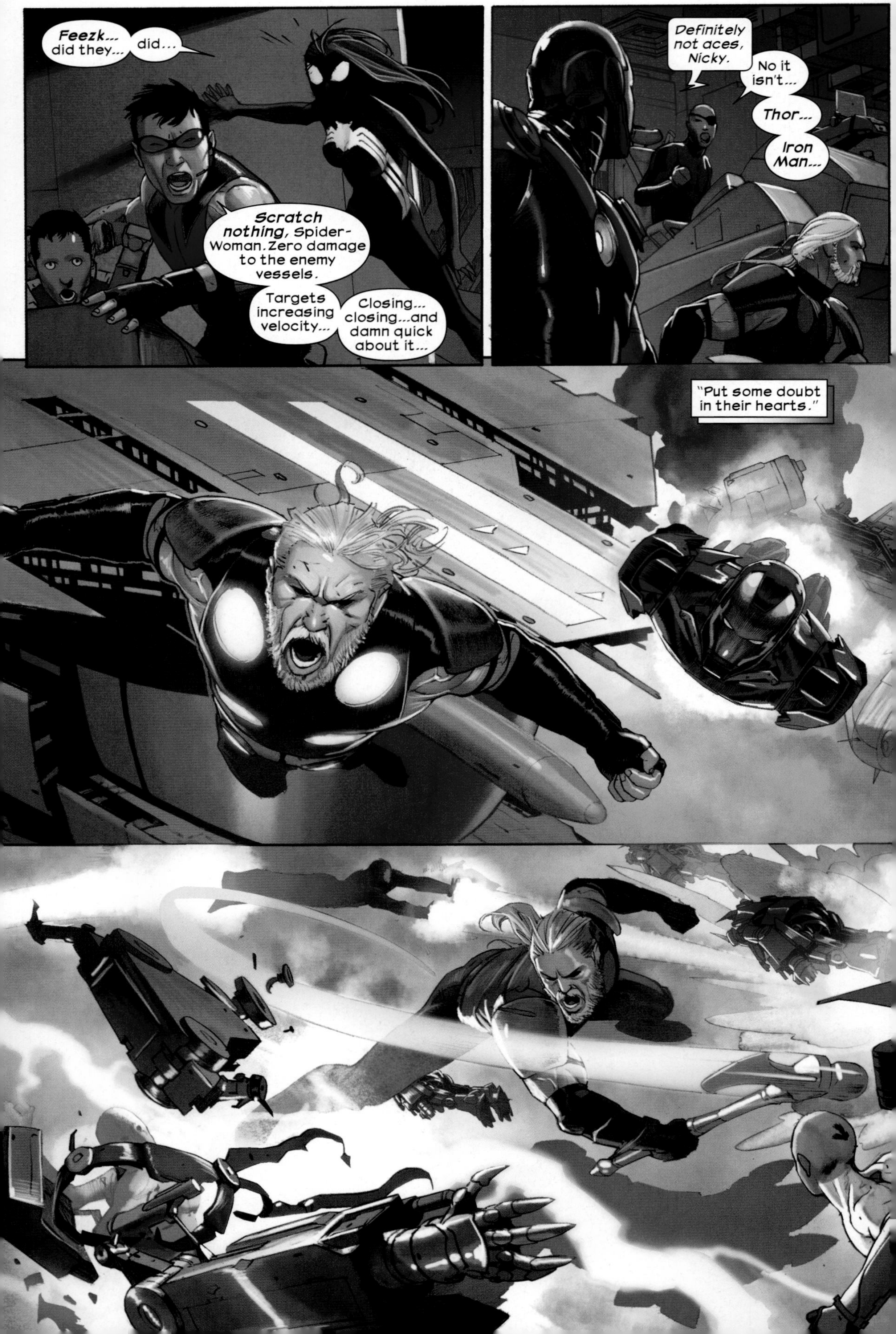
Feezk... did they...
did...
Scratch nothing, Spider-Woman. Zero damage to the enemy vessels.
Targets increasing velocity...
Closing... closing...and damn quick about it...
Definitely not aces, Nicky.
No it isn't...
Thor...
Iron Man...
"Put some doubt in their hearts."

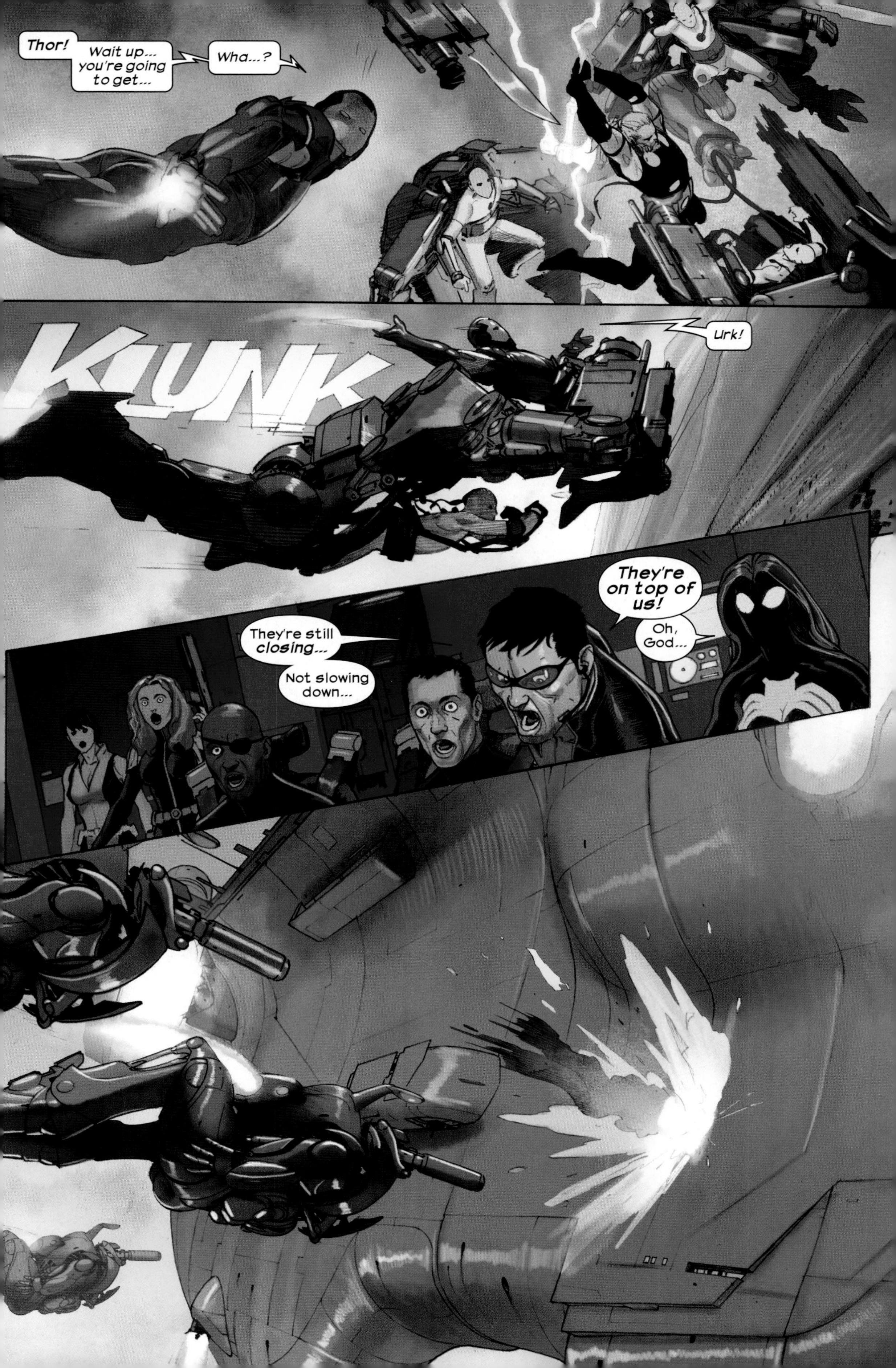
Thor!
Wait up... you're going to get...
Wha...?
KLUNK
Urk!
They're still closing...
Not slowing down...
They're on top of us!
Oh, God...

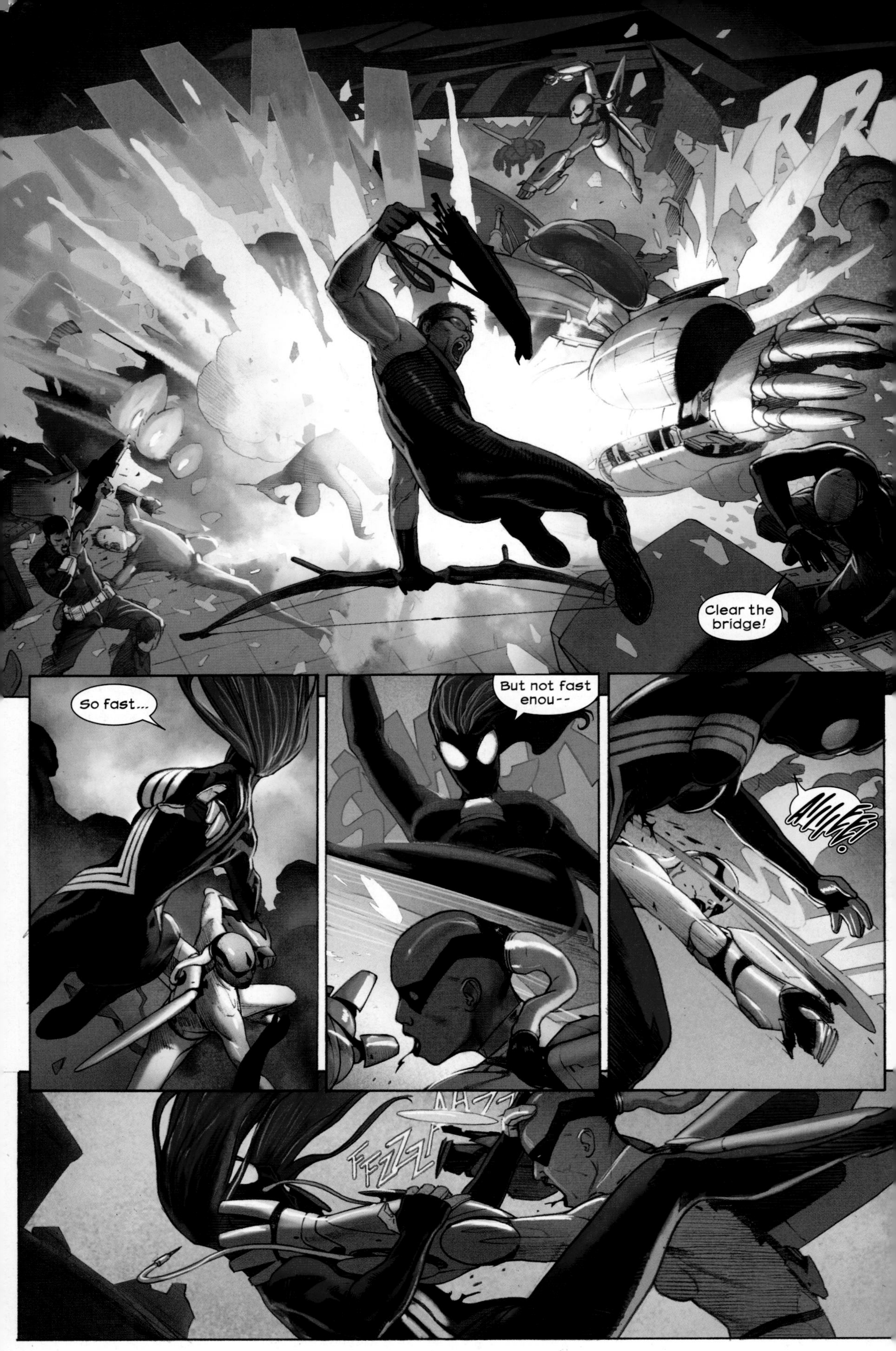
Clear the bridge!
So fast...
But not fast enou--

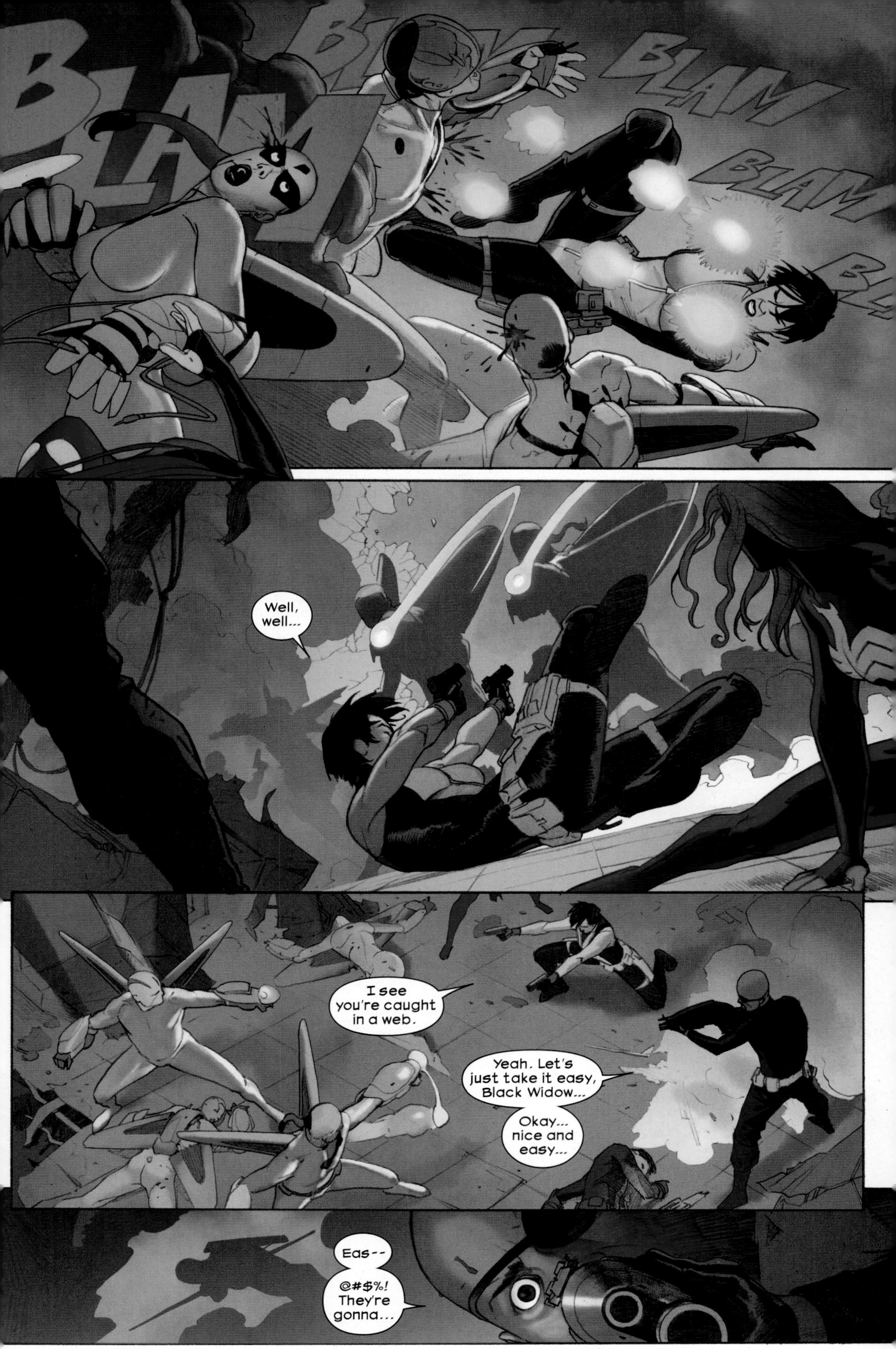
BLAM
BLAM
BLAM
BLAM
BL
Well, well...
I see you're caught in a web.
Yeah. Let's just take it easy, Black Widow...
Okay... nice and easy...
Eas--
@#$%! They're gonna...

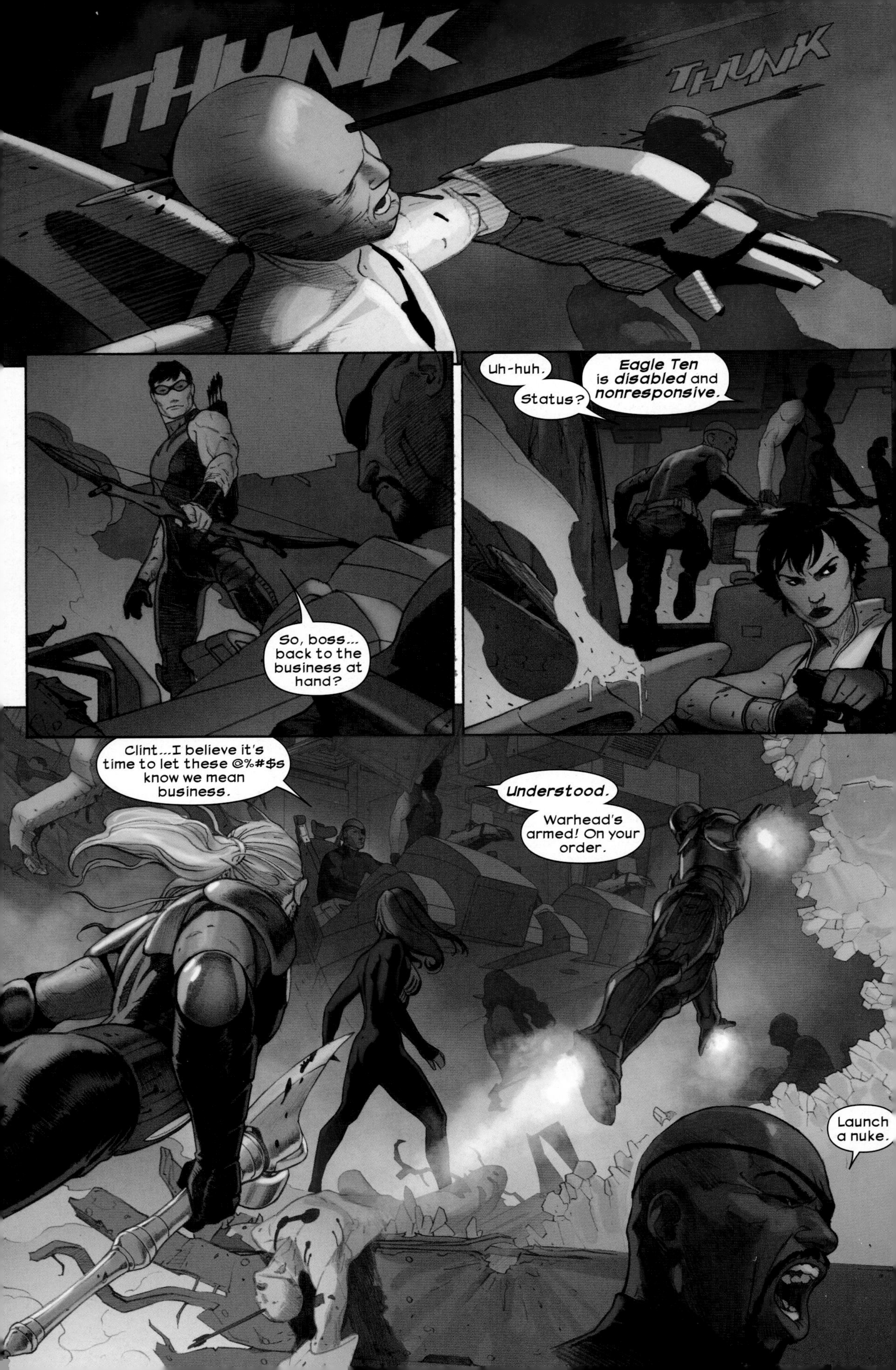
THUNK
THUNK
Uh-huh.
Status?
Eagle Ten is disabled and nonresponsive.
So, boss... back to the business at hand?
Clint...I believe it's time to let these @%#$s know we mean business.
Understood.
Warhead's armed! On your order.
Launch a nuke.

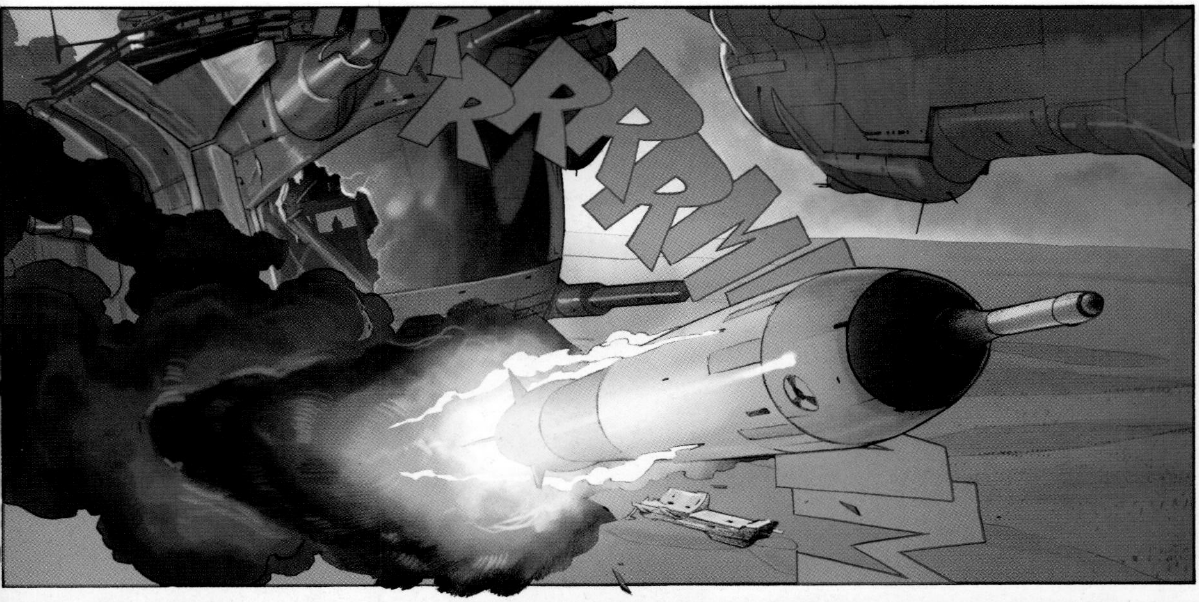

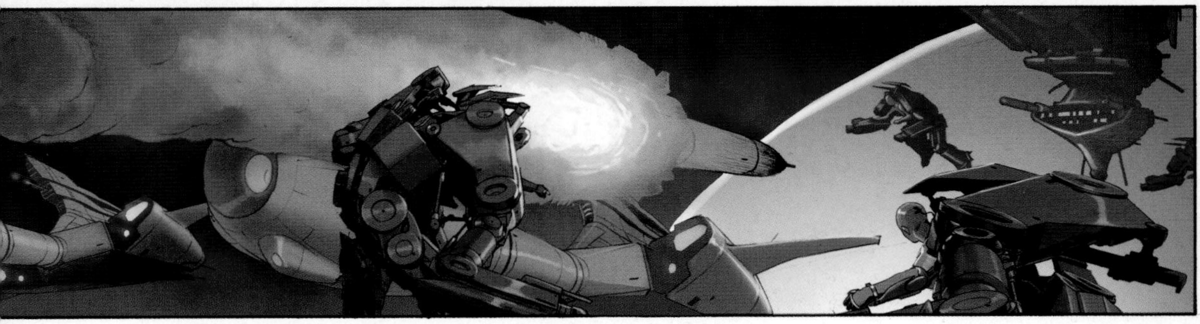

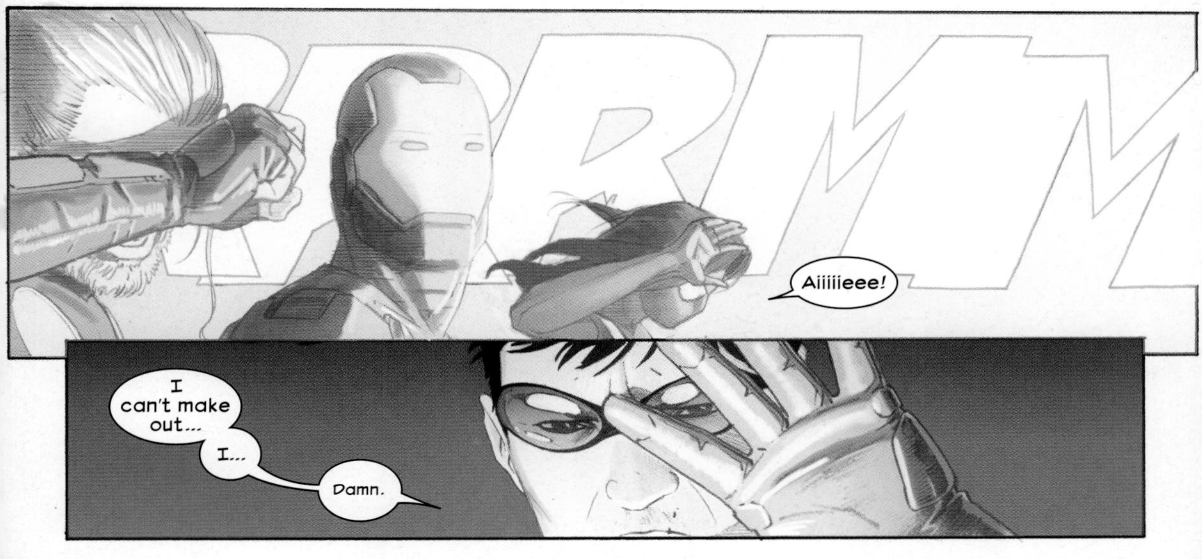
Aiiiiieee!
I can't make out...
I...
Damn.

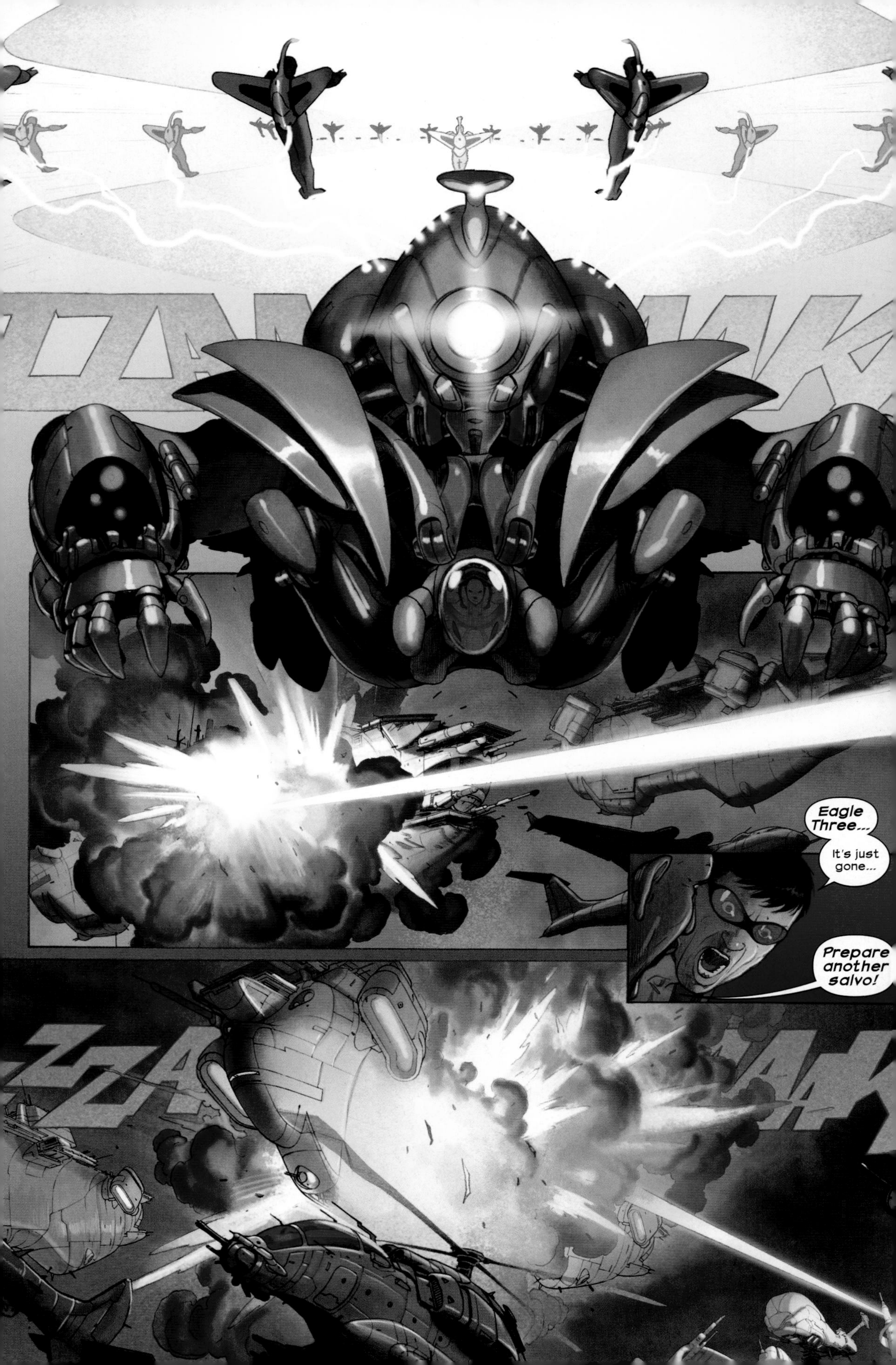
Eagle Three...
It's just gone...
Prepare another salvo!

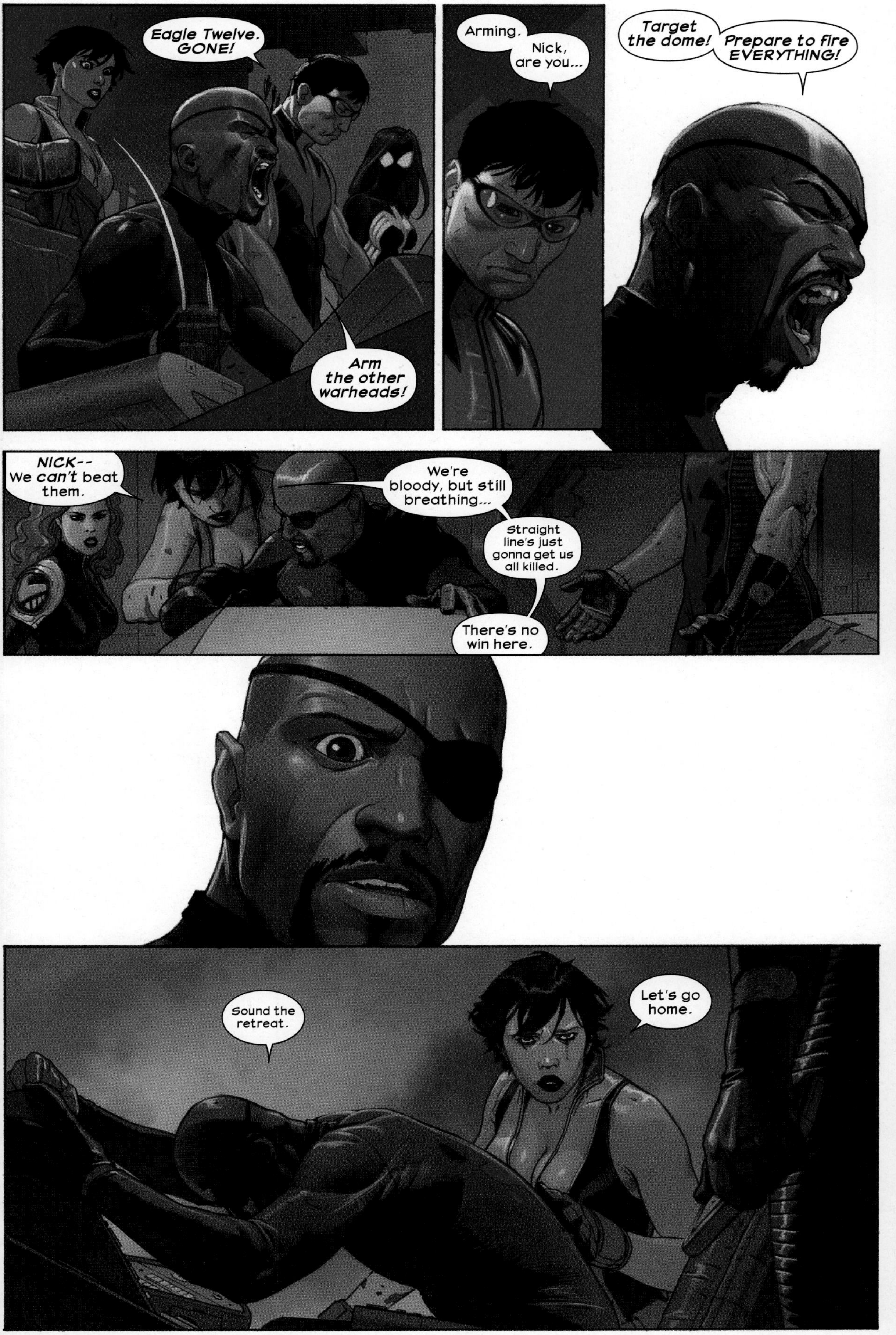
Eagle Twelve. GONE!
Arm the other warheads!
Arming.
Nick, are you...
Target the dome!
Prepare to fire EVERYTHING!
NICK-- We can't beat them.
We're bloody, but still breathing...
Straight line's just gonna get us all killed.
There's no win here.
Sound the retreat.
Let's go home.

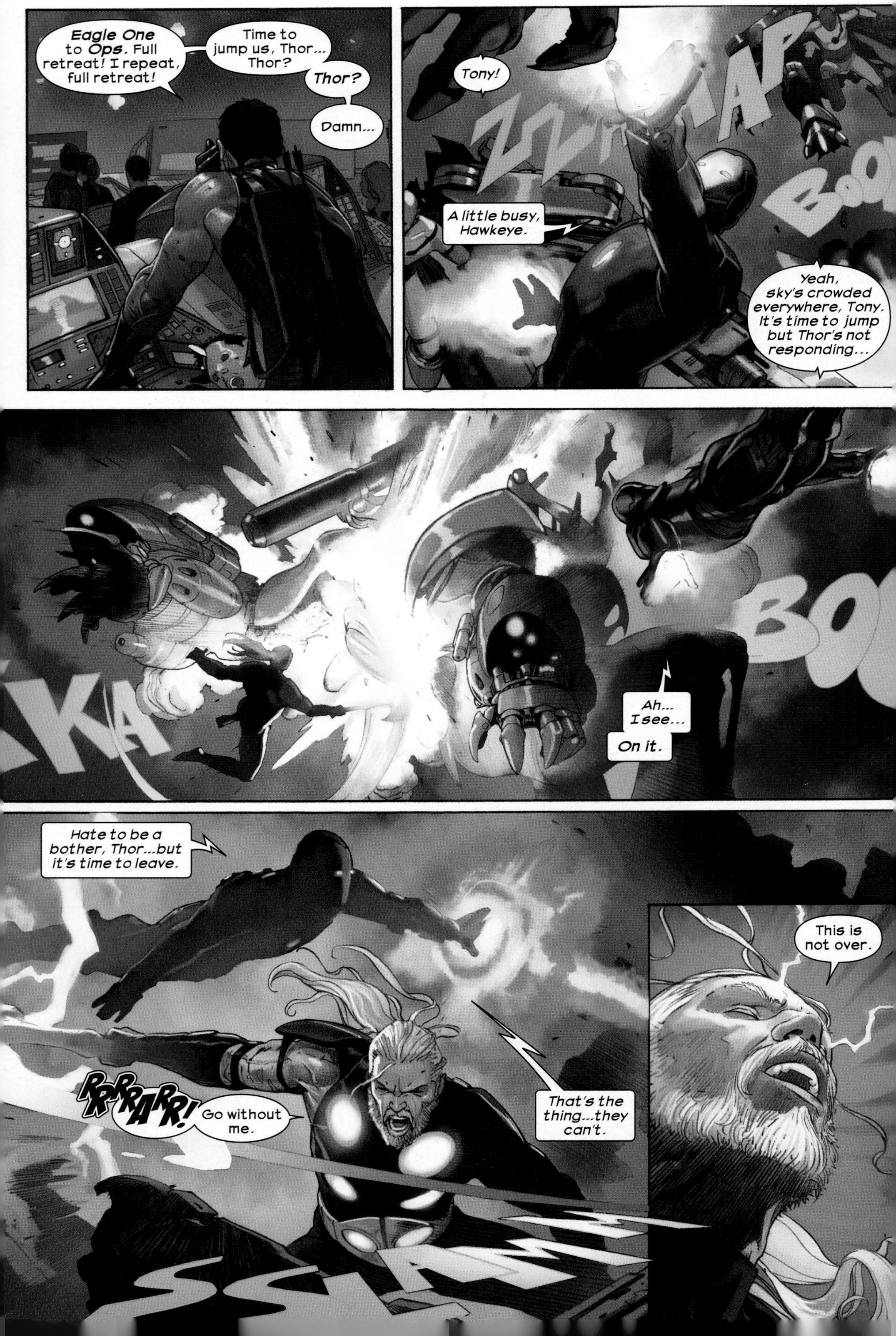
Eagle One to Ops. Full retreat! I repeat, full retreat!
Time to jump us, Thor... Thor?
Thor?
Damn...
Tony!
ZZZRAP
A little busy, Hawkeye.
BOO
Yeah, sky's crowded everywhere, Tony. It's time to jump but Thor's not responding...
KA
BOO
Ah... I see...
On it.
Hate to be a bother, Thor...but it's time to leave.
RRRRARR!
Go without me.
That's the thing...they can't.
This is not over.

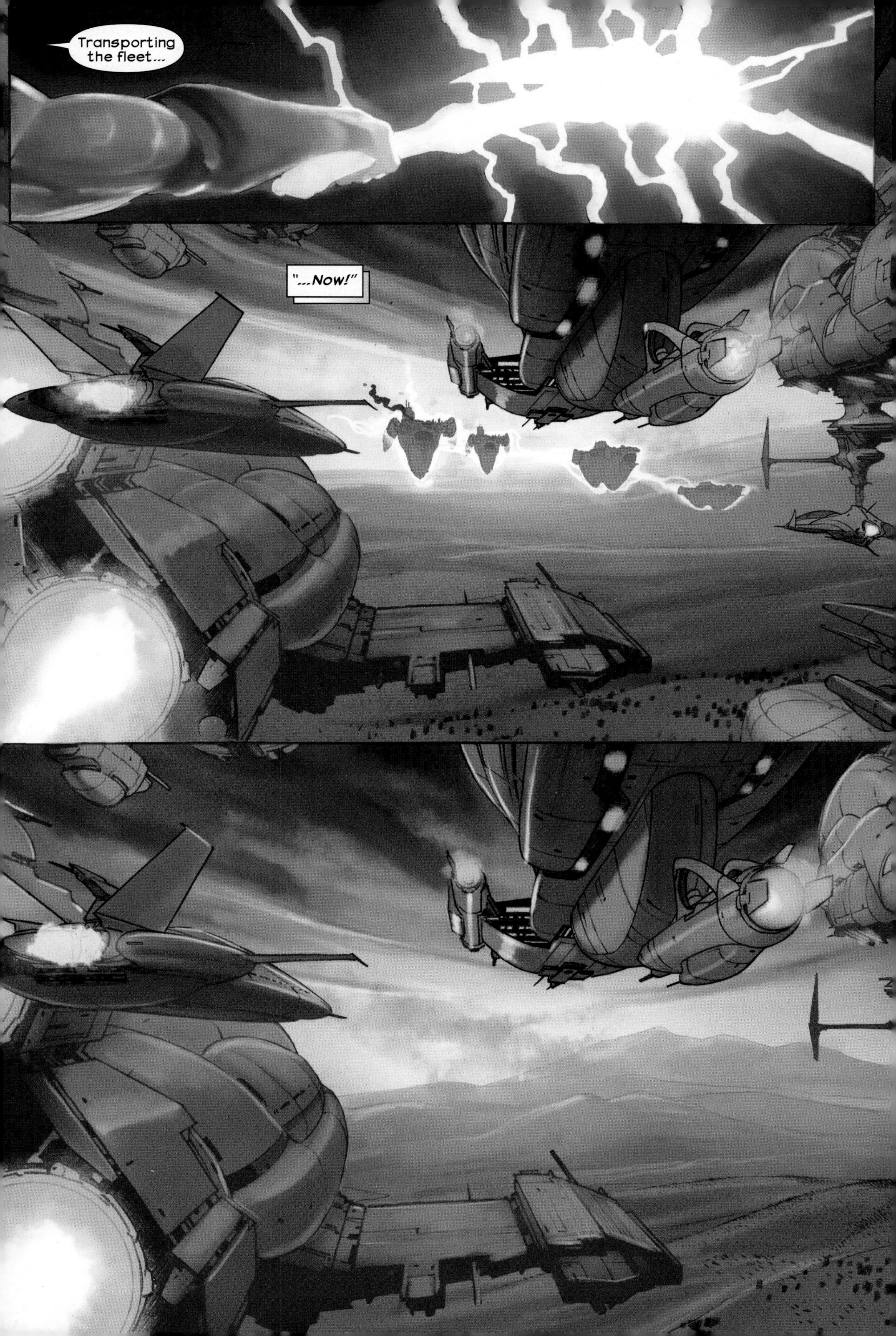
Transporting the fleet...
"...Now!"

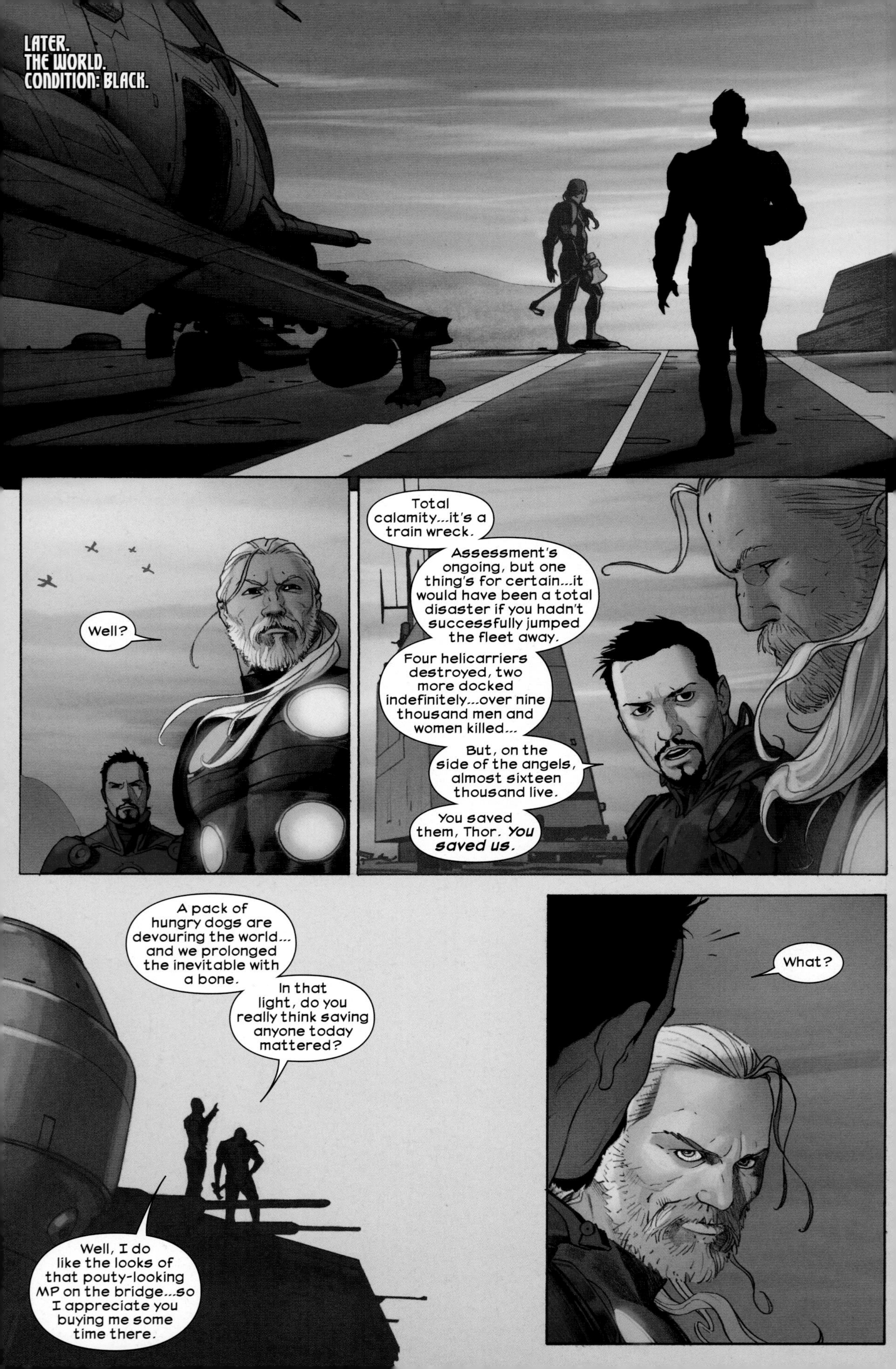
LATER.
THE WORLD.
CONDITION: BLACK.
Well?
Total calamity...it's a train wreck.
Assessment's ongoing, but one thing's for certain...it would have been a total disaster if you hadn't successfully jumped the fleet away.
Four helicarriers destroyed, two more docked indefinitely...over nine thousand men and women killed...
But, on the side of the angels, almost sixteen thousand live.
You saved them, Thor. You saved us.
A pack of hungry dogs are devouring the world... and we prolonged the inevitable with a bone.
In that light, do you really think saving anyone today mattered?
Well, I do like the looks of that pouty-looking MP on the bridge...so I appreciate you buying me some time there.
What?

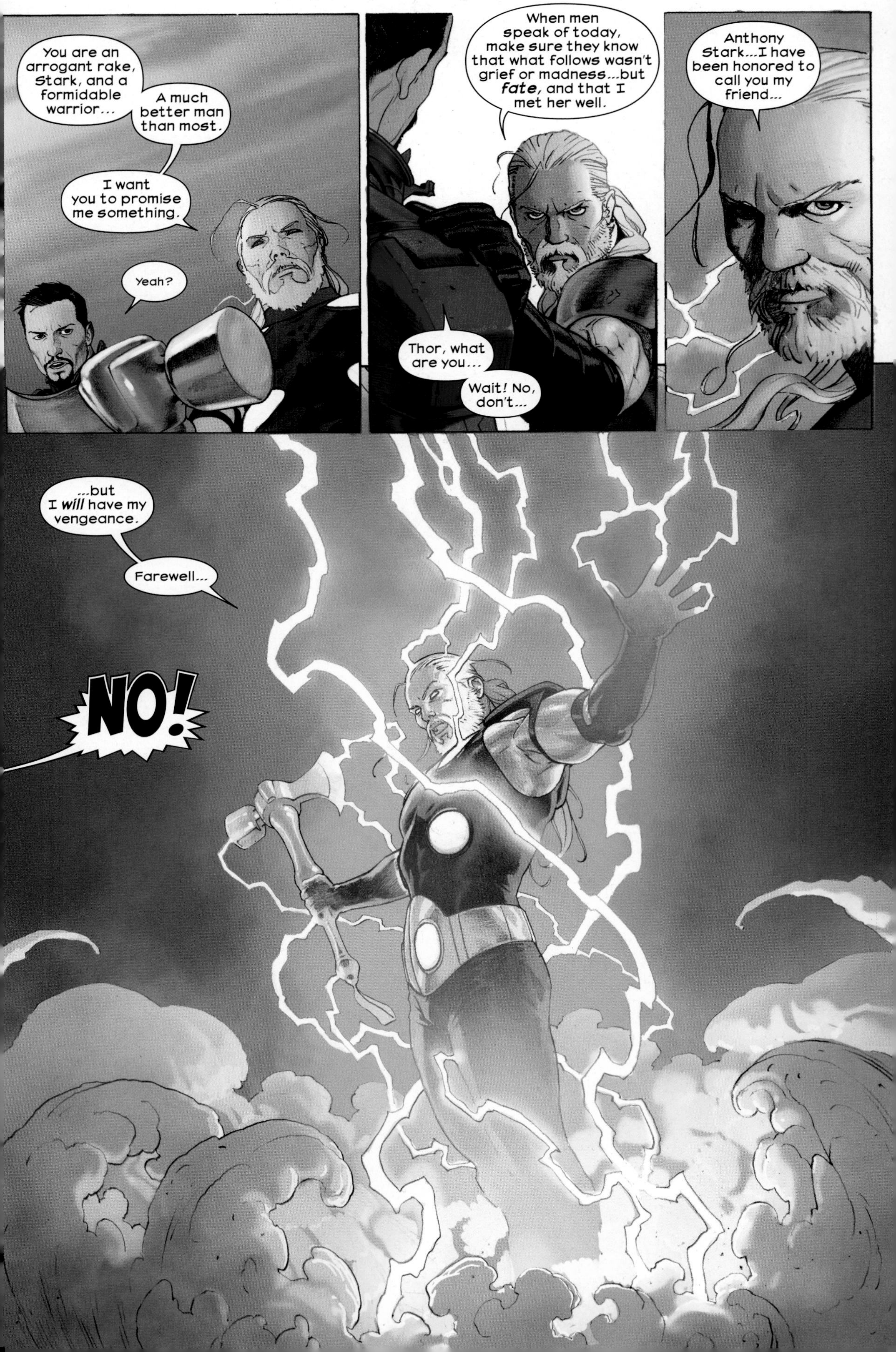
You are an arrogant rake, Stark, and a formidable warrior...
A much better man than most.
I want you to promise me something.
Yeah?
When men speak of today, make sure they know that what follows wasn't grief or madness...but *fate*, and that I met her well.
Thor, what are you...
Wait! No, don't...
Anthony Stark...I have been honored to call you my friend...
...but I *will* have my vengeance.
Farewell...
NO!

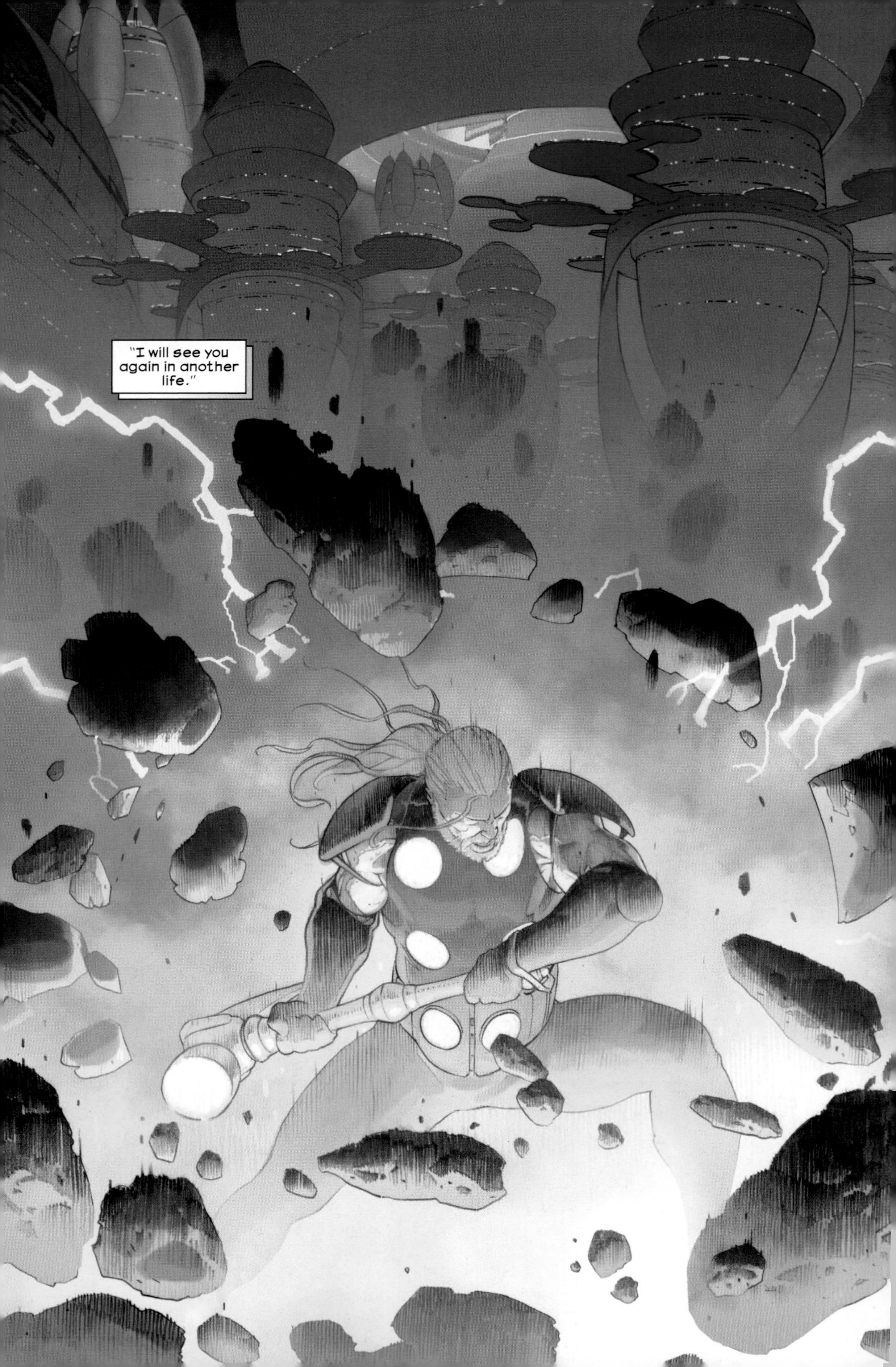
"I will see you again in another life."

#4 VARIANT
BY CHRIS STEVENS

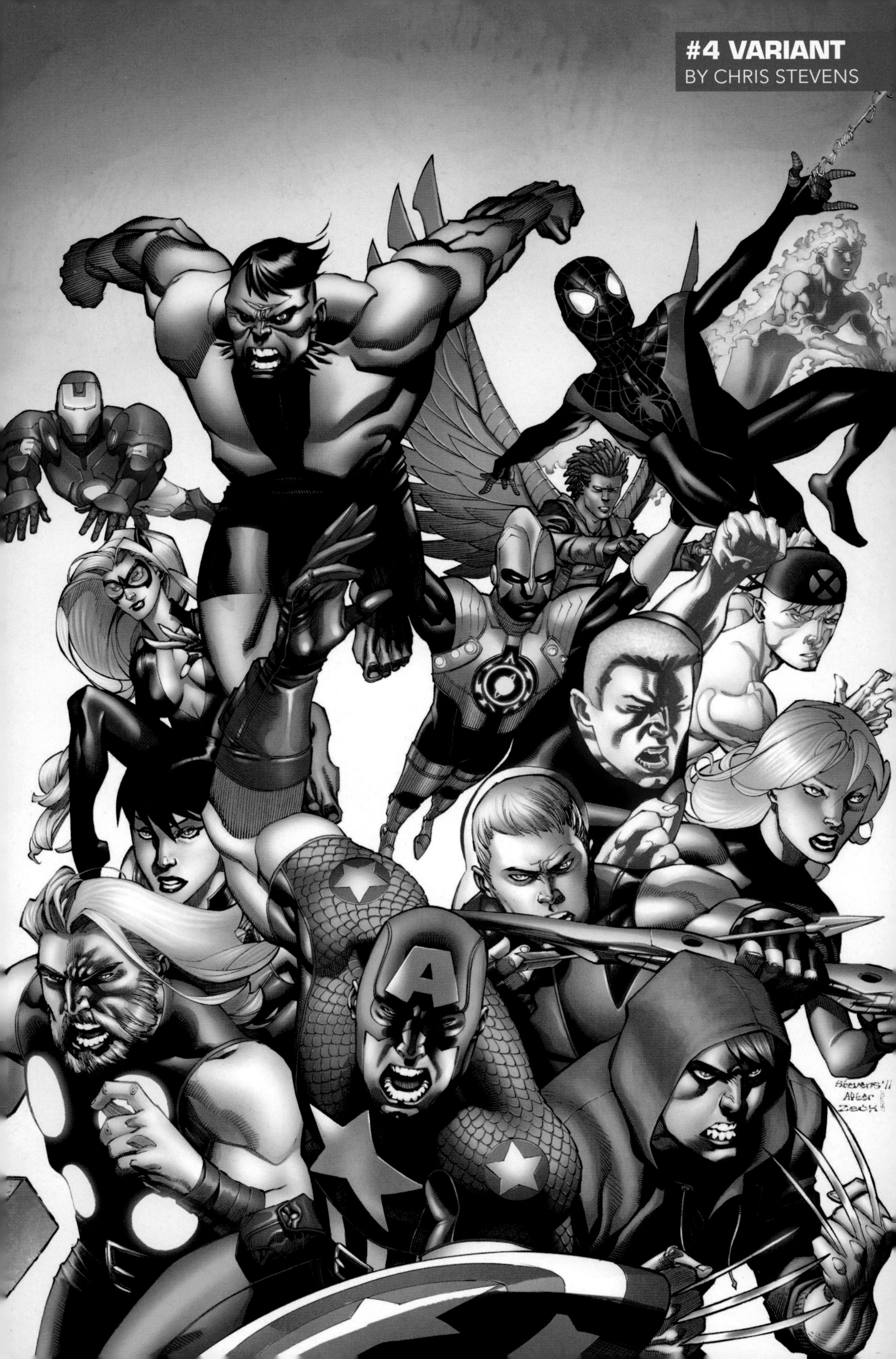
Stevens'11
After
Zeck

4

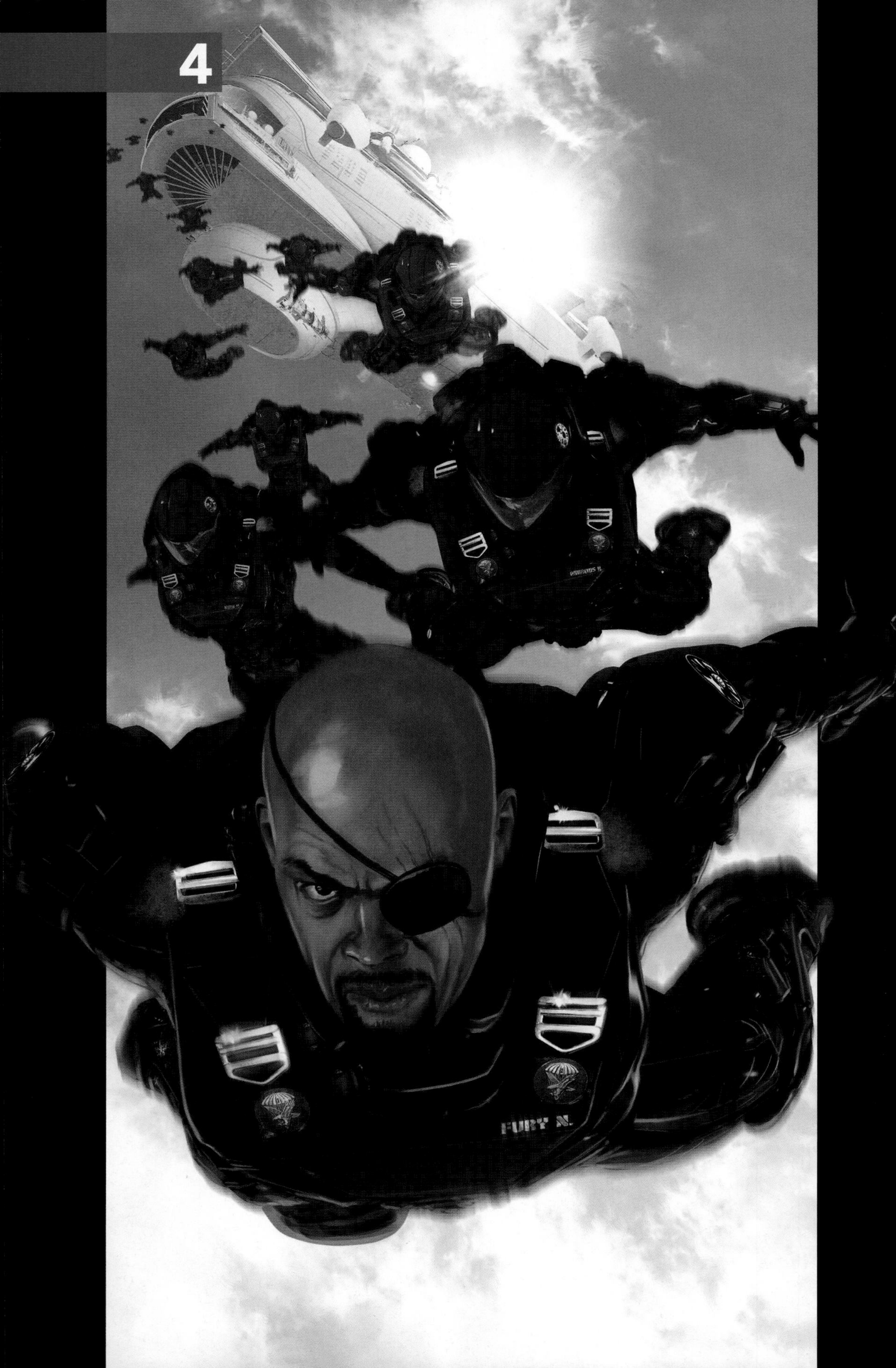
FURY N.

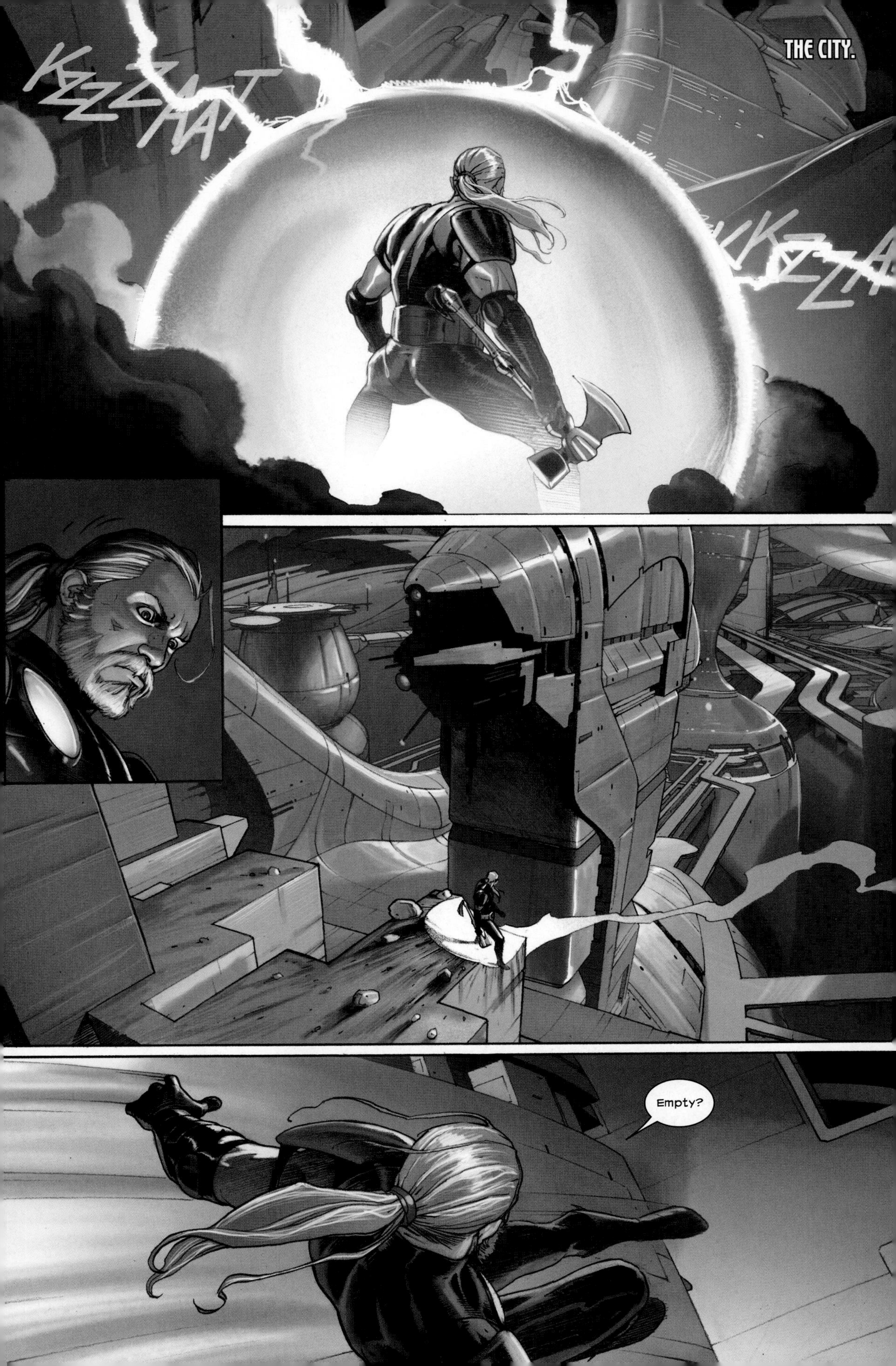
THE CITY.
KZZZAAT
KKZZZA
Empty?

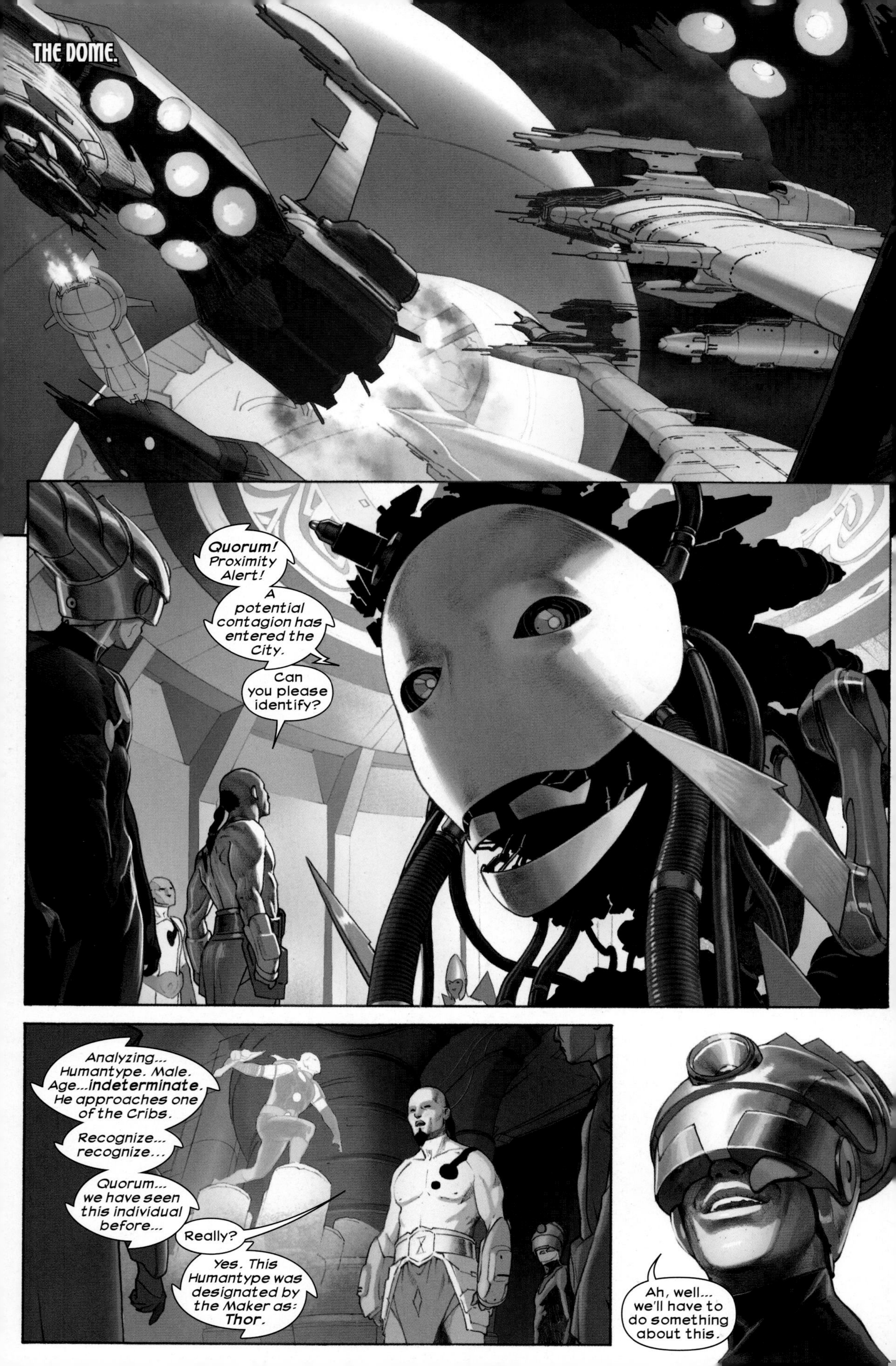
THE DOME.
Quorum! Proximity Alert!
A potential contagion has entered the City.
Can you please identify?
Analyzing... Humantype. Male. Age...indeterminate. He approaches one of the Cribs.
Recognize... recognize...
Quorum... we have seen this individual before...
Really?
Yes. This Humantype was designated by the Maker as: Thor.
Ah, well... we'll have to do something about this.

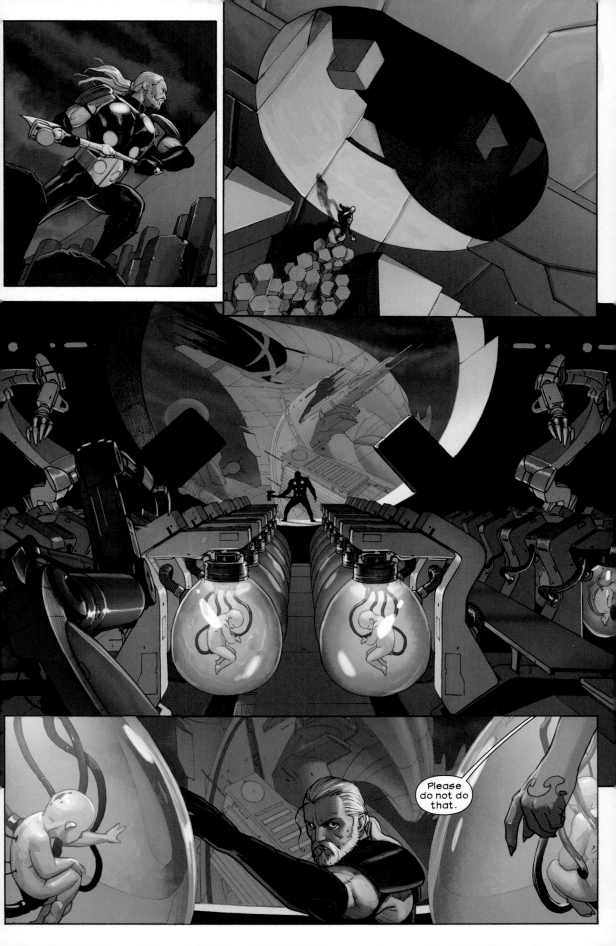

Please do not do that.

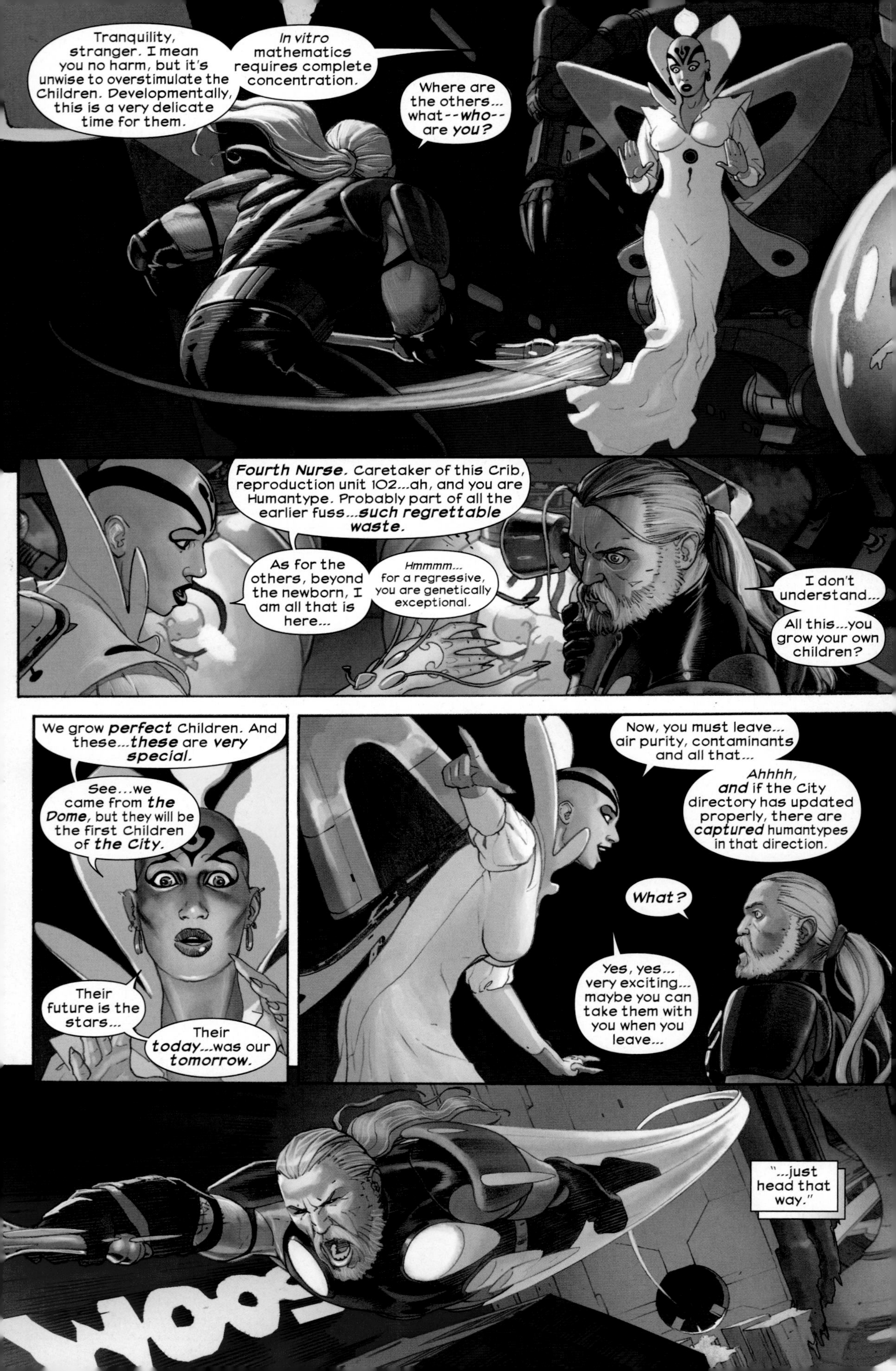

Tranquility, stranger. I mean you no harm, but it's unwise to overstimulate the Children. Developmentally, this is a very delicate time for them.
In vitro mathematics requires complete concentration.
Where are the others... what--*who*--are *you*?
Fourth Nurse. Caretaker of this Crib, reproduction unit 102...ah, and you are Humantype. Probably part of all the earlier fuss...***such regrettable waste.***
As for the others, beyond the newborn, I am all that is here...
Hmmmm... for a regressive, you are genetically exceptional.
I don't understand...
All this...you grow your own children?
We grow ***perfect*** Children. And these...***these*** are ***very special.***
See...we came from ***the Dome,*** but they will be the first Children of ***the City.***
Their future is the stars...
Their ***today***...was our ***tomorrow.***
Now, you must leave... air purity, contaminants and all that...
Ahhhh, ***and*** if the City directory has updated properly, there are ***captured*** humantypes in that direction.
What?
Yes, yes... very exciting... maybe you can take them with you when you leave...
"...just head that way."

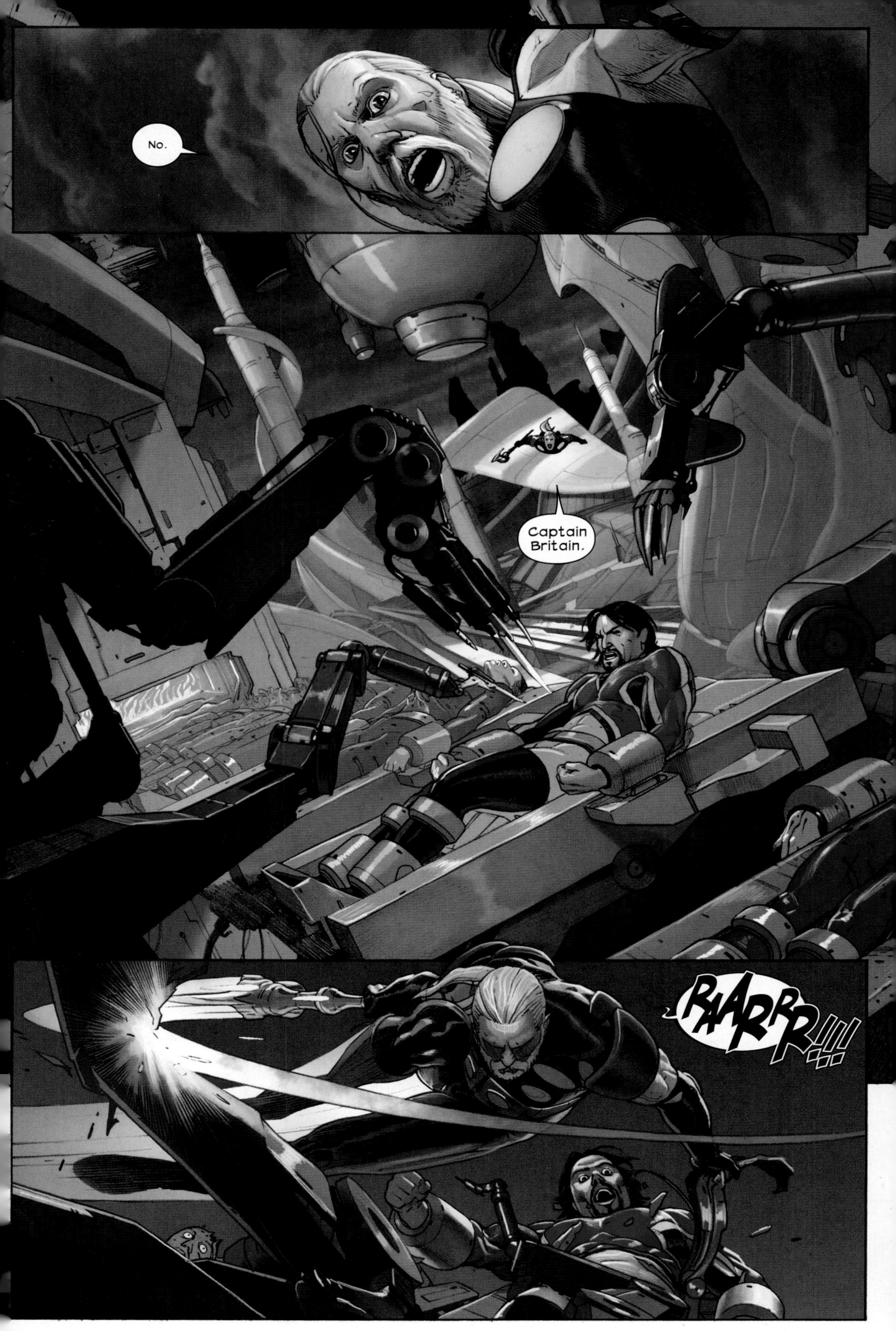
No.
Captain Britain.
RAARRR!!!!

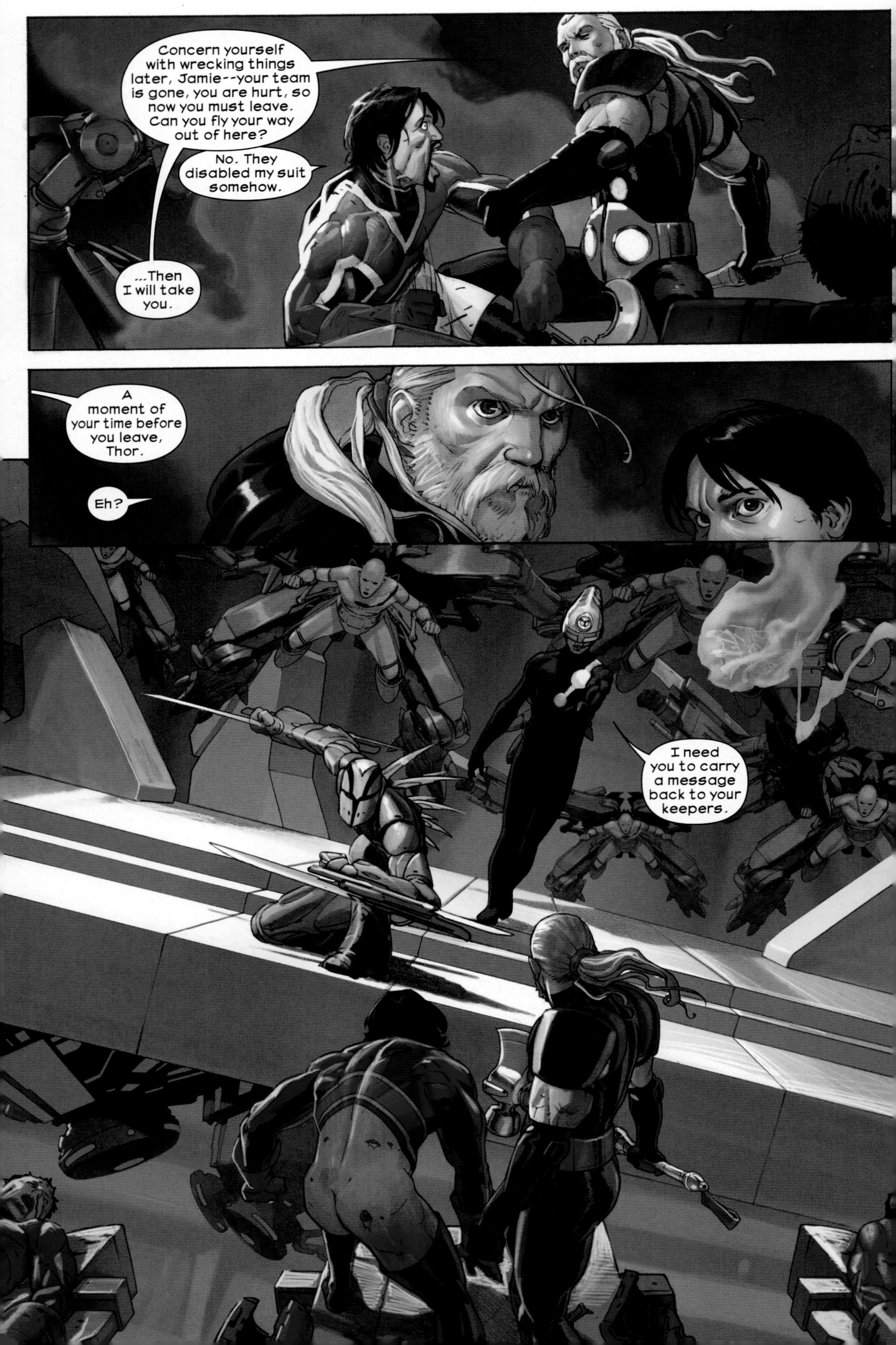
Concern yourself with wrecking things later, Jamie--your team is gone, you are hurt, so now you must leave. Can you fly your way out of here?
No. They disabled my suit somehow.
...Then I will take you.
A moment of your time before you leave, Thor.
Eh?
I need you to carry a message back to your keepers.

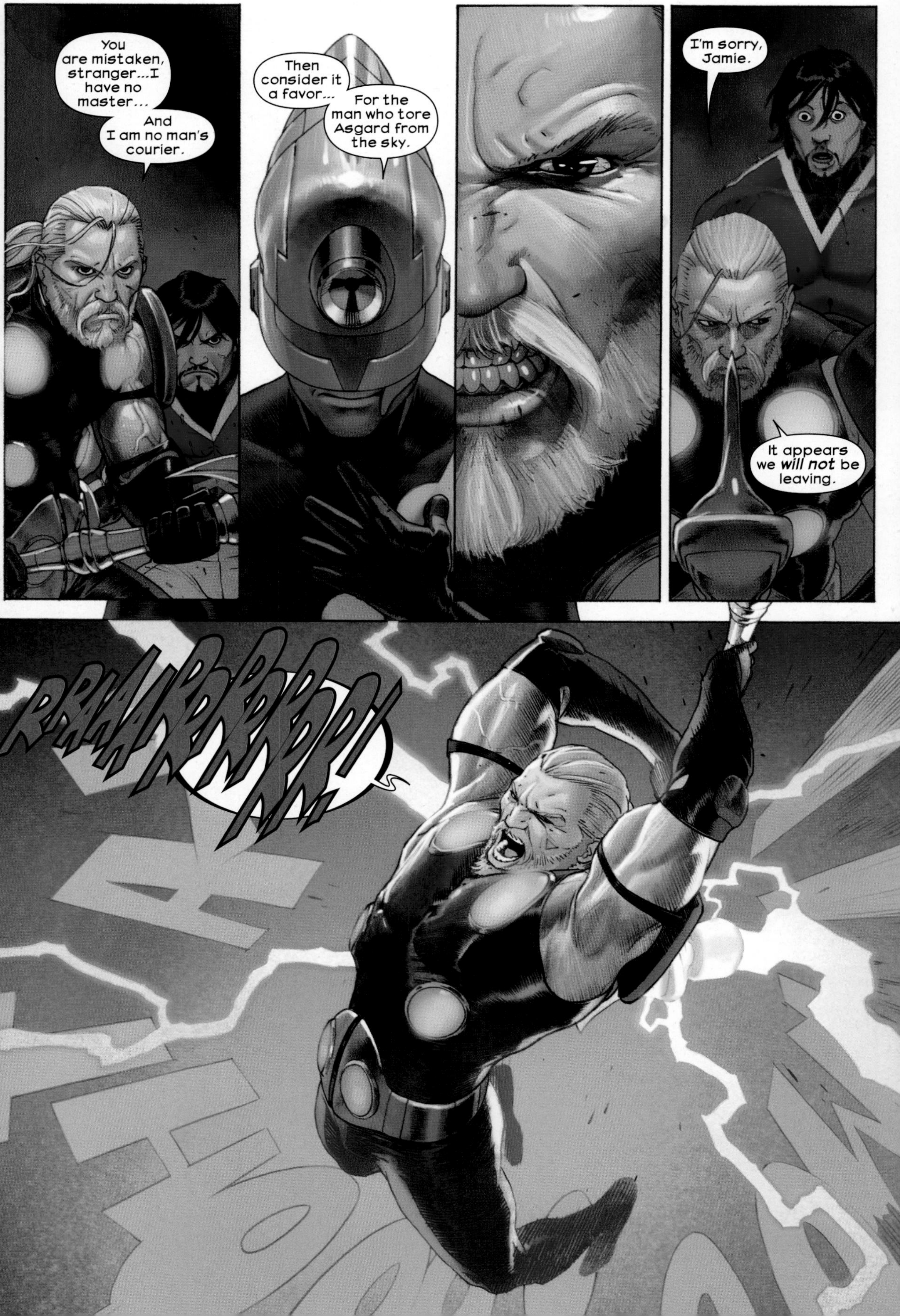
You are mistaken, stranger...I have no master...
And I am no man's courier.
Then consider it a favor...
For the man who tore Asgard from the sky.
I'm sorry, Jamie.
It appears we *will not* be leaving.
RRAAAARRRRR!

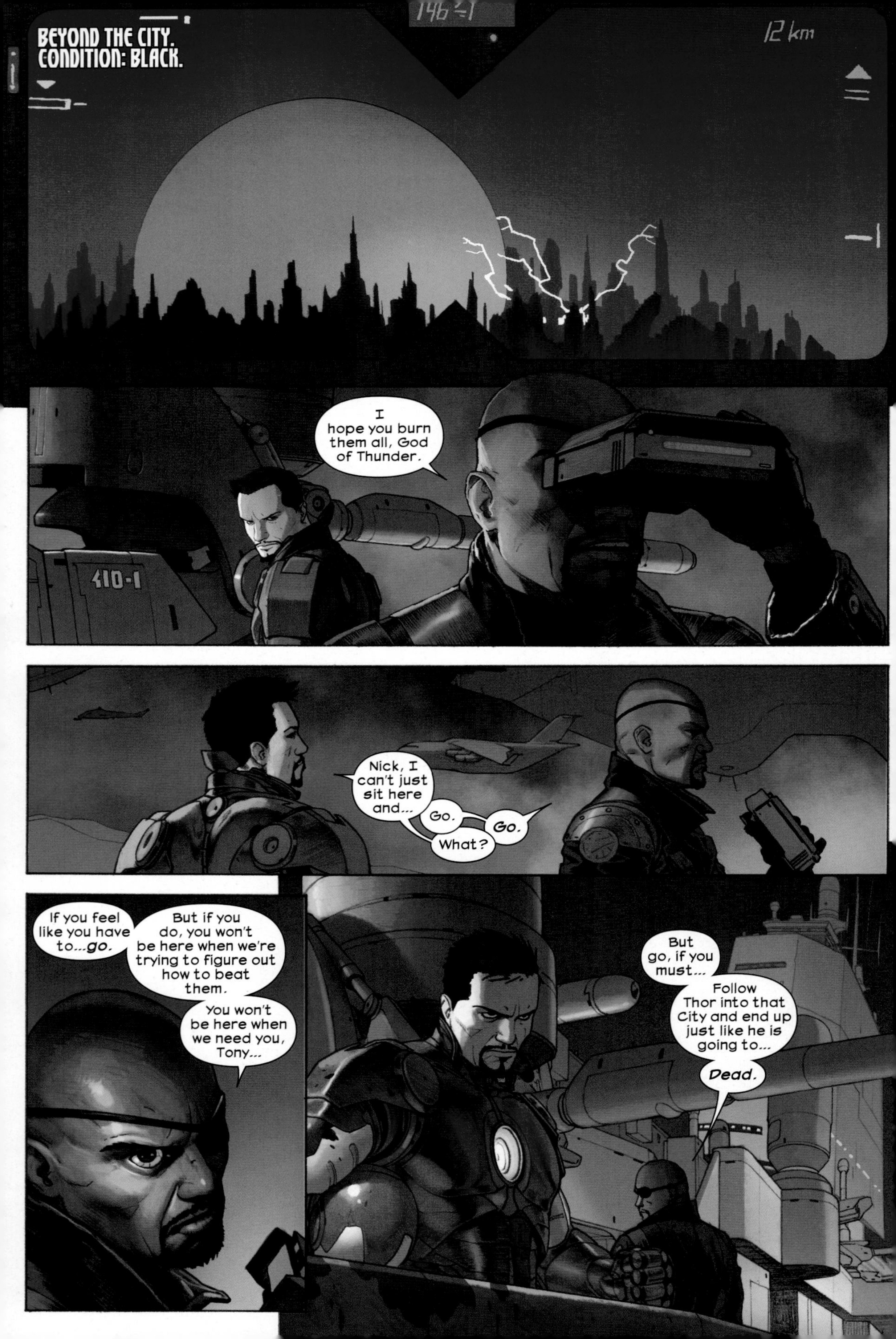

BEYOND THE CITY.
CONDITION: BLACK.
146
12 km
410-1
I hope you burn them all, God of Thunder.
Nick, I can't just sit here and...
Go.
What?
Go.
If you feel like you have to...go.
But if you do, you won't be here when we're trying to figure out how to beat them.
You won't be here when we need you, Tony...
But go, if you must...
Follow Thor into that City and end up just like he is going to...
Dead.

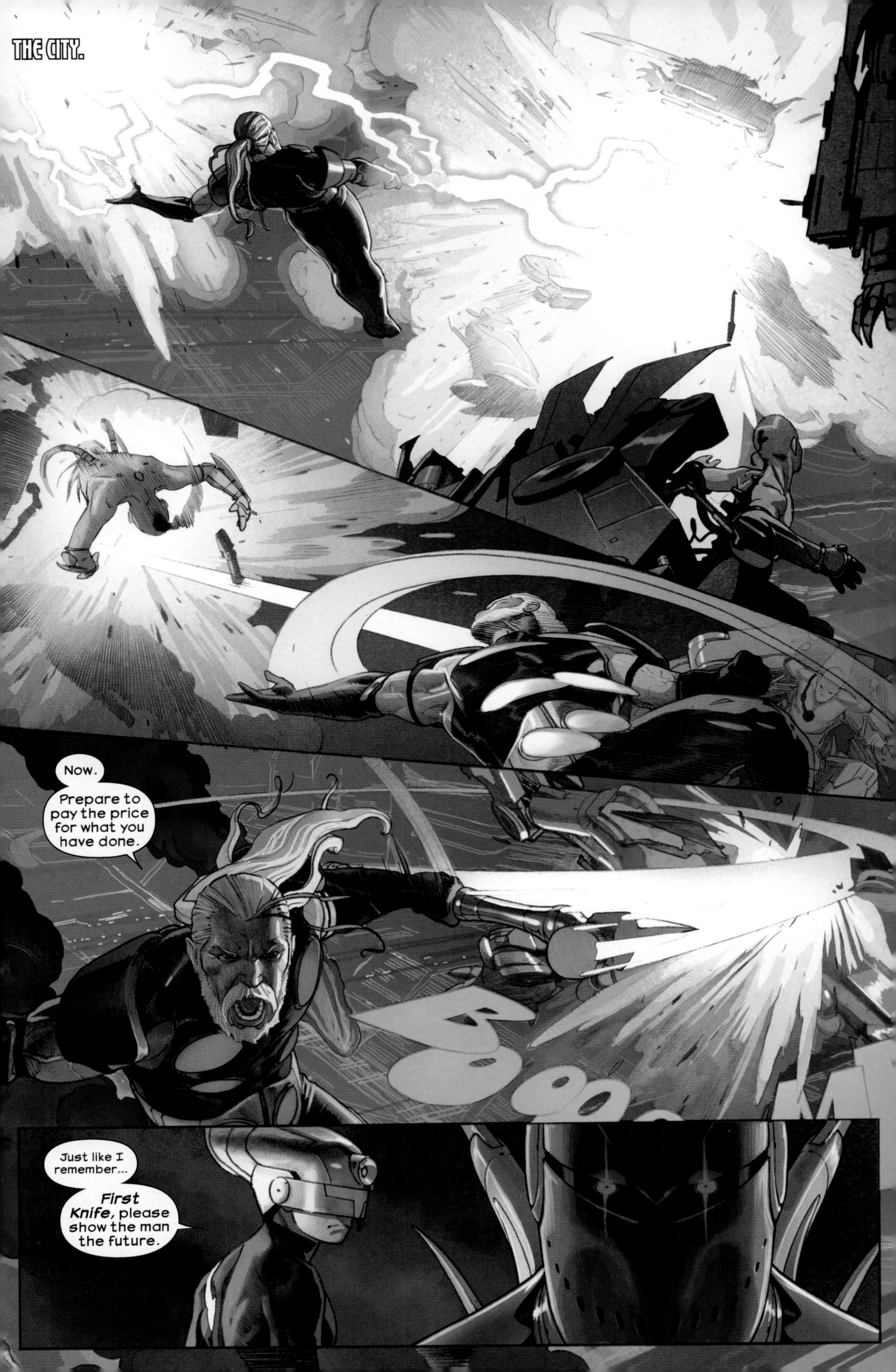
THE CITY.
Now.
Prepare to pay the price for what you have done.
Just like I remember...
First Knife, please show the man the future.

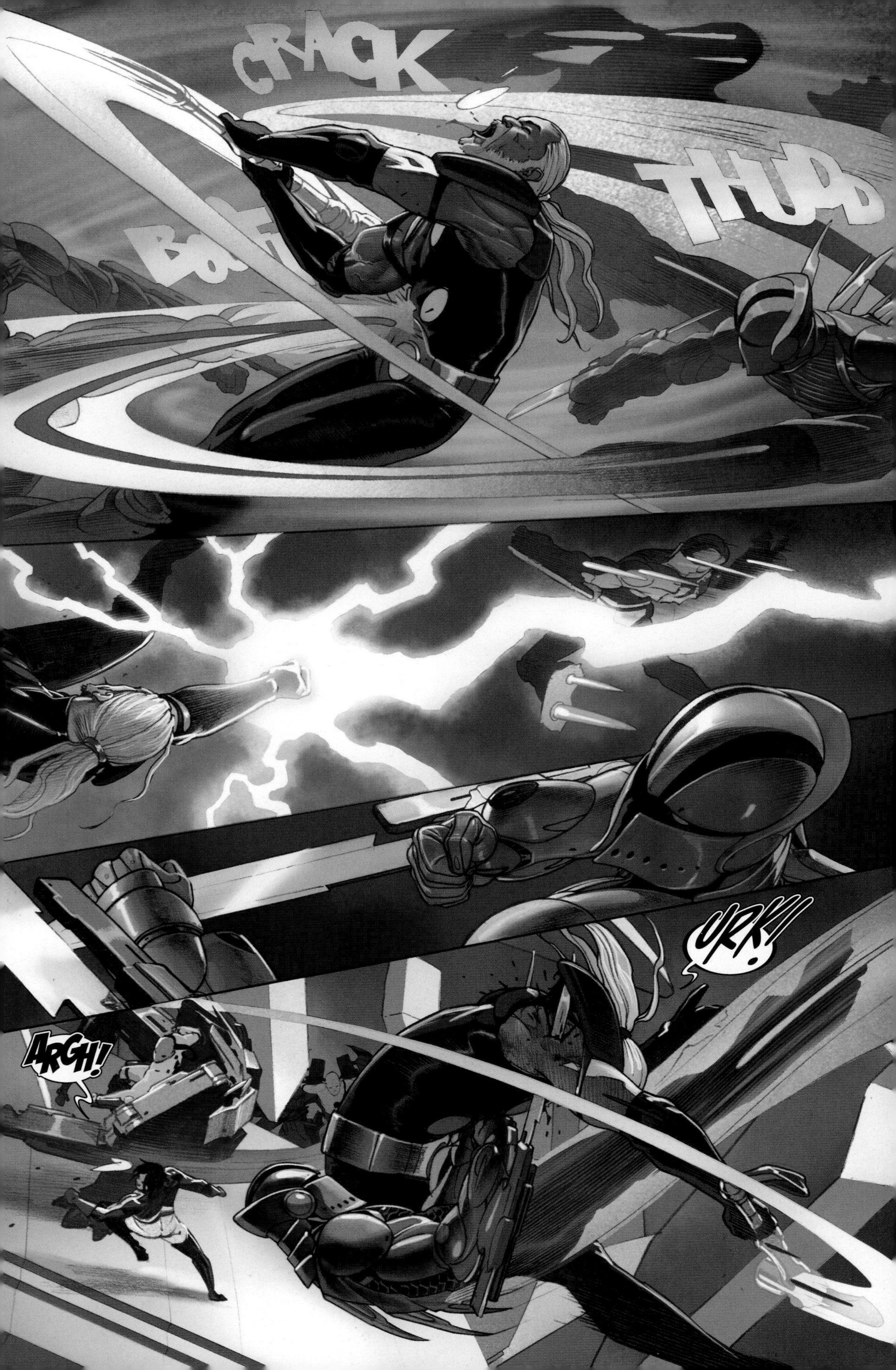
CRACK
THUD
BOOF
URK!!
ARGH!

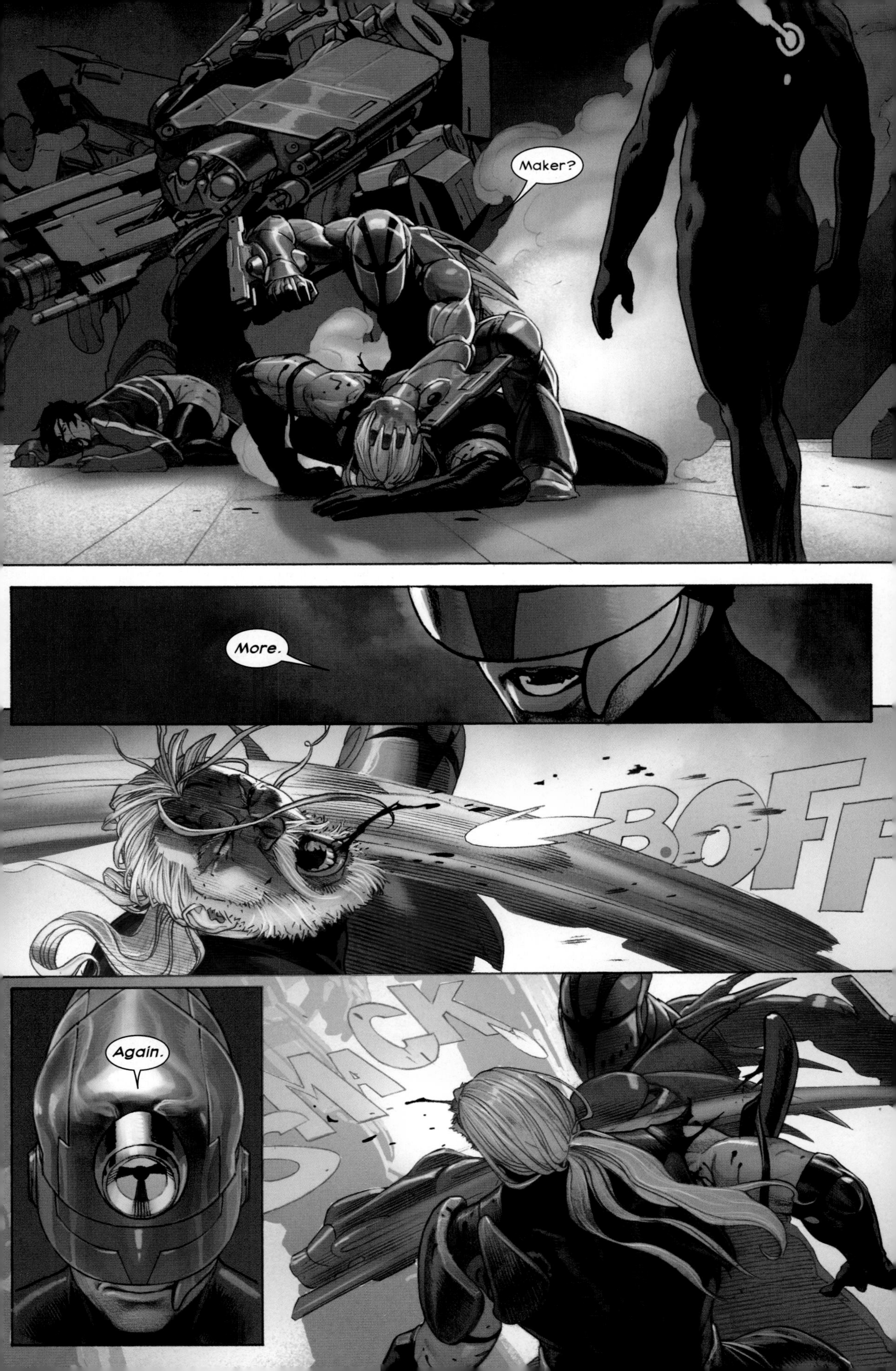
Maker?
More.
BOFF
Again.
SMACK

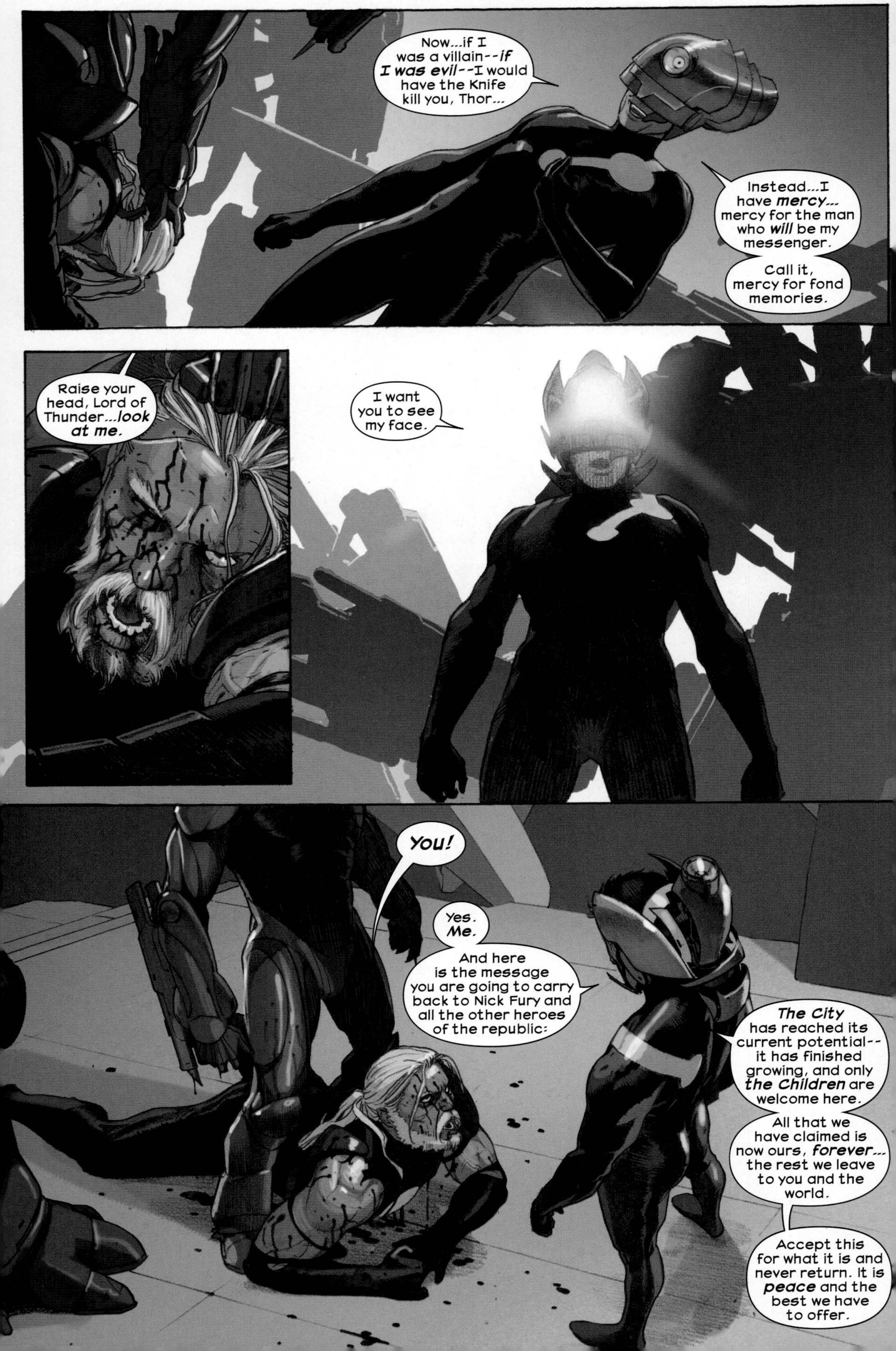

Now...if I was a villain--*if I was evil*--I would have the Knife kill you, Thor...
Instead...I have ***mercy***... mercy for the man who ***will*** be my messenger.
Call it, mercy for fond memories.
Raise your head, Lord of Thunder...***look at me.***
I want you to see my face.
You!
Yes. ***Me.***
And here is the message you are going to carry back to Nick Fury and all the other heroes of the republic:
The City has reached its current potential--it has finished growing, and only ***the Children*** are welcome here.
All that we have claimed is now ours, ***forever***... the rest we leave to you and the world.
Accept this for what it is and never return. It is ***peace*** and the best we have to offer.

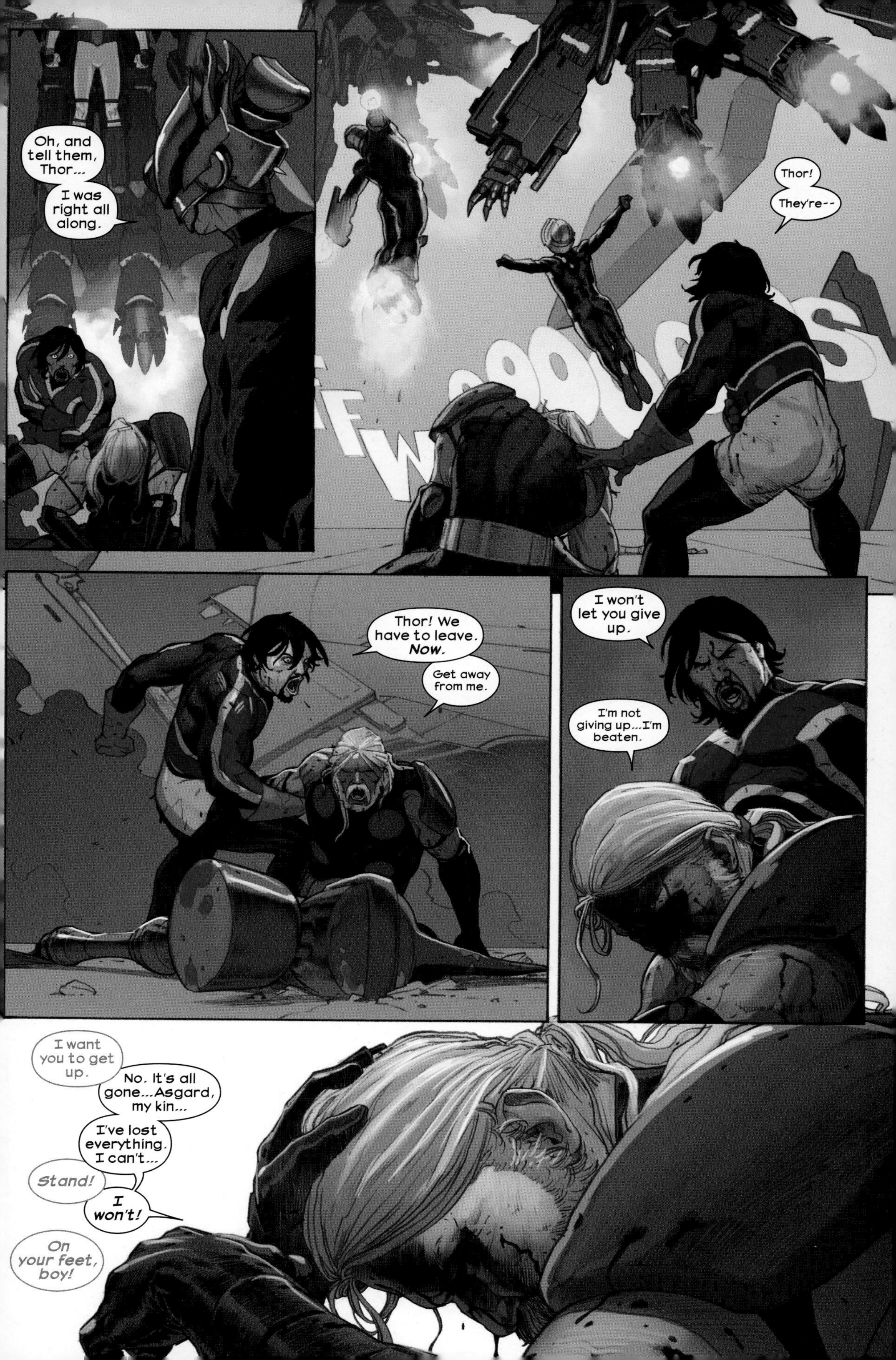
Oh, and tell them, Thor...
I was right all along.
Thor!
They're--
Thor! We have to leave. Now.
Get away from me.
I won't let you give up.
I'm not giving up...I'm beaten.
I want you to get up.
No. It's all gone...Asgard, my kin...
I've lost everything. I can't...
Stand!
I won't!
On your feet, boy!

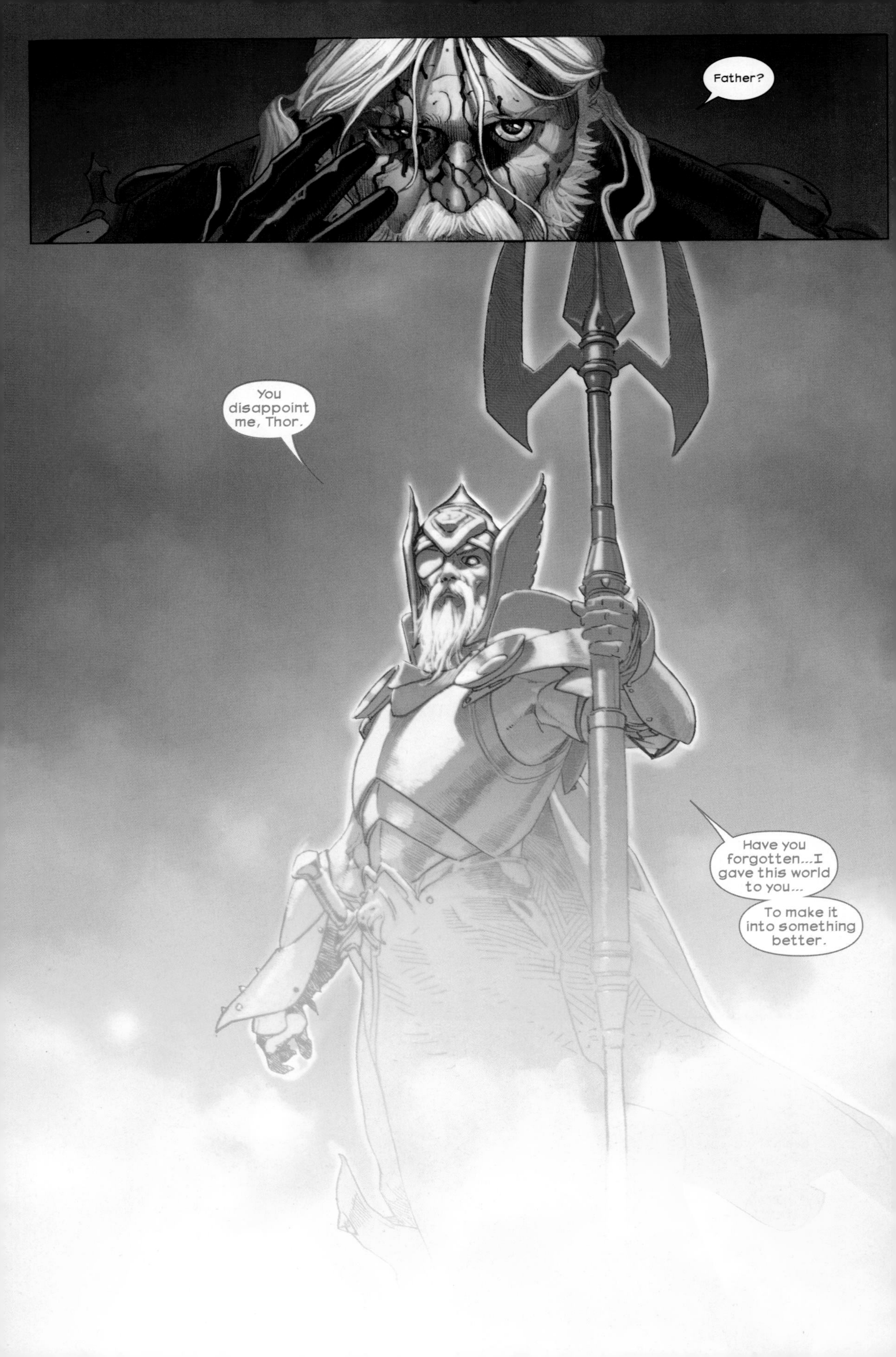
Father?
You disappoint me, Thor.
Have you forgotten...I gave this world to you...
To make it into something better.

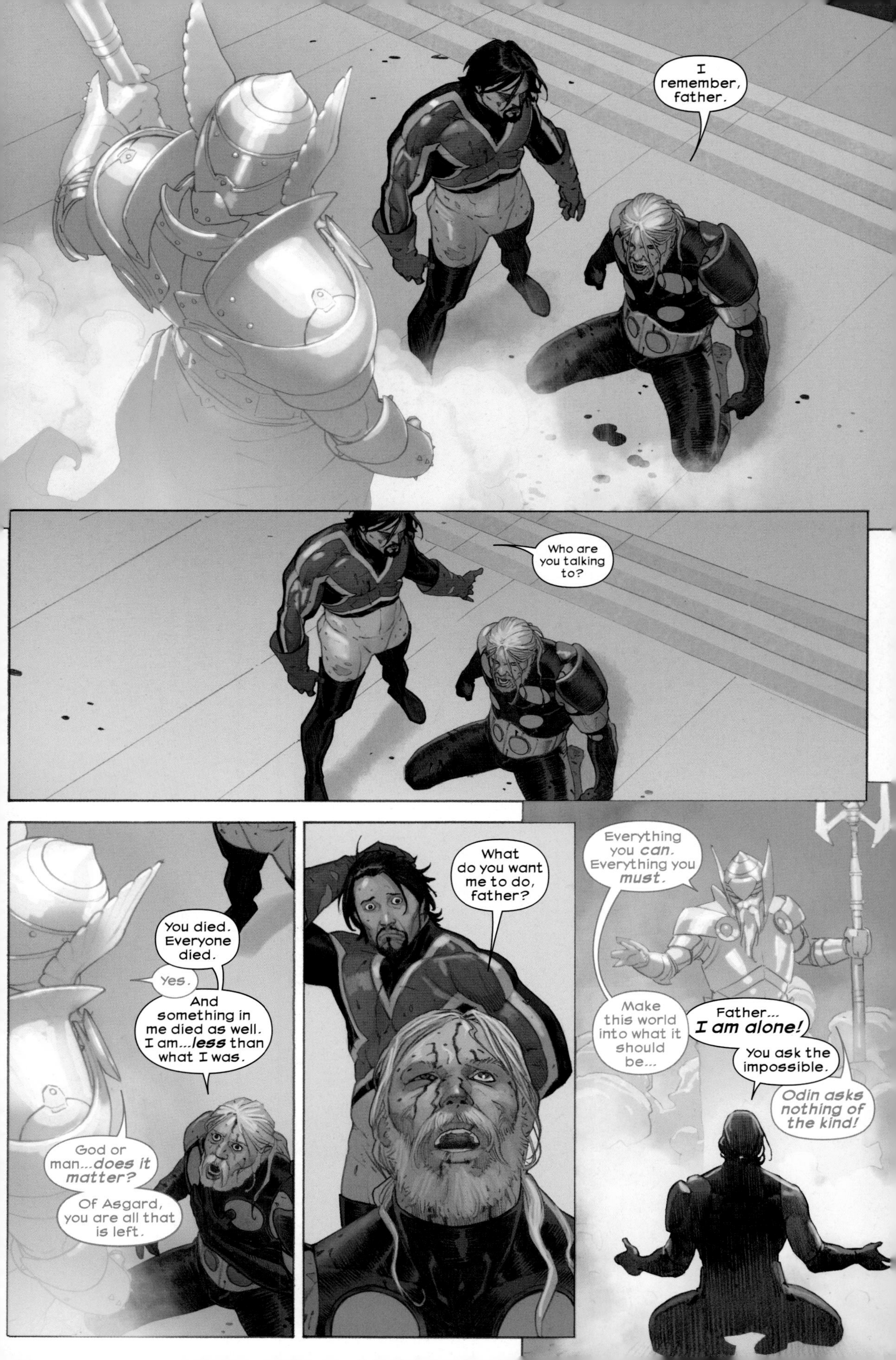
I remember, father.
Who are you talking to?
You died. Everyone died.
Yes.
And something in me died as well. I am...*less* than what I was.
God or man...*does it matter?*
Of Asgard, you are all that is left.
What do you want me to do, father?
Everything you *can*. Everything you *must*.
Make this world into what it should be...
Father... *I am alone!*
You ask the impossible.
Odin asks nothing of the kind!

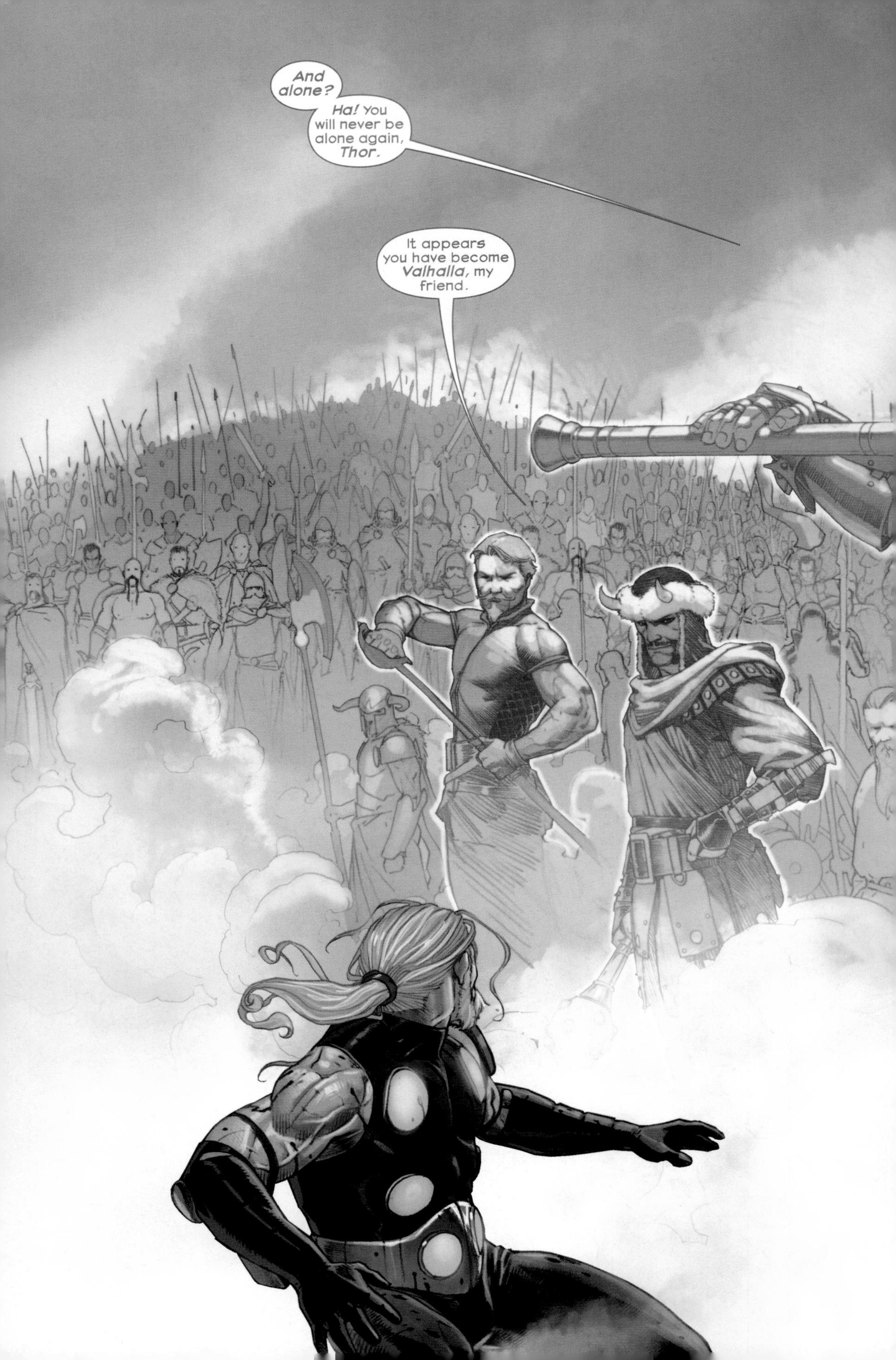

And alone?
Ha! You will never be alone again, Thor.
It appears you have become Valhalla, my friend.

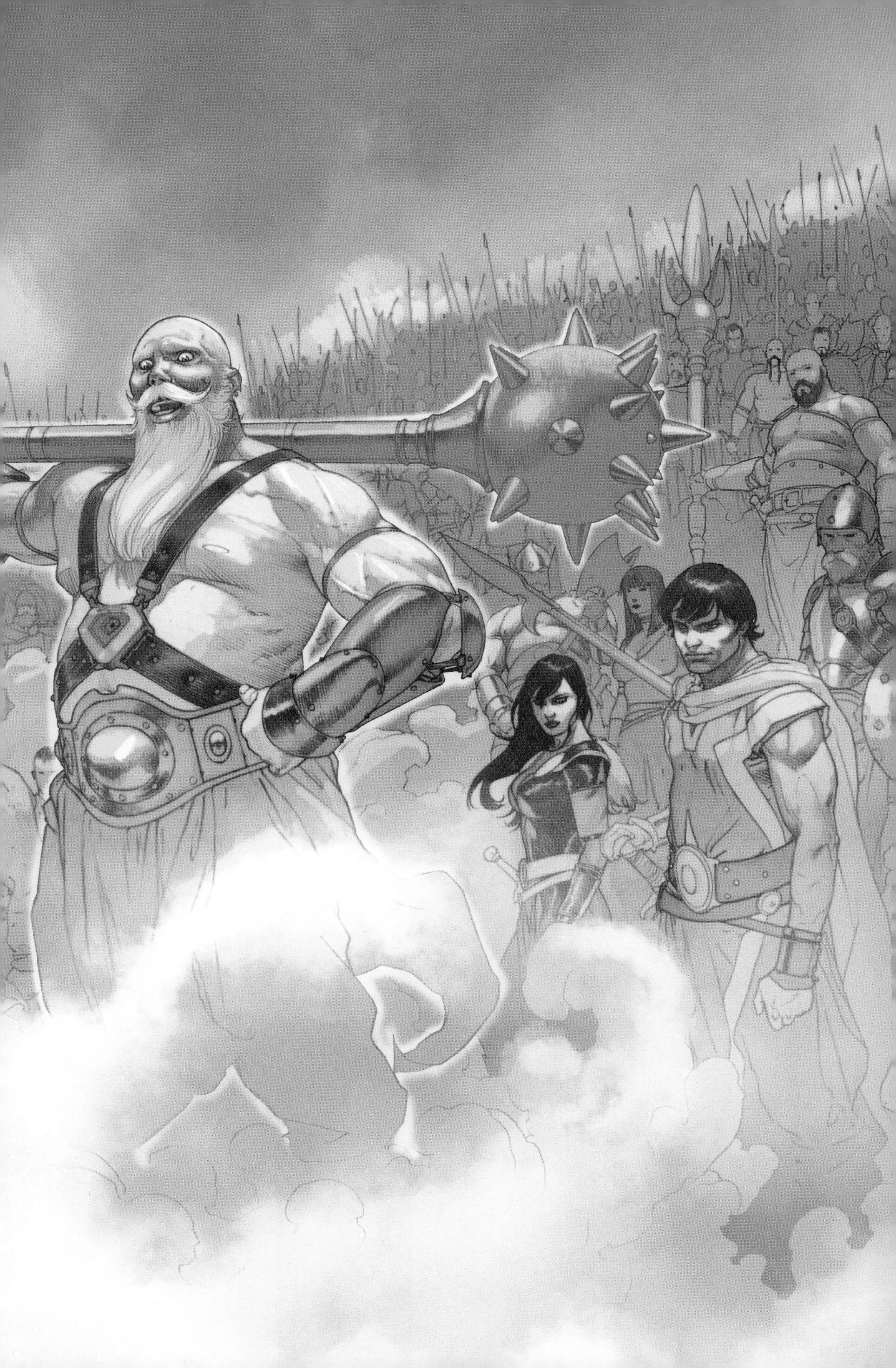

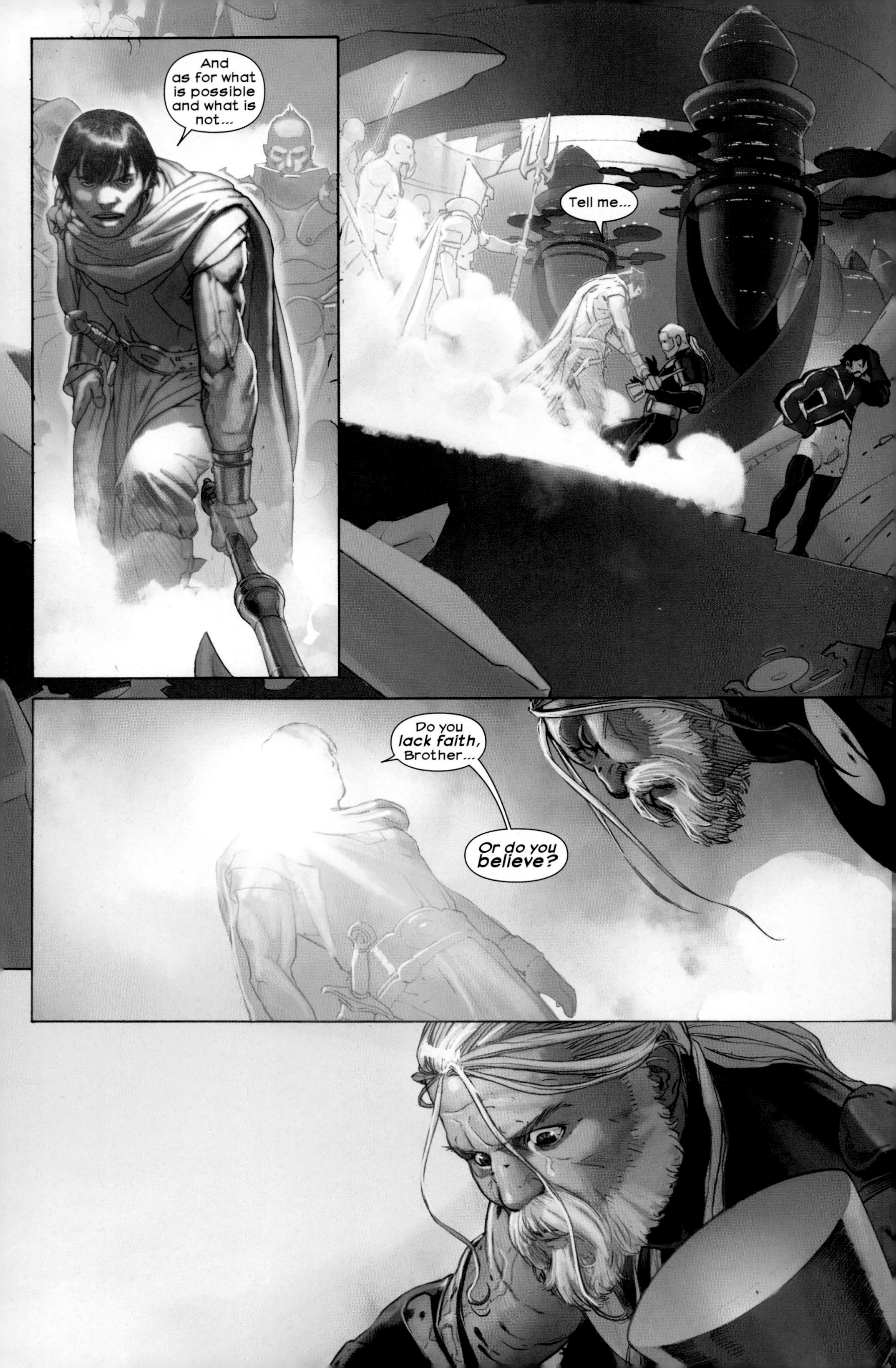
And as for what is possible and what is not...
Tell me...
Do you lack faith, Brother...
Or do you believe?

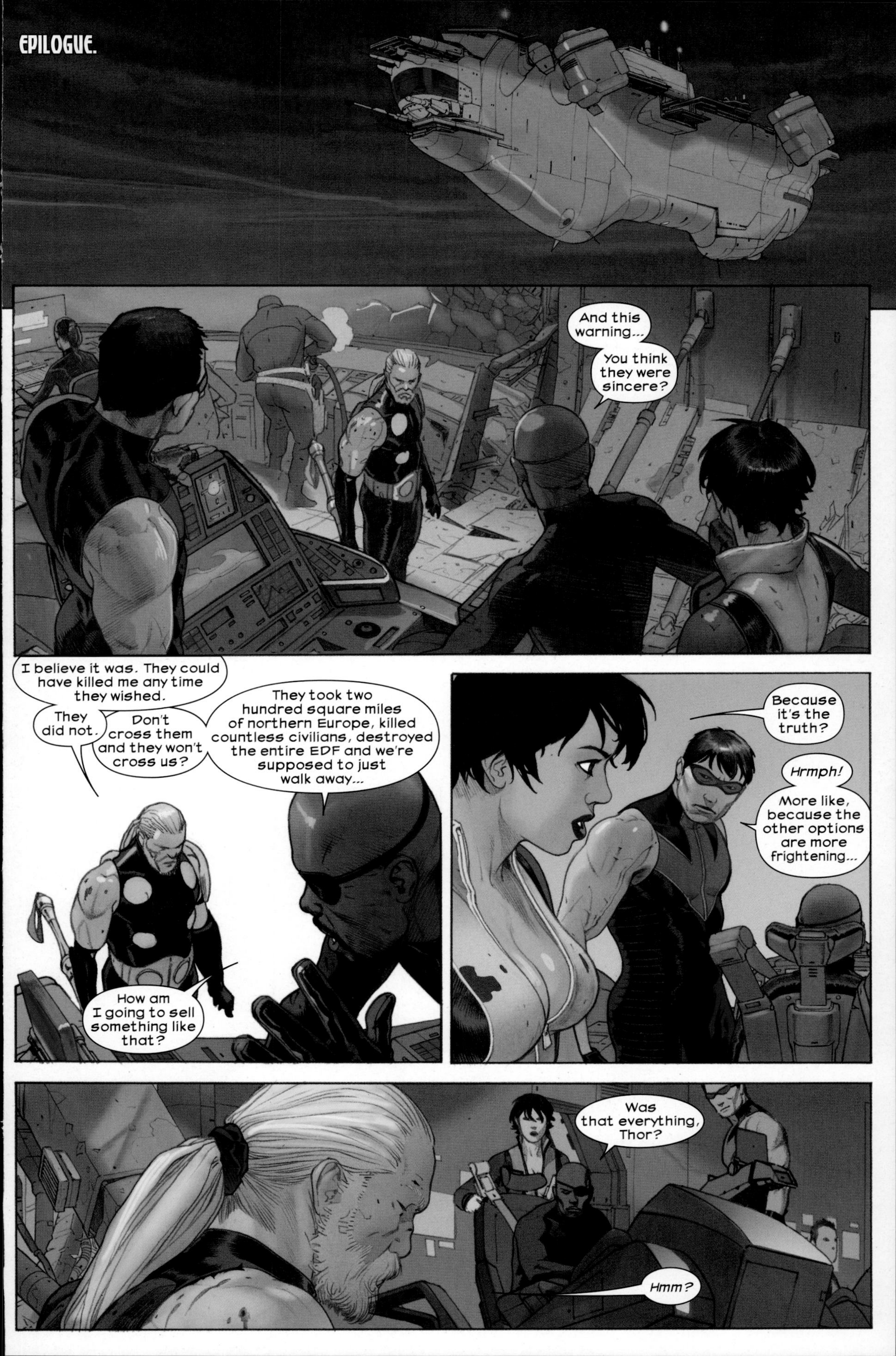
EPILOGUE.
And this warning...
You think they were sincere?
I believe it was. They could have killed me any time they wished.
They did not.
Don't cross them and they won't cross us?
They took two hundred square miles of northern Europe, killed countless civilians, destroyed the entire EDF and we're supposed to just walk away...
How am I going to sell something like that?
Because it's the truth?
Hrmph!
More like, because the other options are more frightening...
Was that everything, Thor?
Hmm?

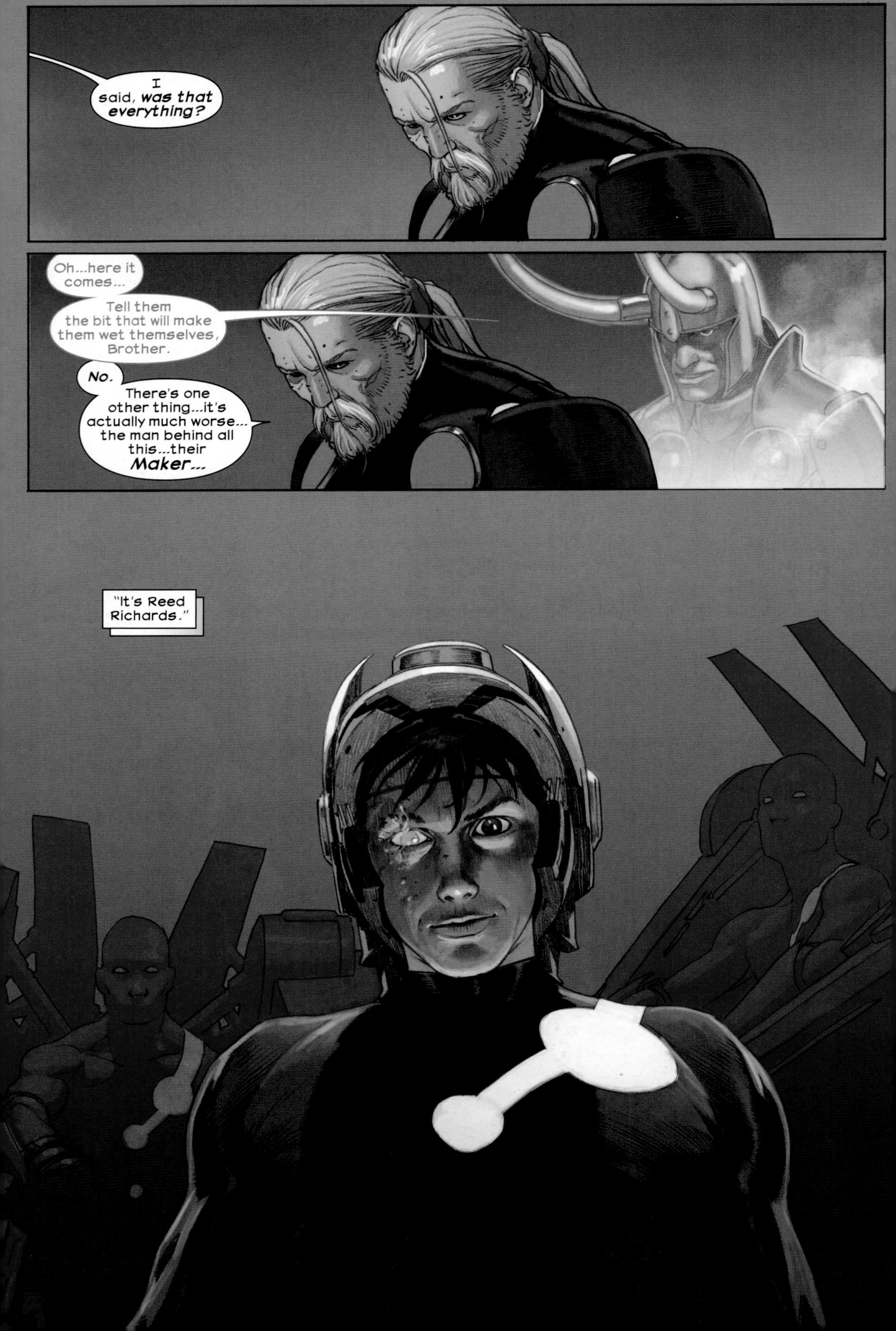
I said, *was that everything?*
Oh...here it comes...
Tell them the bit that will make them wet themselves, Brother.
No.
There's one other thing...it's actually much worse...the man behind all this...their *Maker*...
"It's Reed Richards."

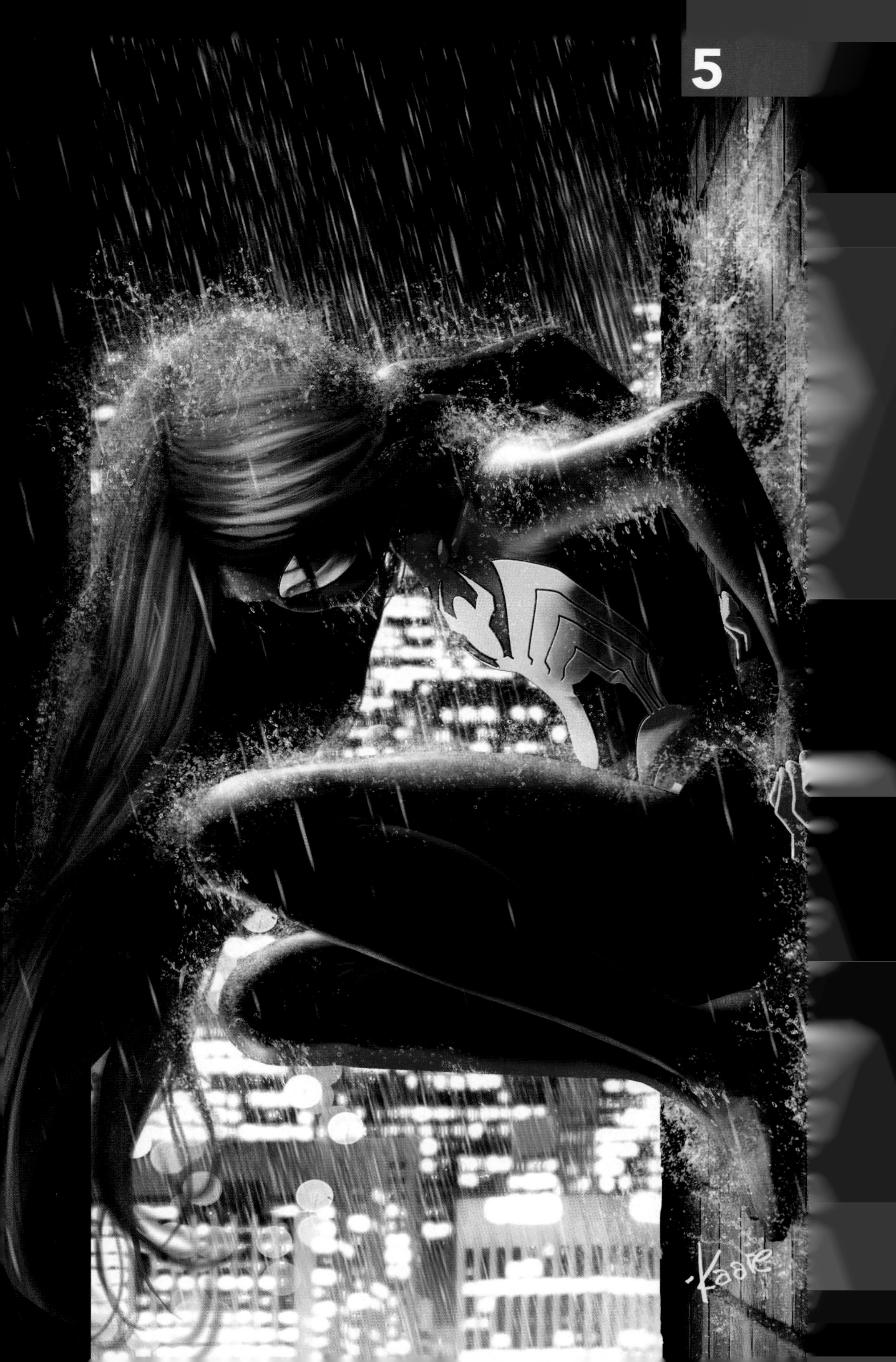
5
Kaare

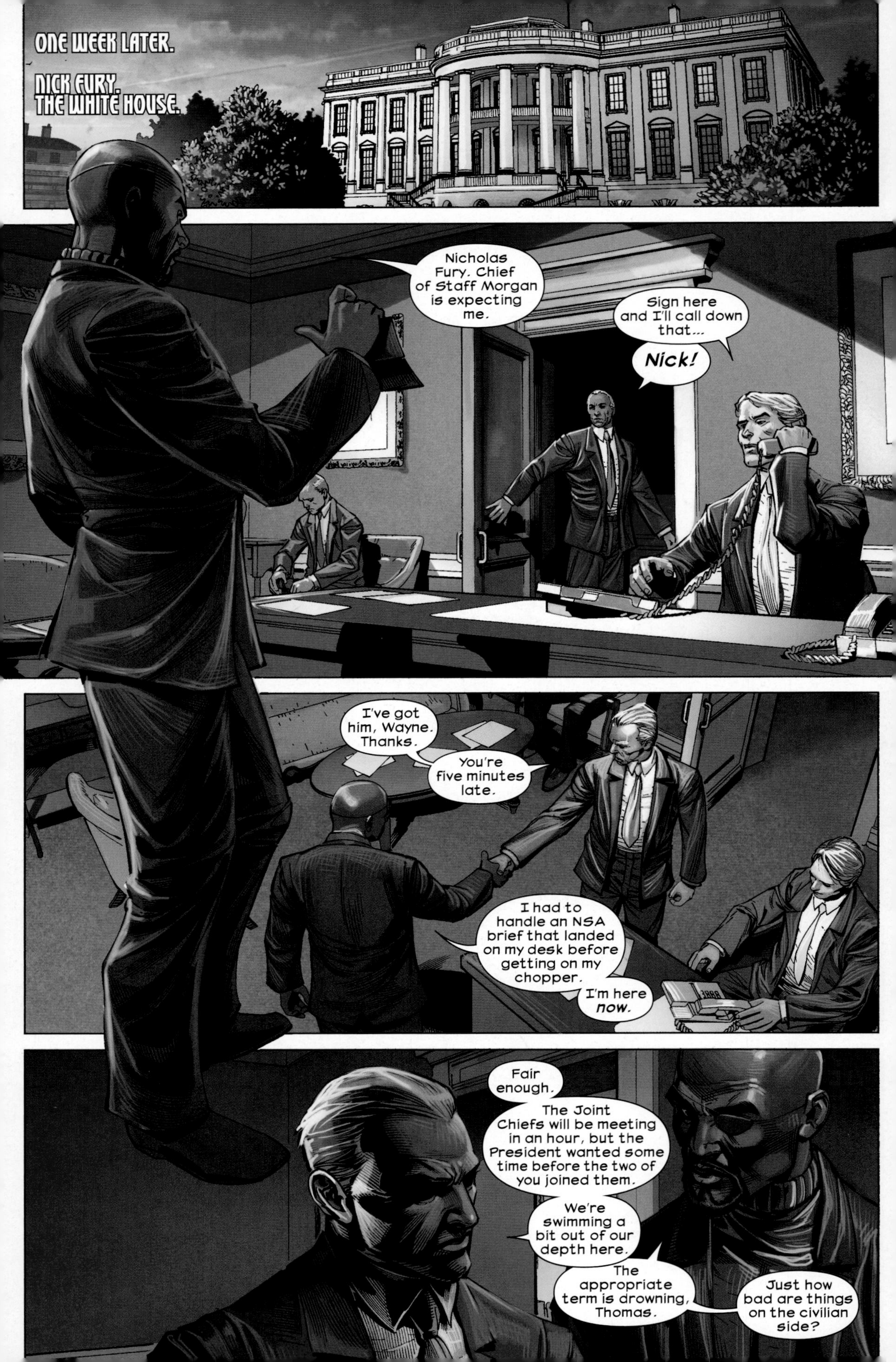
ONE WEEK LATER.
NICK FURY. THE WHITE HOUSE.
Nicholas Fury. Chief of Staff Morgan is expecting me.
Sign here and I'll call down that...
Nick!
I've got him, Wayne. Thanks.
You're five minutes late.
I had to handle an NSA brief that landed on my desk before getting on my chopper.
I'm here now.
Fair enough.
The Joint Chiefs will be meeting in an hour, but the President wanted some time before the two of you joined them.
We're swimming a bit out of our depth here.
The appropriate term is drowning, Thomas.
Just how bad are things on the civilian side?

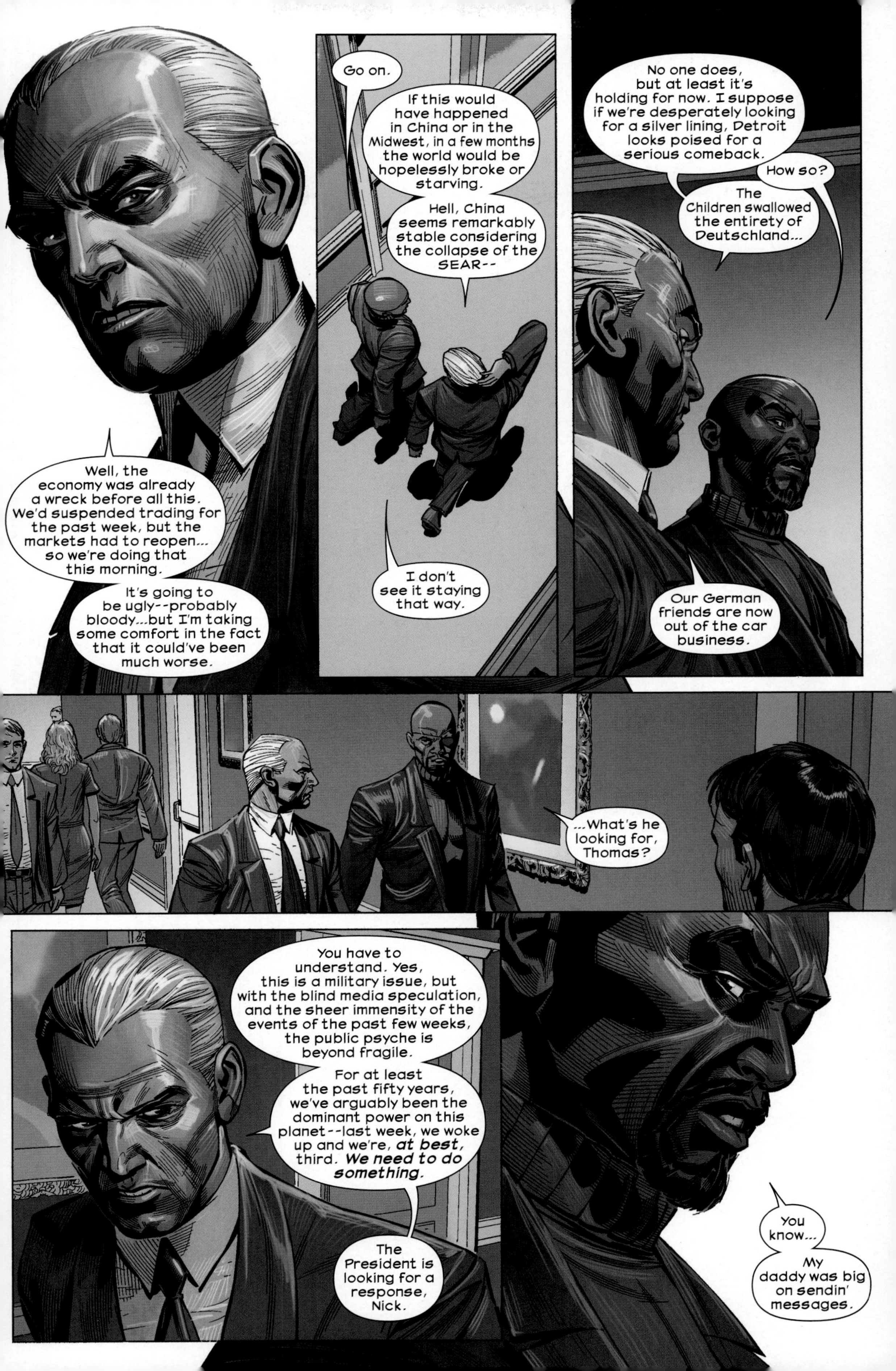
Well, the economy was already a wreck before all this. We'd suspended trading for the past week, but the markets had to reopen... so we're doing that this morning.
It's going to be ugly--probably bloody...but I'm taking some comfort in the fact that it could've been much worse.
Go on.
If this would have happened in China or in the Midwest, in a few months the world would be hopelessly broke or starving.
Hell, China seems remarkably stable considering the collapse of the SEAR--
I don't see it staying that way.
No one does, but at least it's holding for now. I suppose if we're desperately looking for a silver lining, Detroit looks poised for a serious comeback.
How so?
The Children swallowed the entirety of Deutschland...
Our German friends are now out of the car business.
...What's he looking for, Thomas?
You have to understand. Yes, this is a military issue, but with the blind media speculation, and the sheer immensity of the events of the past few weeks, the public psyche is beyond fragile.
For at least the past fifty years, we've arguably been the dominant power on this planet--last week, we woke up and we're, ***at best,*** third. ***We need to do something.***
The President is looking for a response, Nick.
You know...
My daddy was big on sendin' messages.

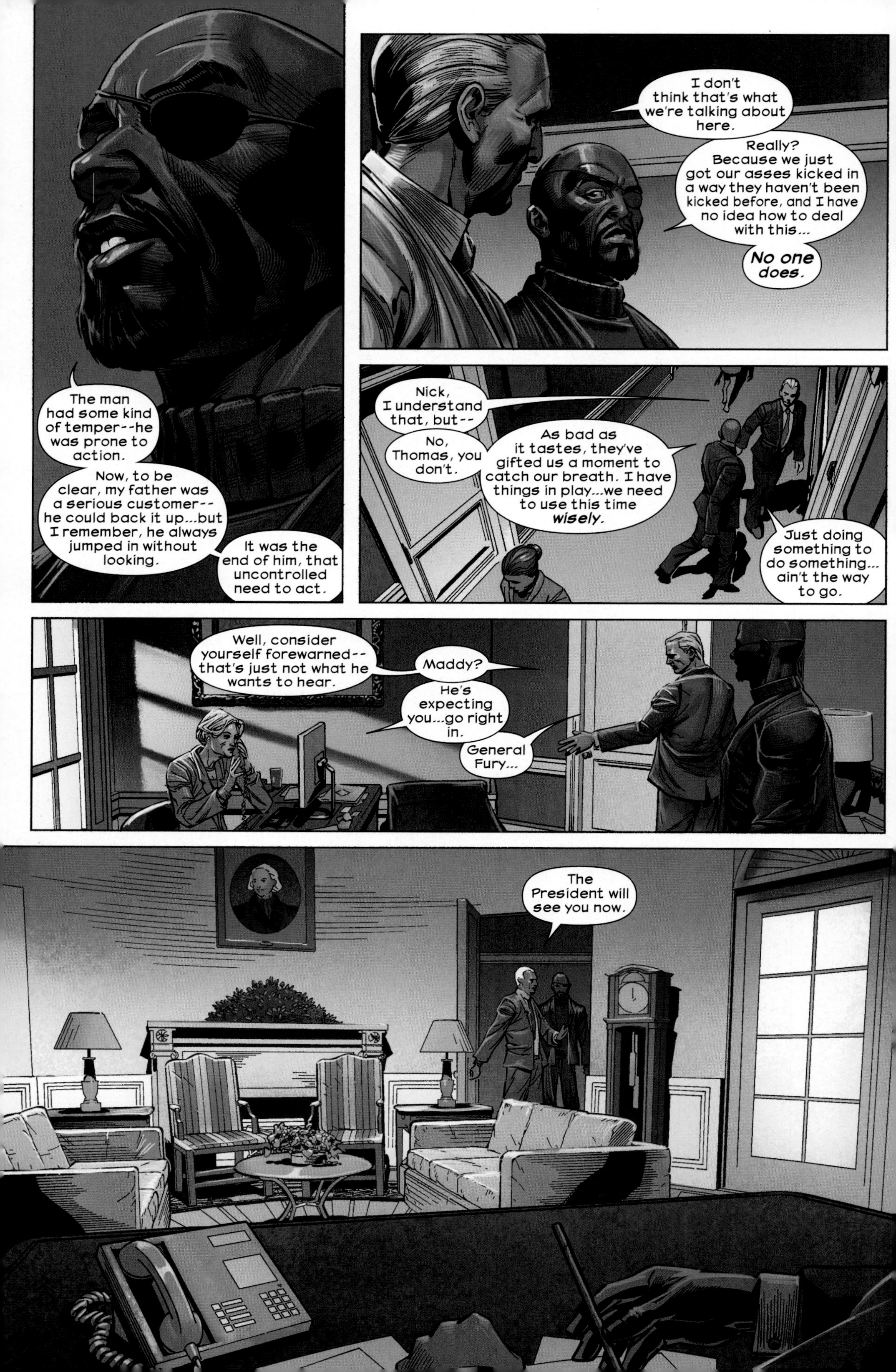
The man had some kind of temper--he was prone to action.
Now, to be clear, my father was a serious customer--he could back it up...but I remember, he always jumped in without looking.
It was the end of him, that uncontrolled need to act.
I don't think that's what we're talking about here.
Really? Because we just got our asses kicked in a way they haven't been kicked before, and I have no idea how to deal with this...
No one does.
Nick, I understand that, but--
No, Thomas, you don't.
As bad as it tastes, they've gifted us a moment to catch our breath. I have things in play...we need to use this time *wisely.*
Just doing something to do something... ain't the way to go.
Well, consider yourself forewarned--that's just not what he wants to hear.
Maddy?
He's expecting you...go right in.
General Fury...
The President will see you now.

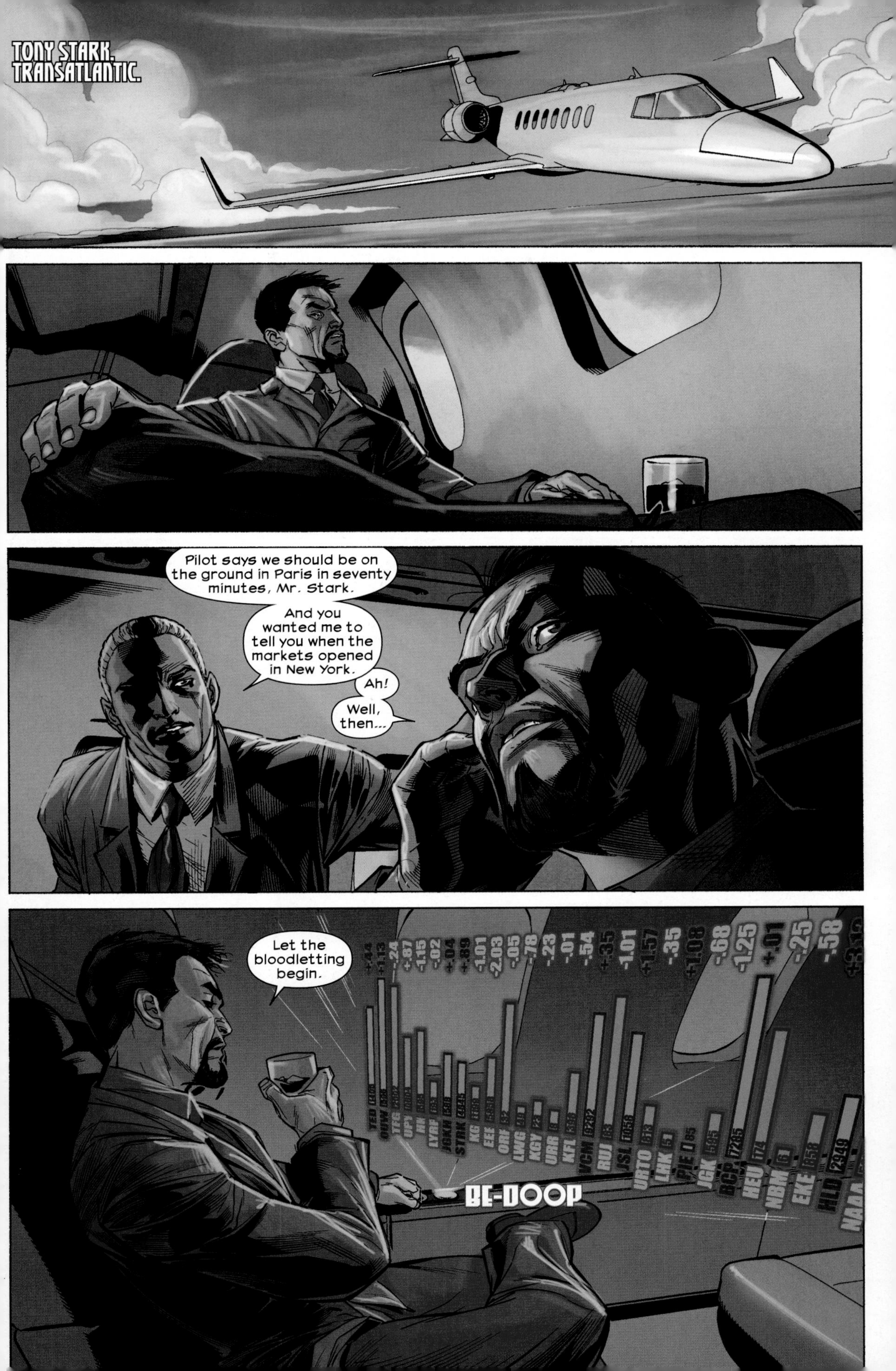
TONY STARK.
TRANSATLANTIC.
Pilot says we should be on the ground in Paris in seventy minutes, Mr. Stark.
And you wanted me to tell you when the markets opened in New York.
Ah!
Well, then...
Let the bloodletting begin.
BE-DOOP

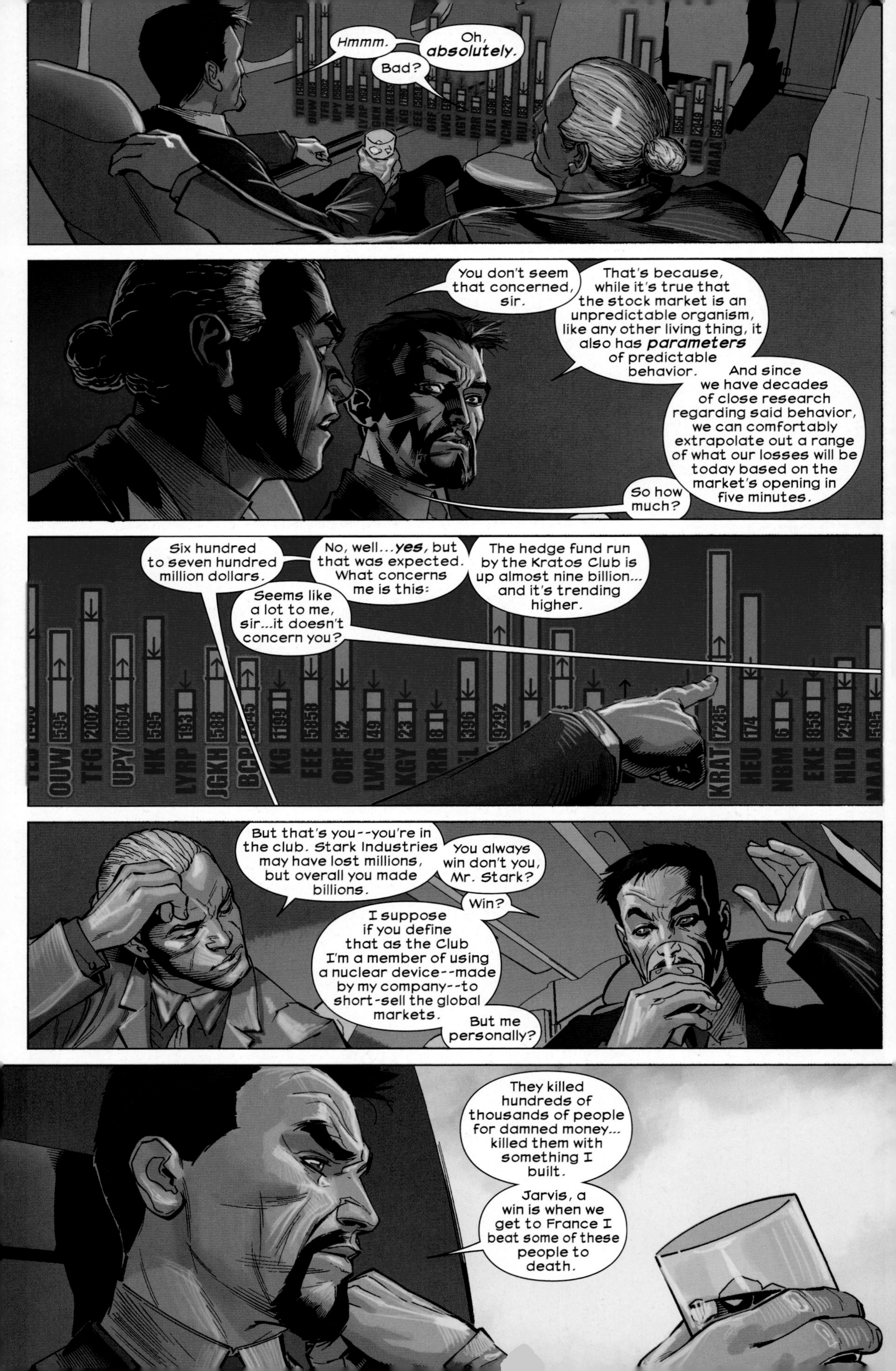
Hmmm.
Oh, *absolutely.*
Bad?
You don't seem that concerned, sir.
That's because, while it's true that the stock market is an unpredictable organism, like any other living thing, it also has ***parameters*** of predictable behavior.
And since we have decades of close research regarding said behavior, we can comfortably extrapolate out a range of what our losses will be today based on the market's opening in five minutes.
So how much?
Six hundred to seven hundred million dollars.
Seems like a lot to me, sir...it doesn't concern you?
No, well... ***yes,*** but that was expected. What concerns me is this:
The hedge fund run by the Kratos Club is up almost nine billion... and it's trending higher.
But that's you--you're in the club. Stark Industries may have lost millions, but overall you made billions.
You always win don't you, Mr. Stark?
Win?
I suppose if you define that as the Club I'm a member of using a nuclear device--made by my company--to short-sell the global markets.
But me personally?
They killed hundreds of thousands of people for damned money... killed them with something I built.
Jarvis, a win is when we get to France I beat some of these people to death.

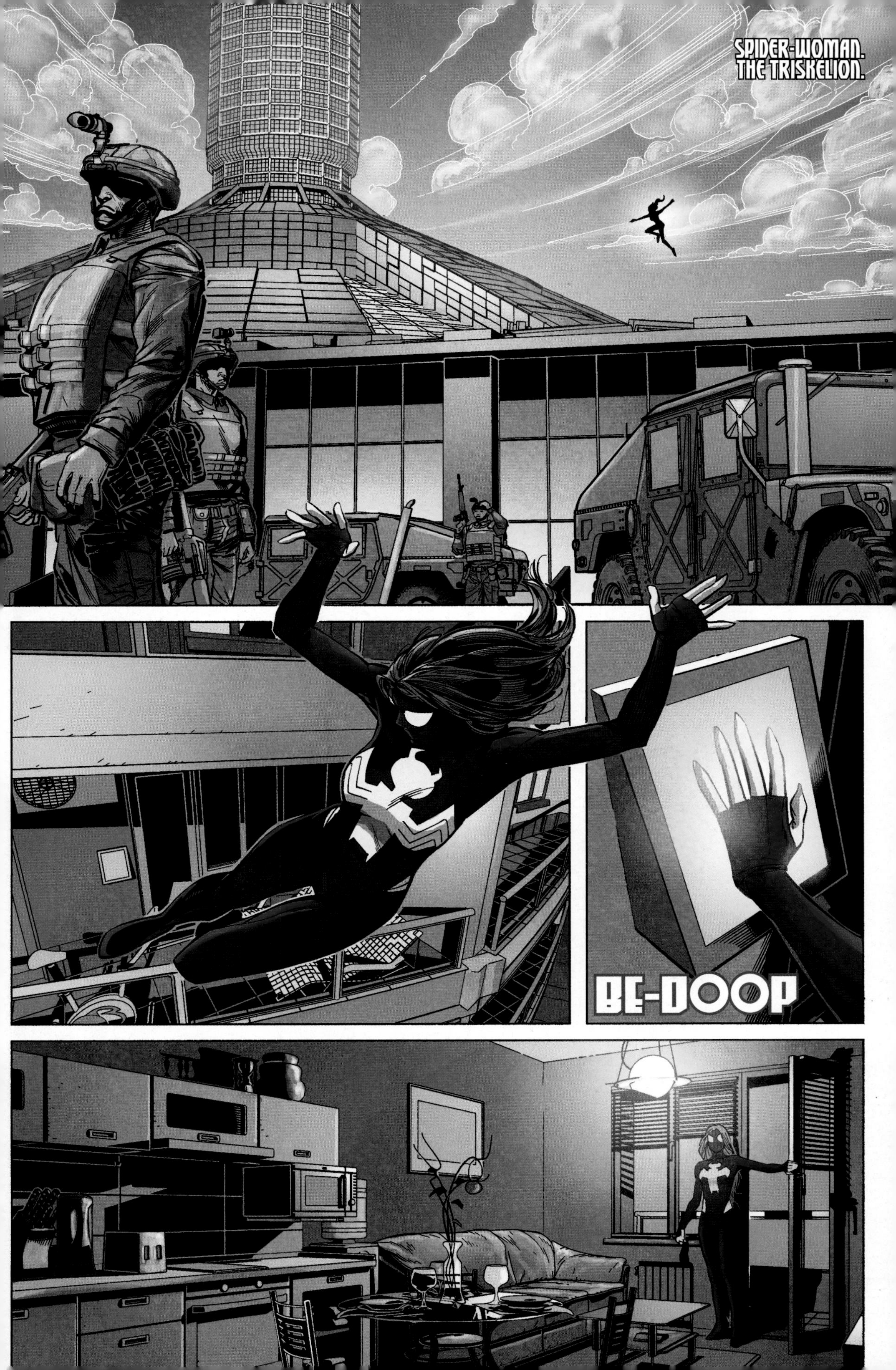
SPIDER-WOMAN.
THE TRISKELION.
BE-DOOP

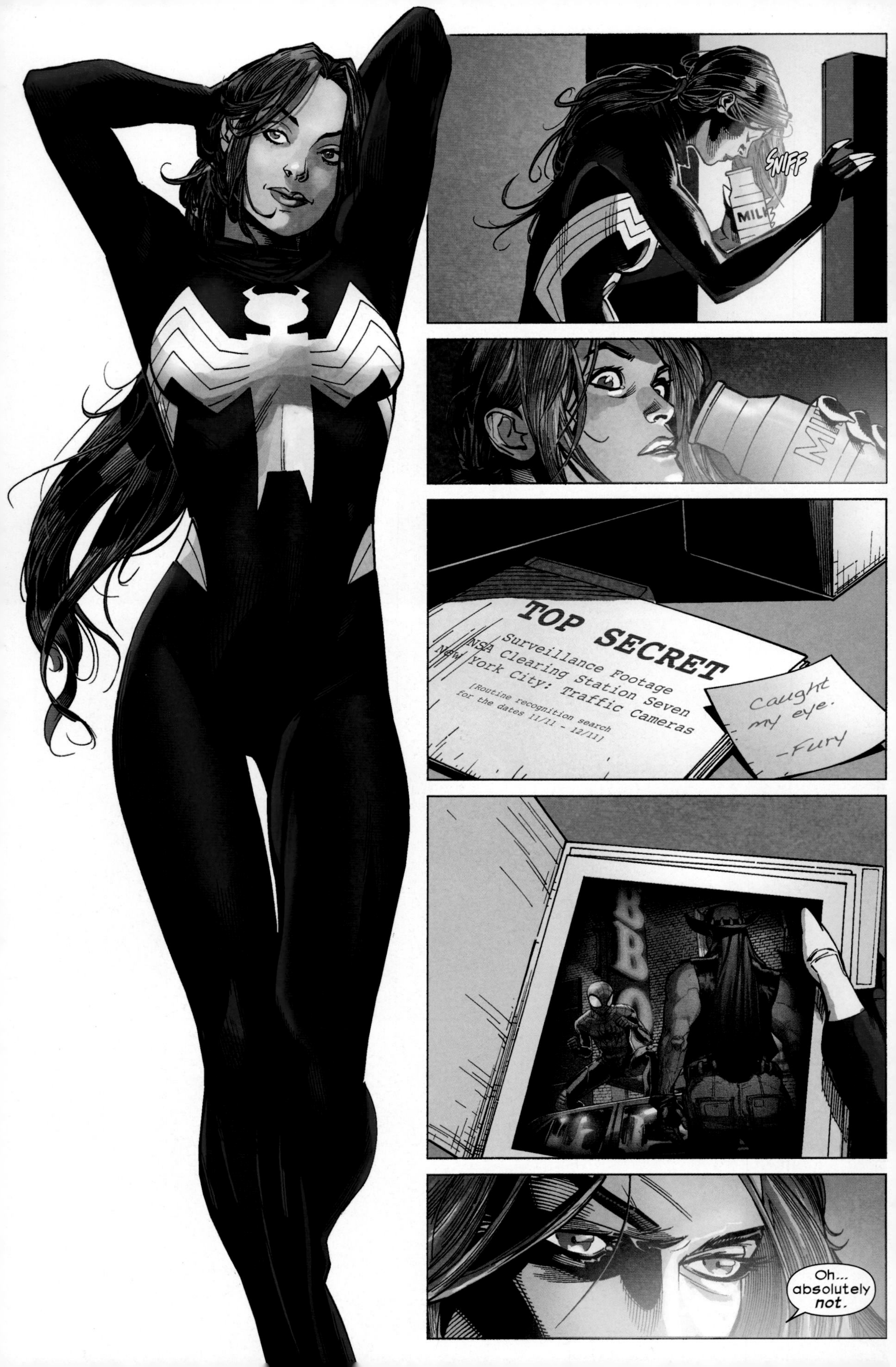
SNIFF
MILK
TOP SECRET
Surveillance Footage
NSA Clearing Station Seven
New York City: Traffic Cameras
[Routine recognition search
for the dates 11/11 - 12/11]
Caught my eye.
-Fury
Oh... absolutely not.

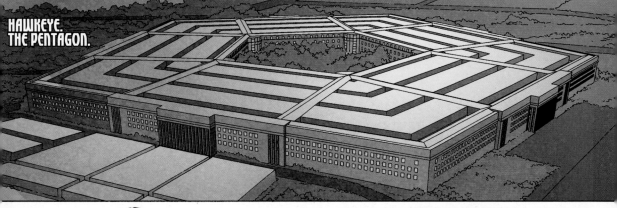

Everyone here?

Director of the FBI stepped out for a phone call, Barton.

He can catch up. Let's go.

My guys are passing out briefing documents for your edification, and it looks like I'm going to have around twenty minutes for you...the floor is yours.

Let it fly.

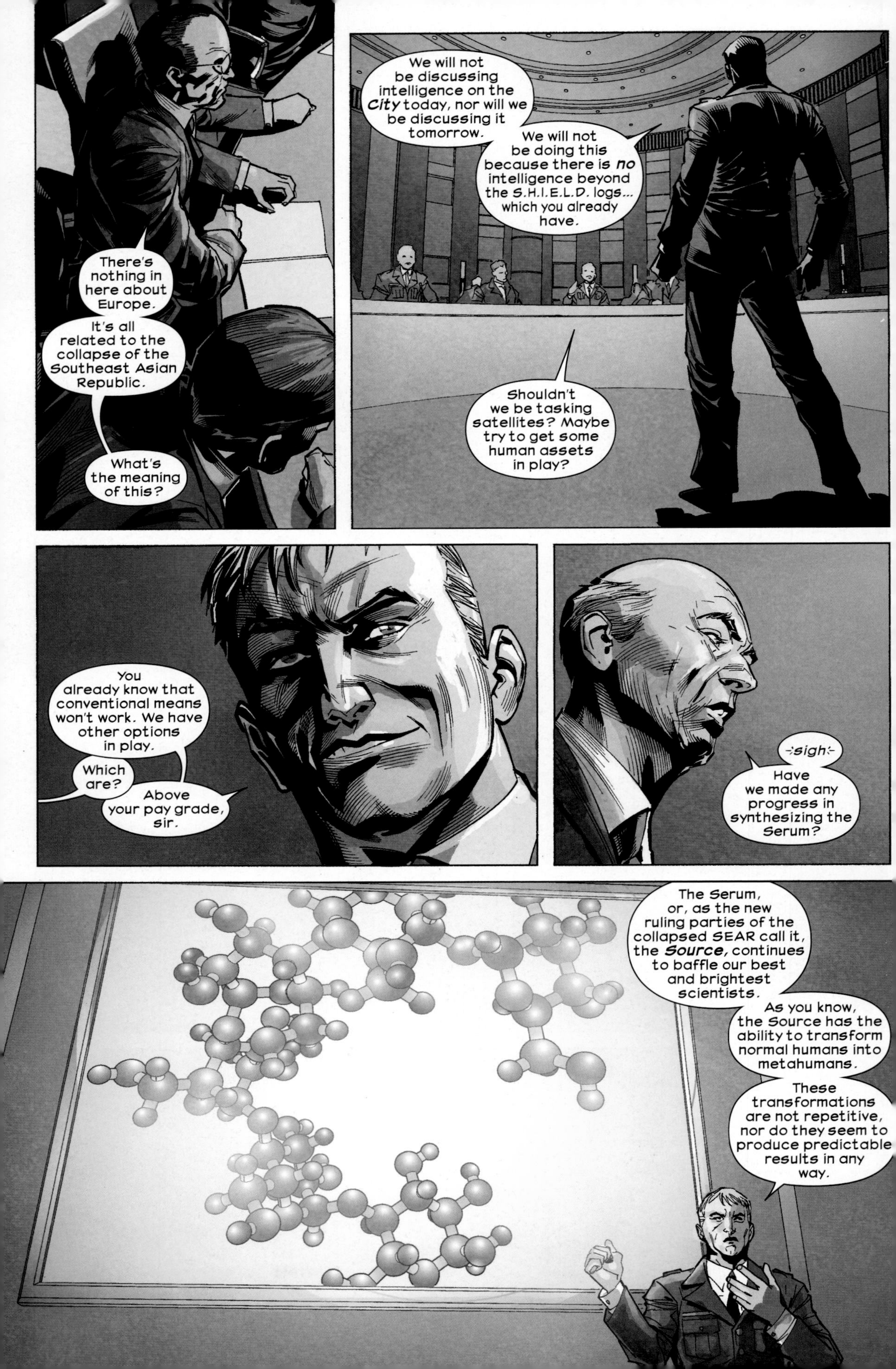
There's nothing in here about Europe.
It's all related to the collapse of the Southeast Asian Republic.
What's the meaning of this?
We will not be discussing intelligence on the City today, nor will we be discussing it tomorrow.
We will not be doing this because there is no intelligence beyond the S.H.I.E.L.D. logs... which you already have.
Shouldn't we be tasking satellites? Maybe try to get some human assets in play?
You already know that conventional means won't work. We have other options in play.
Which are?
Above your pay grade, sir.
-:sigh:-
Have we made any progress in synthesizing the Serum?
The Serum, or, as the new ruling parties of the collapsed SEAR call it, the Source, continues to baffle our best and brightest scientists.
As you know, the Source has the ability to transform normal humans into metahumans.
These transformations are not repetitive, nor do they seem to produce predictable results in any way.

And what do we know about the SEAR government?

While not formally recognized at this point and time, the new government is calling itself Tian.

Right now, there appears to be two factions that have aligned themselves behind one of two brothers.

The Eternals led by Kuan-Yin, and the Celestials led by Shen...

You've met them, yes?

I have. They were... *impressive.*

Talk about the numbers. How many metahumans do they have?

At first, the number was around one hundred thousand.

Since then, the still-human members of Tian have begun taking the *Source* and that number has doubled.

They're also gaining numbers from other places.

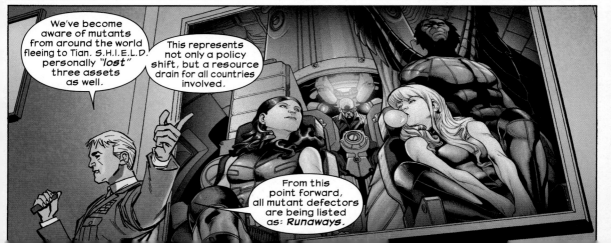

We've become aware of mutants from around the world fleeing to Tian. S.H.I.E.L.D. personally *"lost"* three assets as well.

This represents not only a policy shift, but a resource drain for all countries involved.

From this point forward, all mutant defectors are being listed as: *Runaways.*

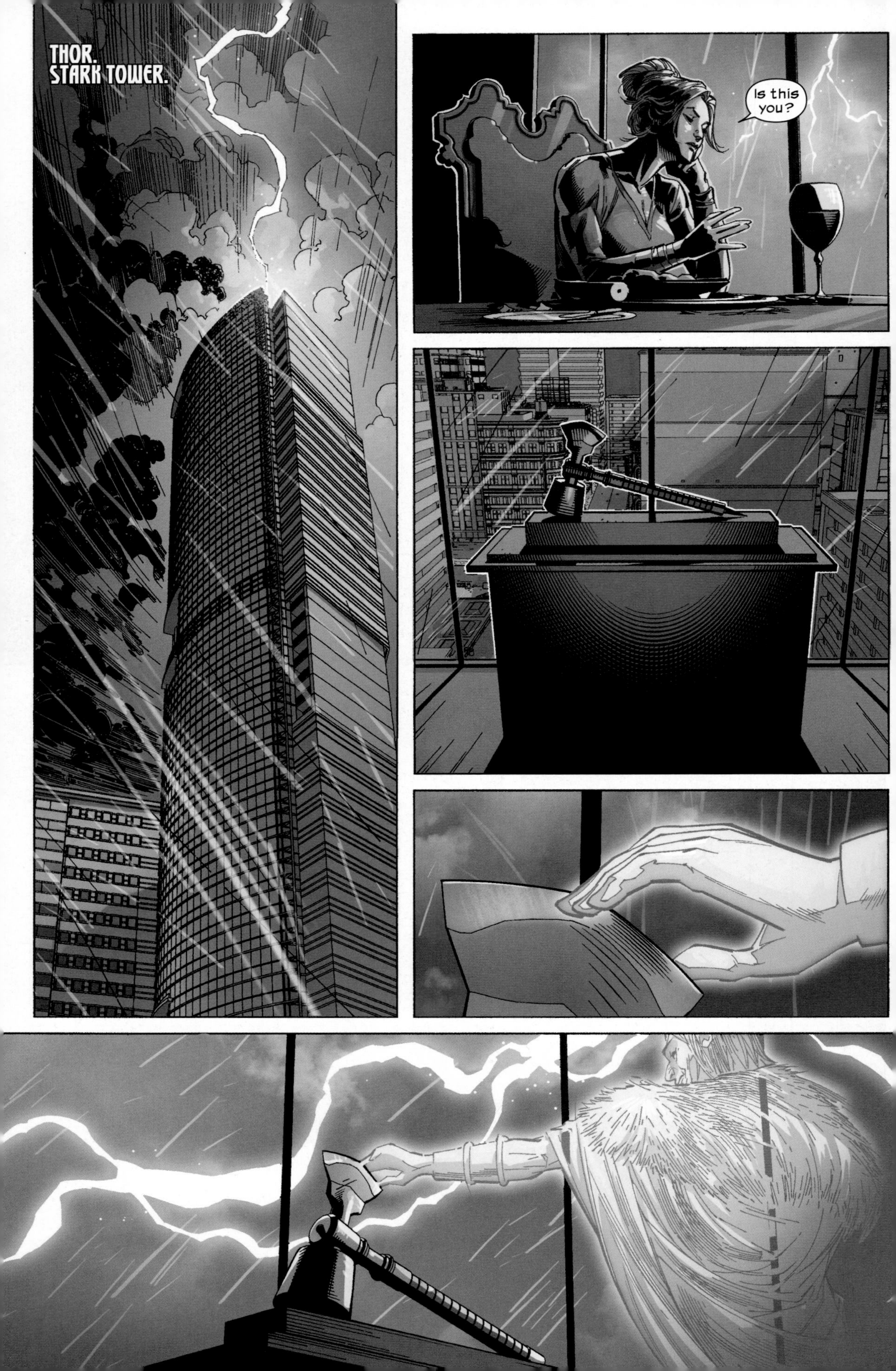
THOR.
STARK TOWER.
Is this you?

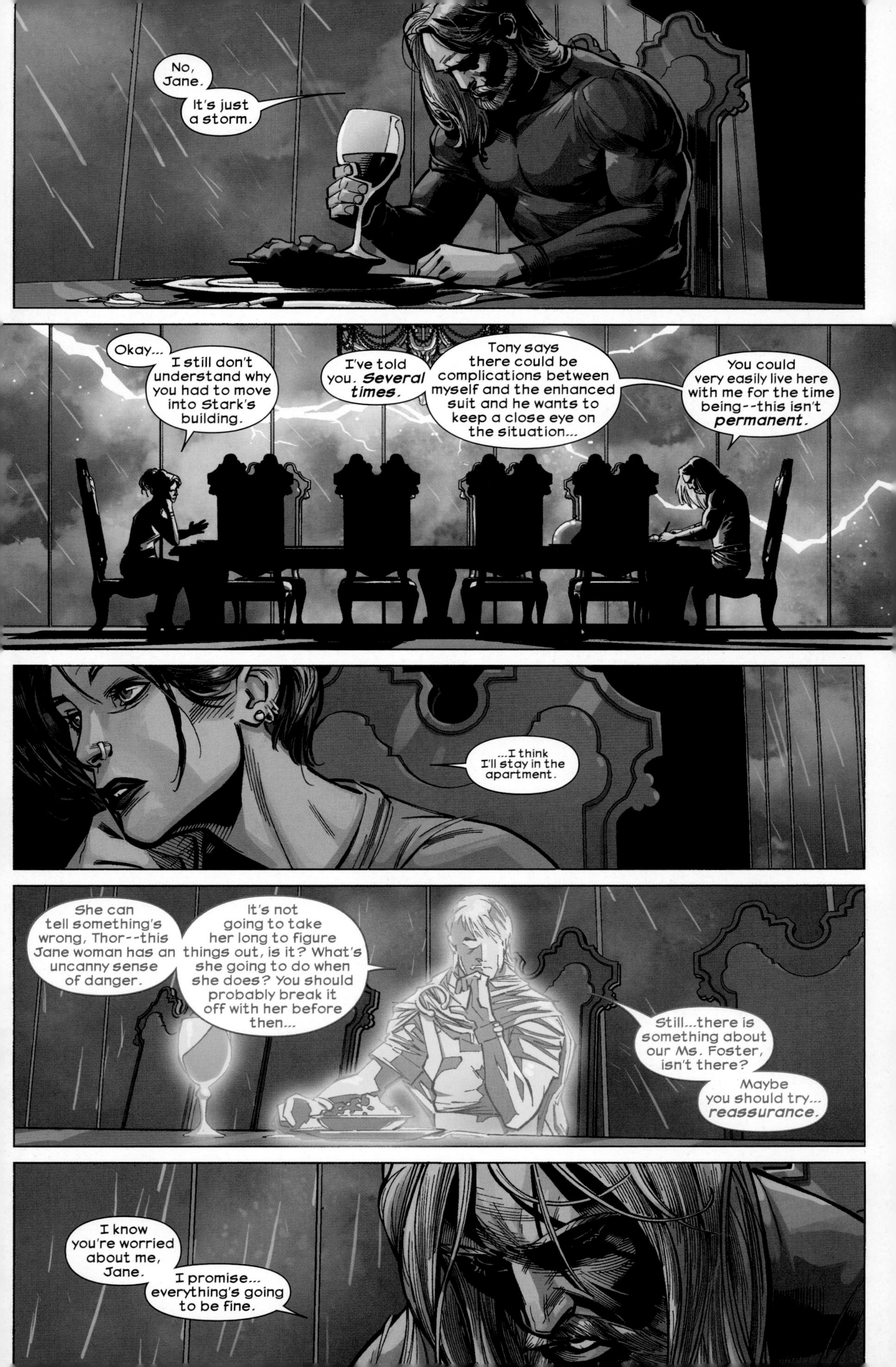
No, Jane.
It's just a storm.
Okay... I still don't understand why you had to move into Stark's building.
I've told you. Several times.
Tony says there could be complications between myself and the enhanced suit and he wants to keep a close eye on the situation...
You could very easily live here with me for the time being--this isn't permanent.
...I think I'll stay in the apartment.
She can tell something's wrong, Thor--this Jane woman has an uncanny sense of danger.
It's not going to take her long to figure things out, is it? What's she going to do when she does? You should probably break it off with her before then...
Still...there is something about our Ms. Foster, isn't there?
Maybe you should try... reassurance.
I know you're worried about me, Jane.
I promise... everything's going to be fine.

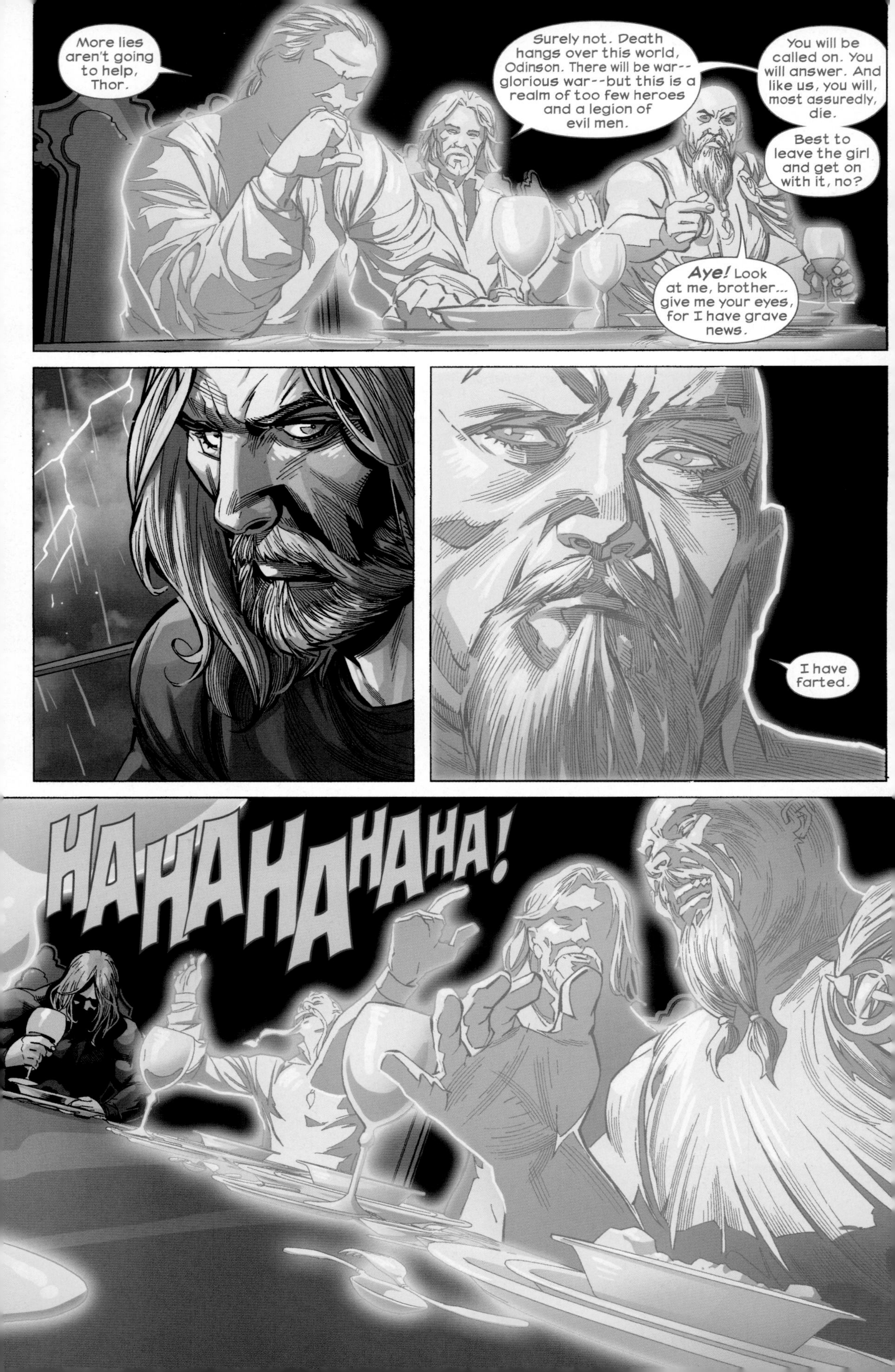
More lies aren't going to help, Thor.
Surely not. Death hangs over this world, Odinson. There will be war--glorious war--but this is a realm of too few heroes and a legion of evil men.
You will be called on. You will answer. And like us, you will, most assuredly, die.
Best to leave the girl and get on with it, no?
Aye! Look at me, brother... give me your eyes, for I have grave news.
I have farted.
HAHAHAHAHAHA!

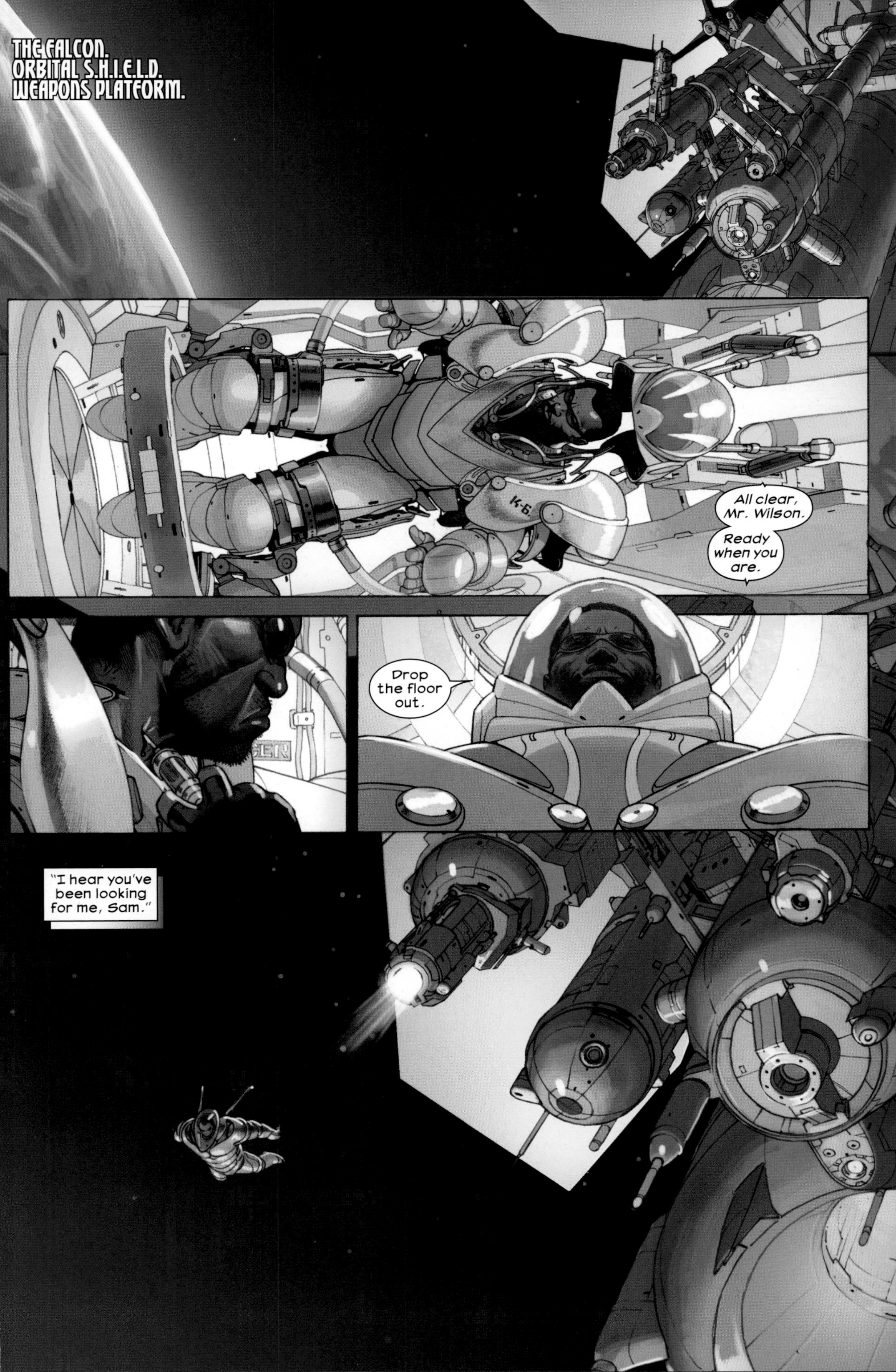
THE FALCON.
ORBITAL S.H.I.E.L.D.
WEAPONS PLATFORM.
All clear, Mr. Wilson.
Ready when you are.
Drop the floor out.
"I hear you've been looking for me, Sam."

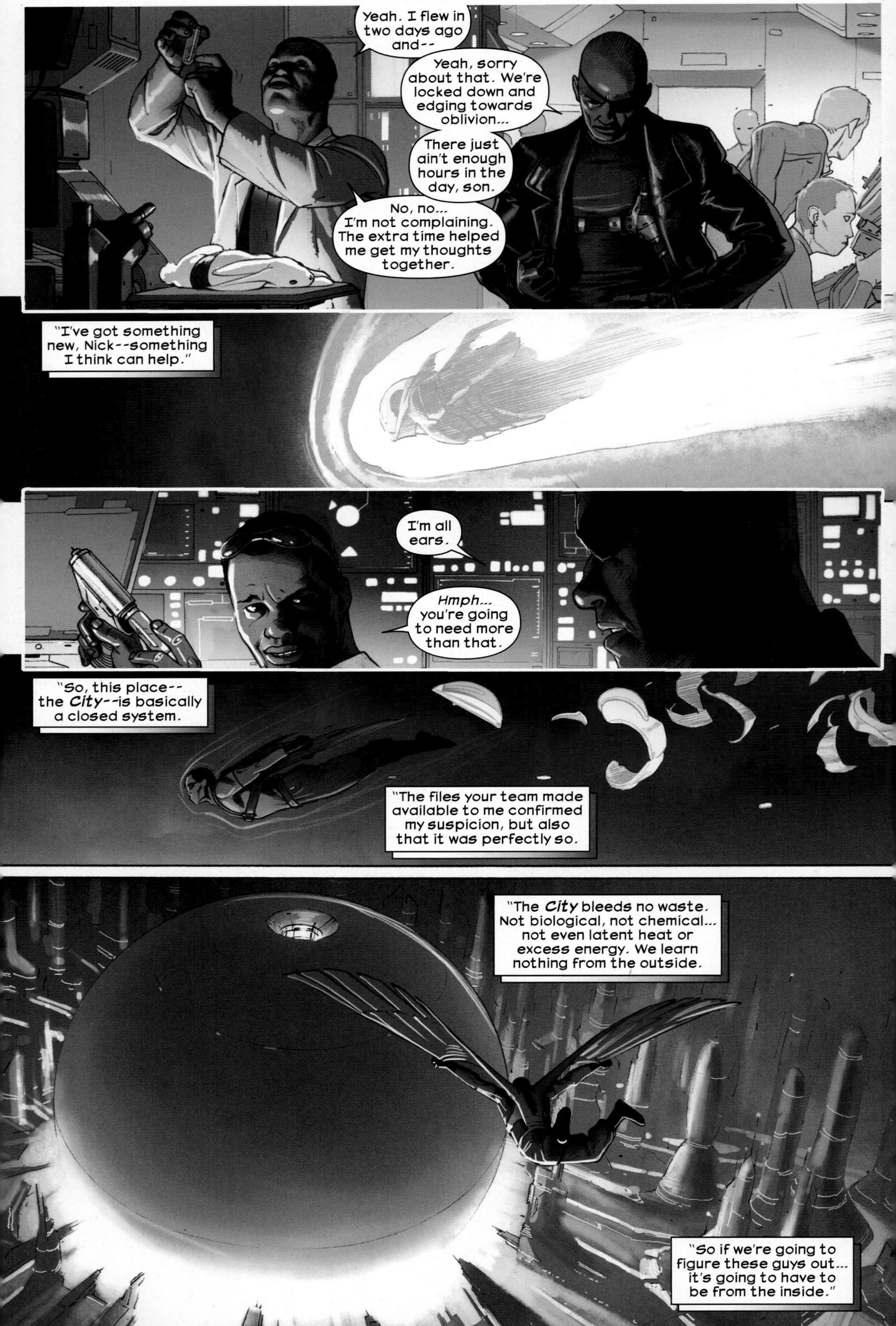

Yeah. I flew in two days ago and--
Yeah, sorry about that. We're locked down and edging towards oblivion...
There just ain't enough hours in the day, son.
No, no... I'm not complaining. The extra time helped me get my thoughts together.
"I've got something new, Nick--something I think can help."
I'm all ears.
Hmph... you're going to need more than that.
"So, this place-- the *City*--is basically a closed system.
"The files your team made available to me confirmed my suspicion, but also that it was perfectly so.
"The *City* bleeds no waste. Not biological, not chemical... not even latent heat or excess energy. We learn nothing from the outside.
"So if we're going to figure these guys out... it's going to have to be from the inside."

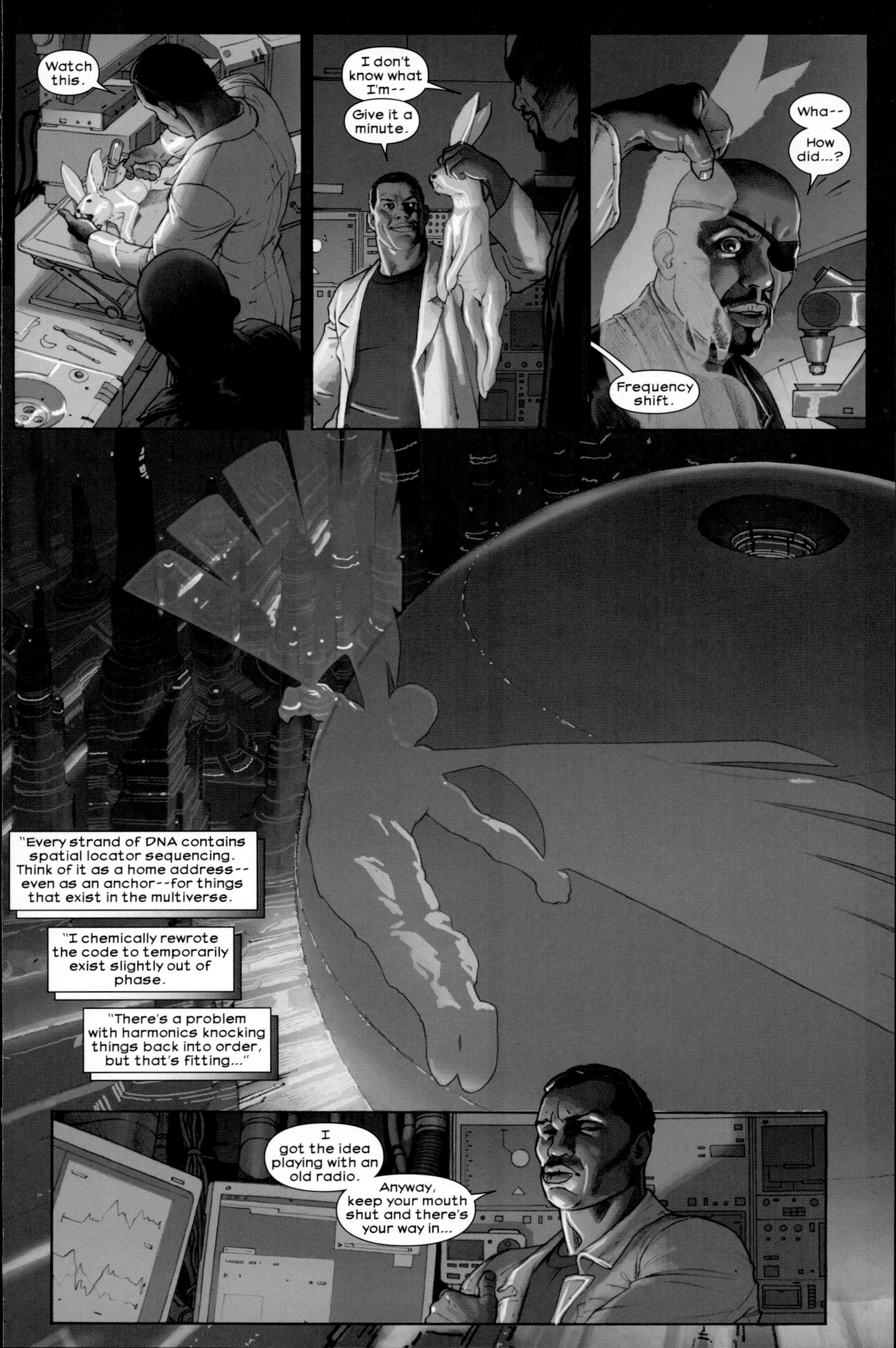
Watch this.
I don't know what I'm--
Give it a minute.
Wha--
How did...?
Frequency shift.
"Every strand of DNA contains spatial locator sequencing. Think of it as a home address--even as an anchor--for things that exist in the multiverse.
"I chemically rewrote the code to temporarily exist slightly out of phase.
"There's a problem with harmonics knocking things back into order, but that's fitting..."
I got the idea playing with an old radio.
Anyway, keep your mouth shut and there's your way in...

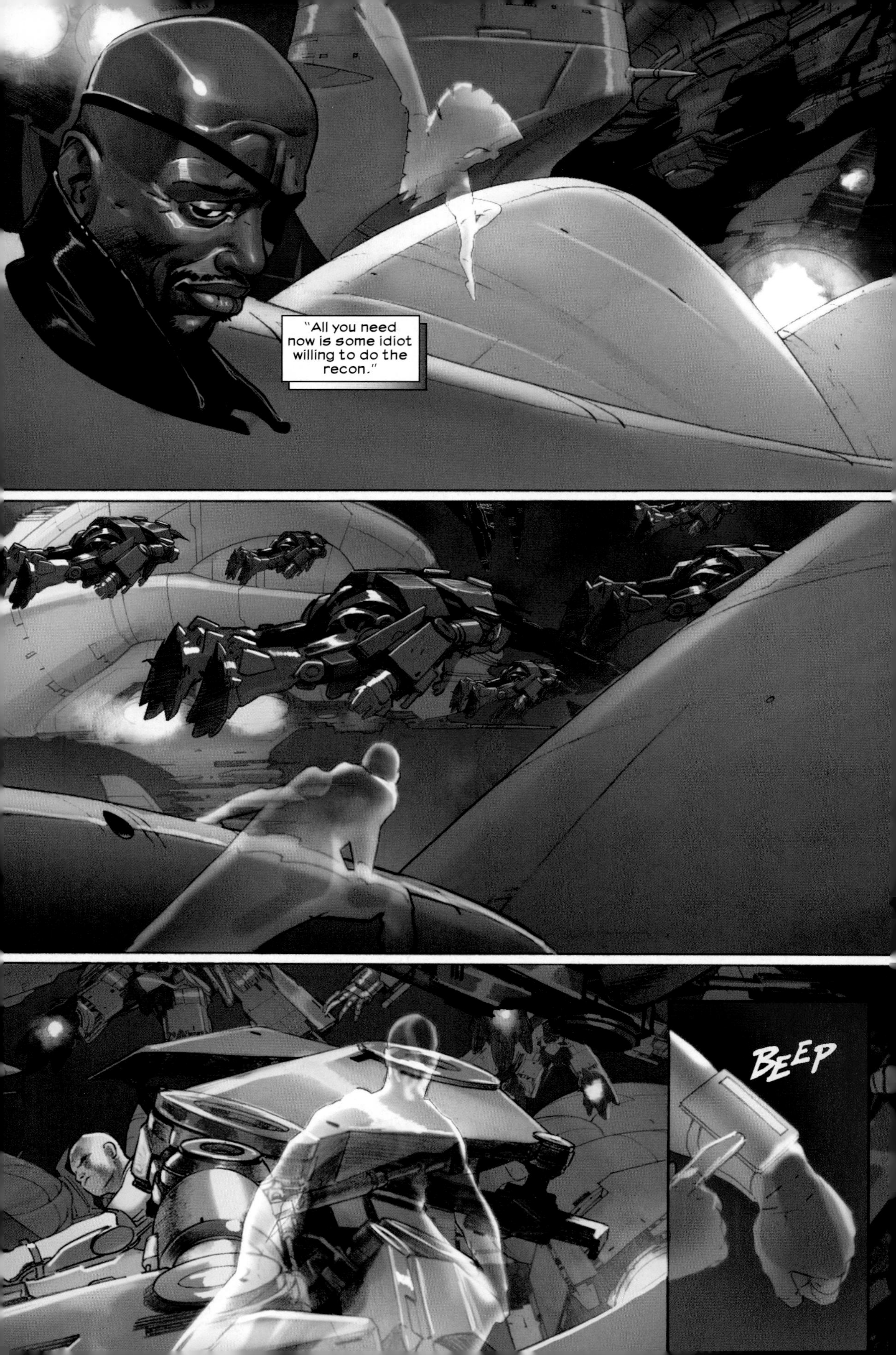
"All you need now is some idiot willing to do the recon."
BEEP

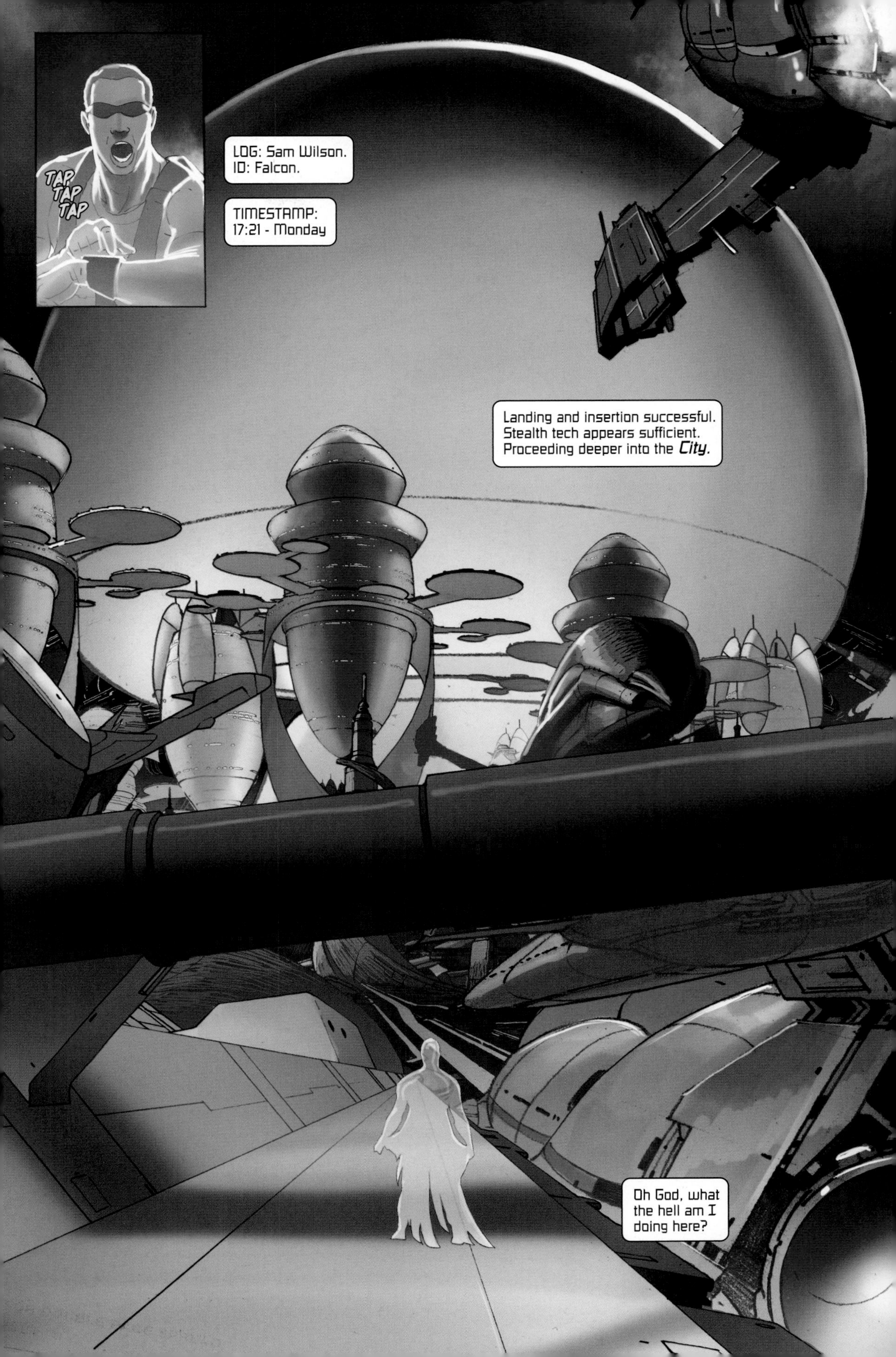
TAP TAP TAP
LOG: Sam Wilson. ID: Falcon.
TIMESTAMP: 17:21 - Monday
Landing and insertion successful. Stealth tech appears sufficient. Proceeding deeper into the *City*.
Oh God, what the hell am I doing here?

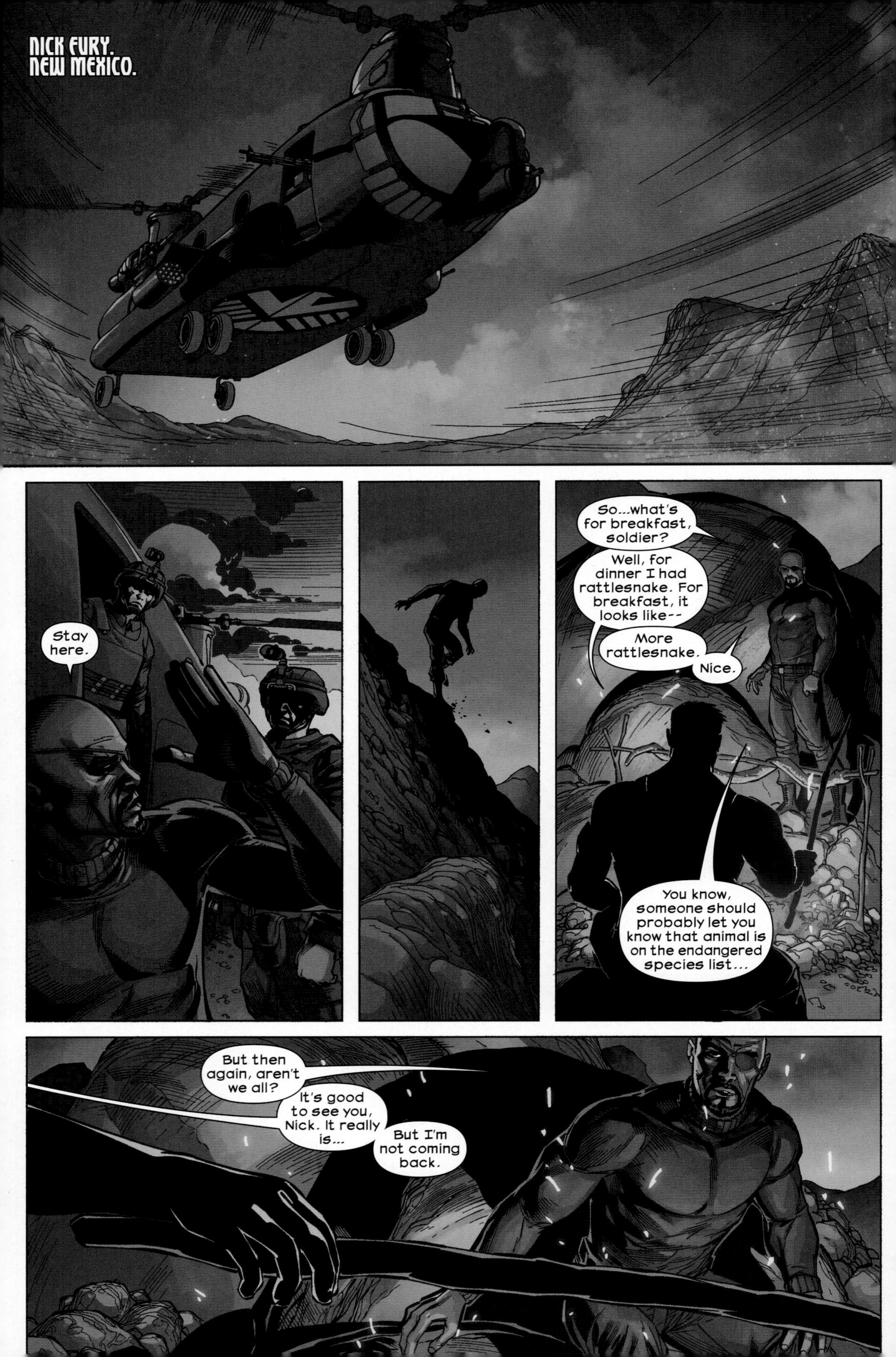
NICK FURY.
NEW MEXICO.
Stay here.
So...what's for breakfast, soldier?
Well, for dinner I had rattlesnake. For breakfast, it looks like--
More rattlesnake.
Nice.
You know, someone should probably let you know that animal is on the endangered species list...
But then again, aren't we all?
It's good to see you, Nick. It really is...
But I'm not coming back.

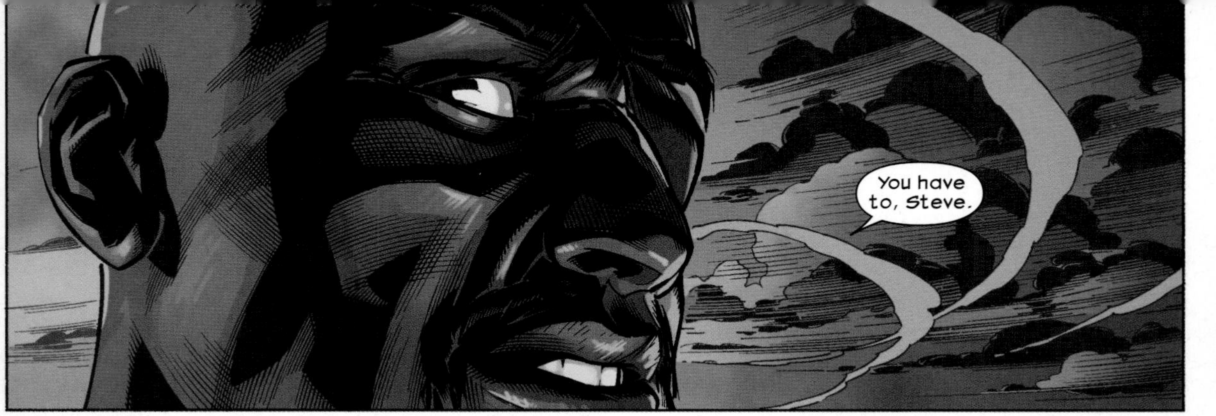
You have to, Steve.

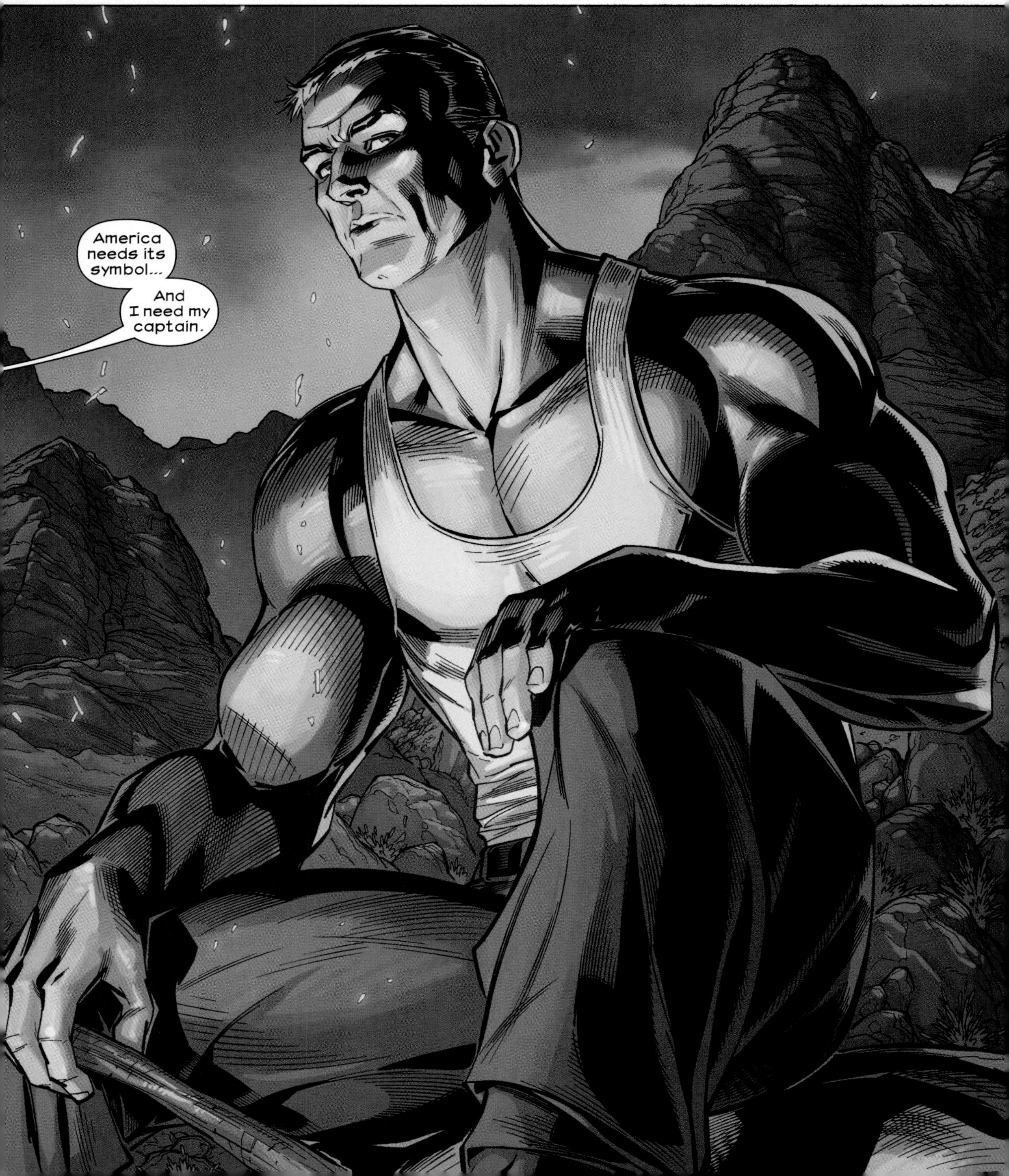
America needs its symbol...
And I need my captain.

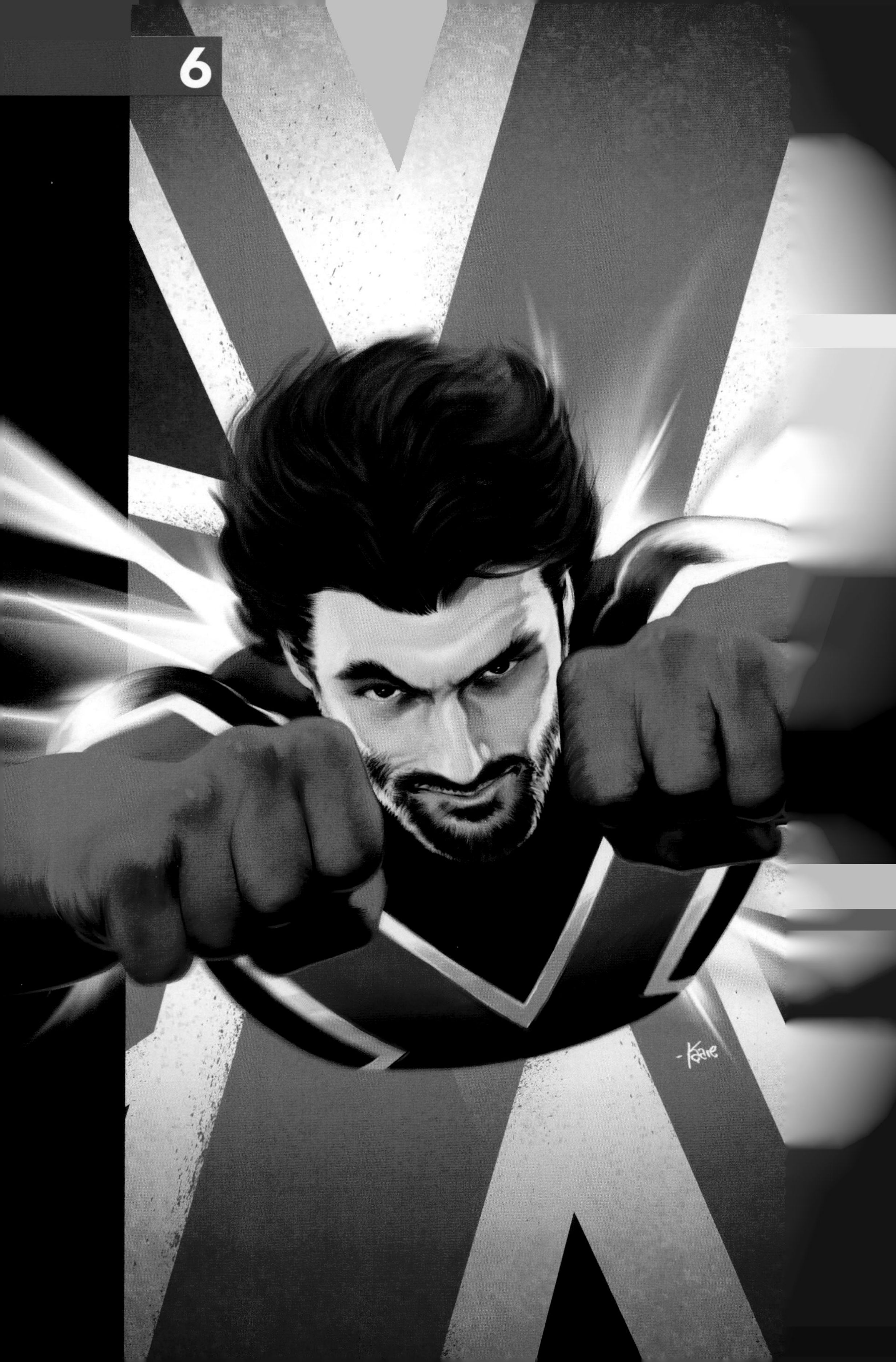
6

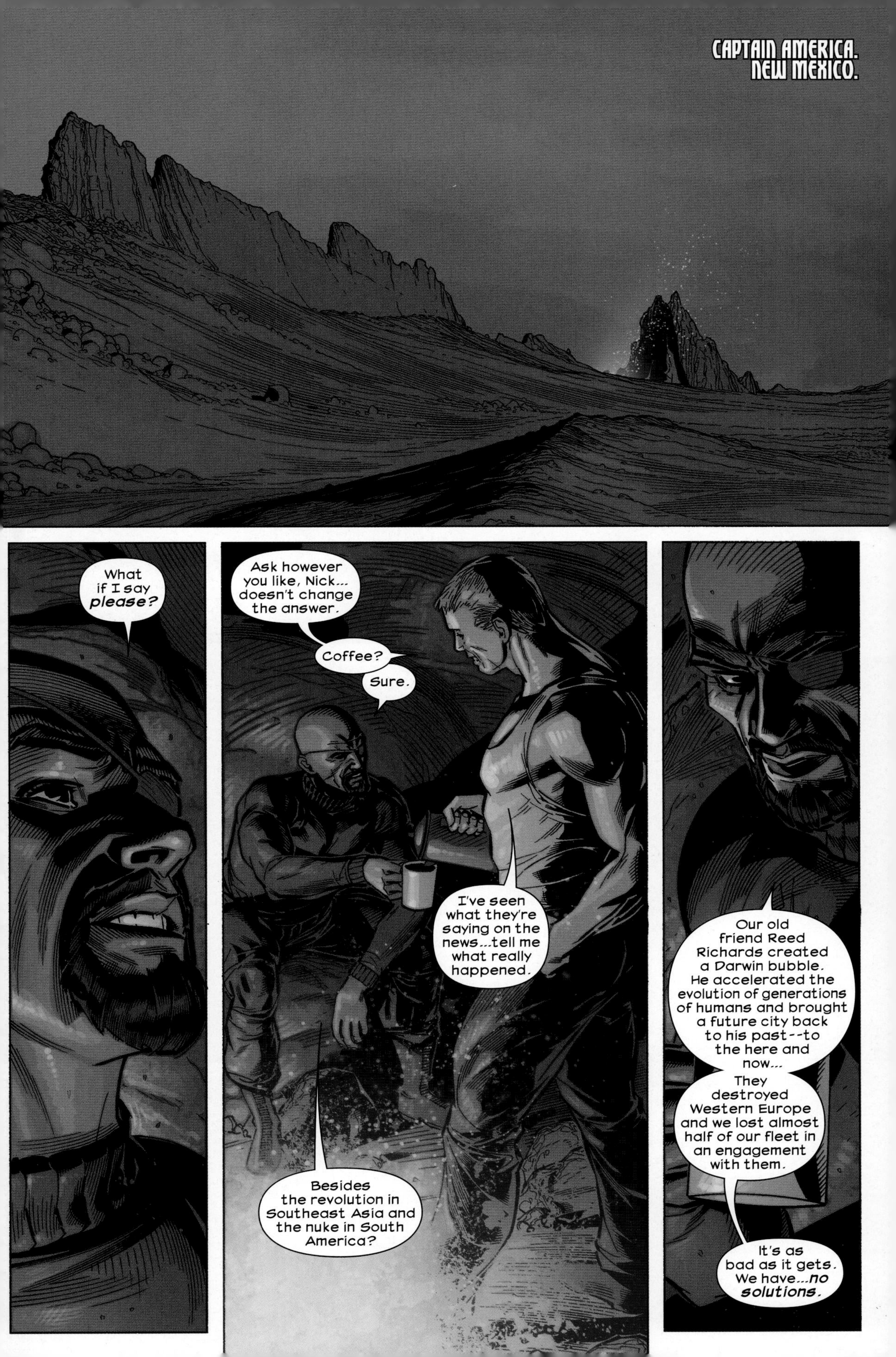
CAPTAIN AMERICA. NEW MEXICO.
What if I say *please?*
Ask however you like, Nick... doesn't change the answer.
Coffee?
Sure.
I've seen what they're saying on the news...tell me what really happened.
Besides the revolution in Southeast Asia and the nuke in South America?
Our old friend Reed Richards created a Darwin bubble. He accelerated the evolution of generations of humans and brought a future city back to his past--to the here and now...
They destroyed Western Europe and we lost almost half of our fleet in an engagement with them.
It's as bad as it gets. We have...*no solutions.*

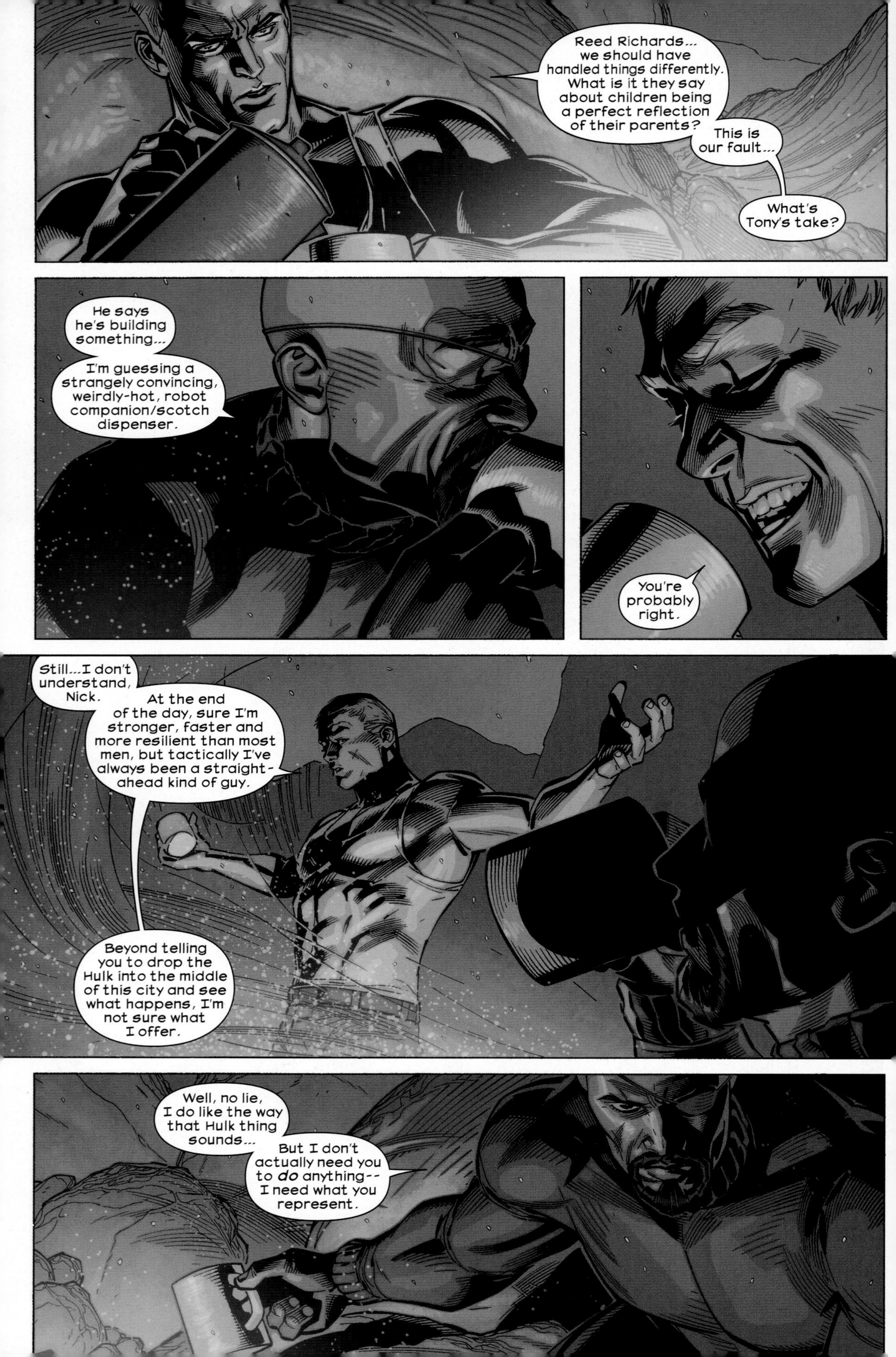
Reed Richards... we should have handled things differently. What is it they say about children being a perfect reflection of their parents?
This is our fault...
What's Tony's take?
He says he's building something...
I'm guessing a strangely convincing, weirdly-hot, robot companion/scotch dispenser.
You're probably right.
Still...I don't understand, Nick.
At the end of the day, sure I'm stronger, faster and more resilient than most men, but tactically I've always been a straight-ahead kind of guy.
Beyond telling you to drop the Hulk into the middle of this city and see what happens, I'm not sure what I offer.
Well, no lie, I do like the way that Hulk thing sounds...
But I don't actually need you to *do* anything-- I need what you represent.

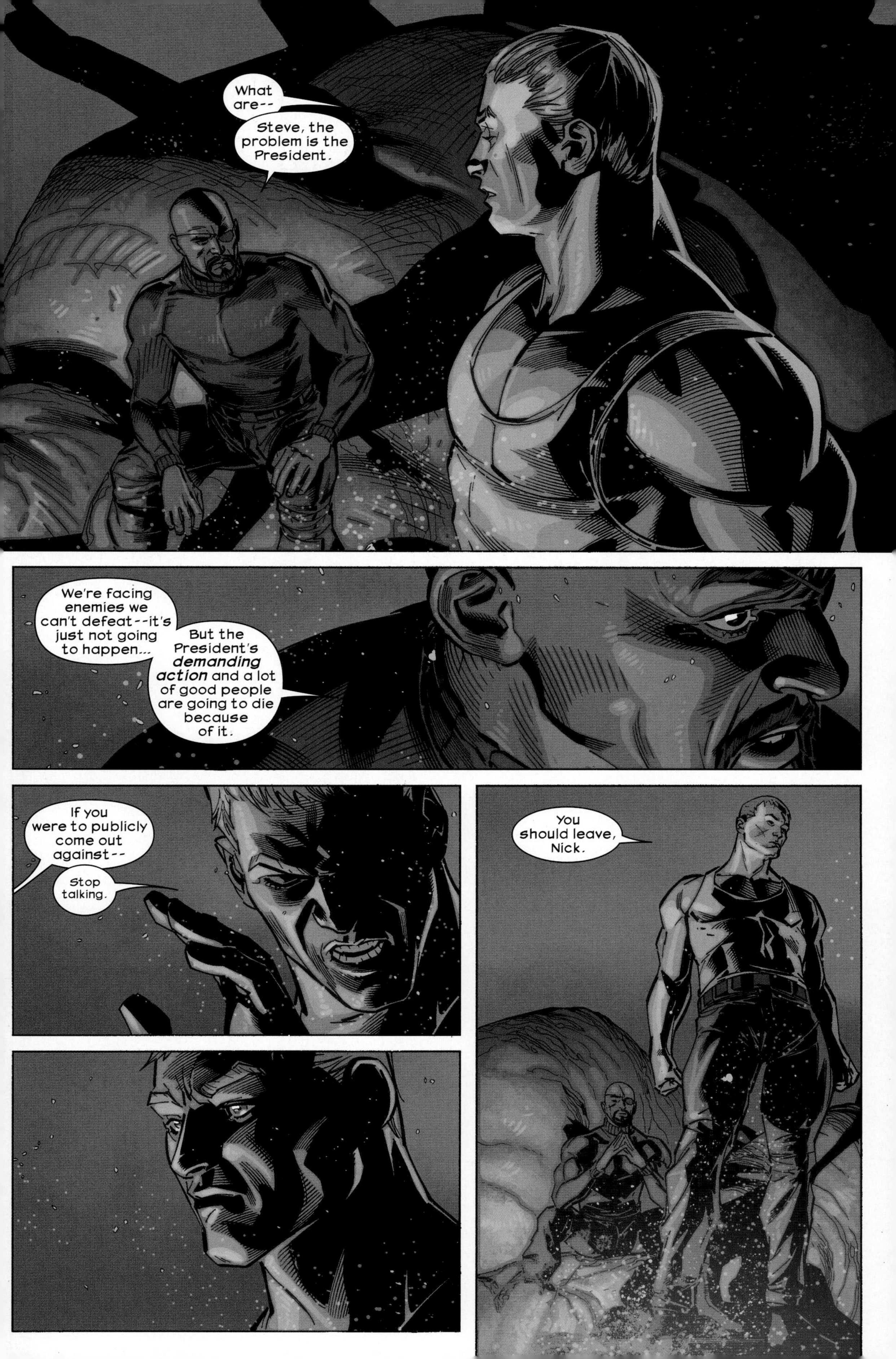
What are--
Steve, the problem is the President.
We're facing enemies we can't defeat--it's just not going to happen...
But the President's *demanding action* and a lot of good people are going to die because of it.
If you were to publicly come out against--
Stop talking.
You should leave, Nick.

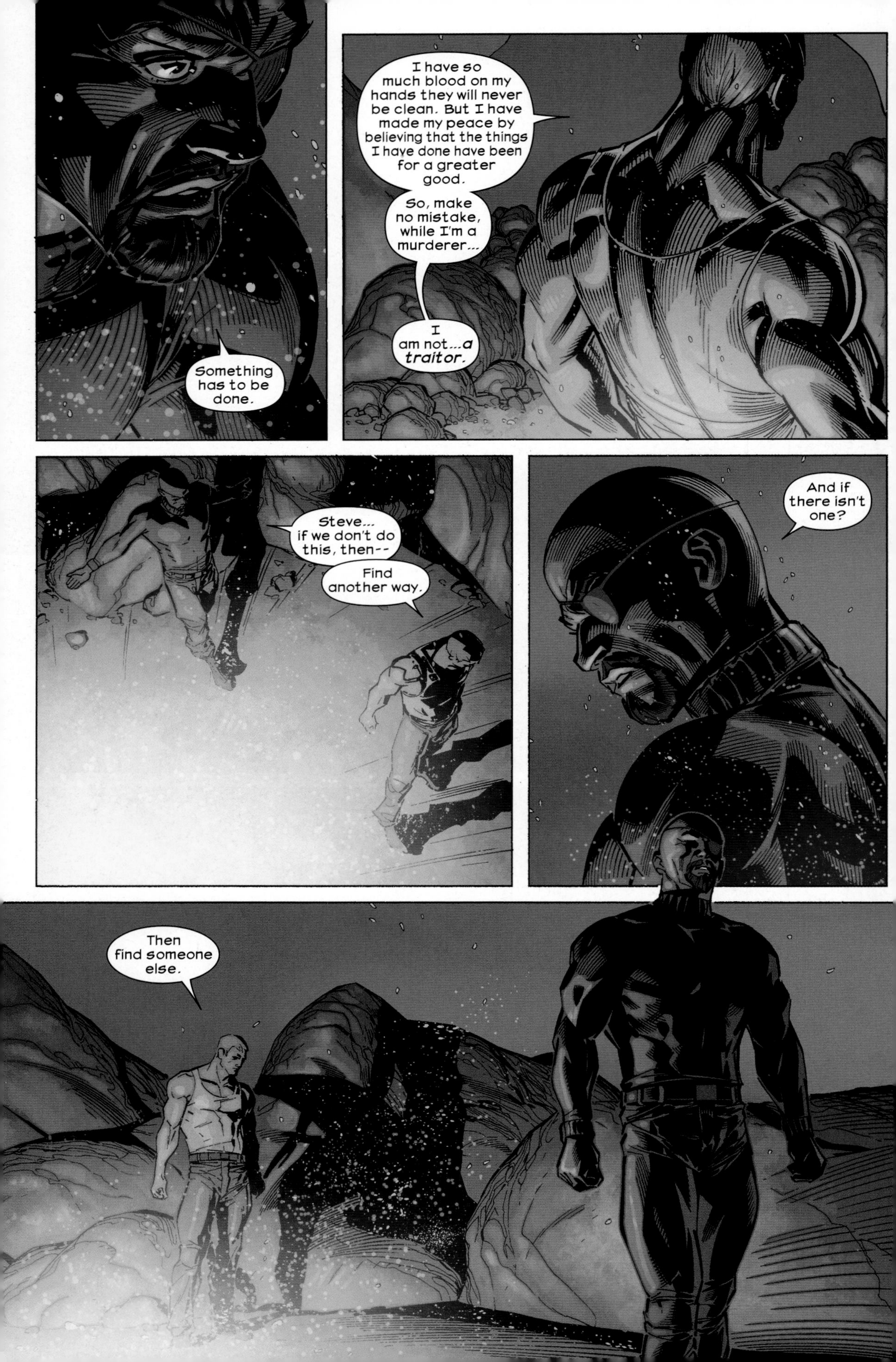
Something has to be done.
I have so much blood on my hands they will never be clean. But I have made my peace by believing that the things I have done have been for a greater good.
So, make no mistake, while I'm a murderer...
I am not...a traitor.
Steve... if we don't do this, then--
Find another way.
And if there isn't one?
Then find someone else.

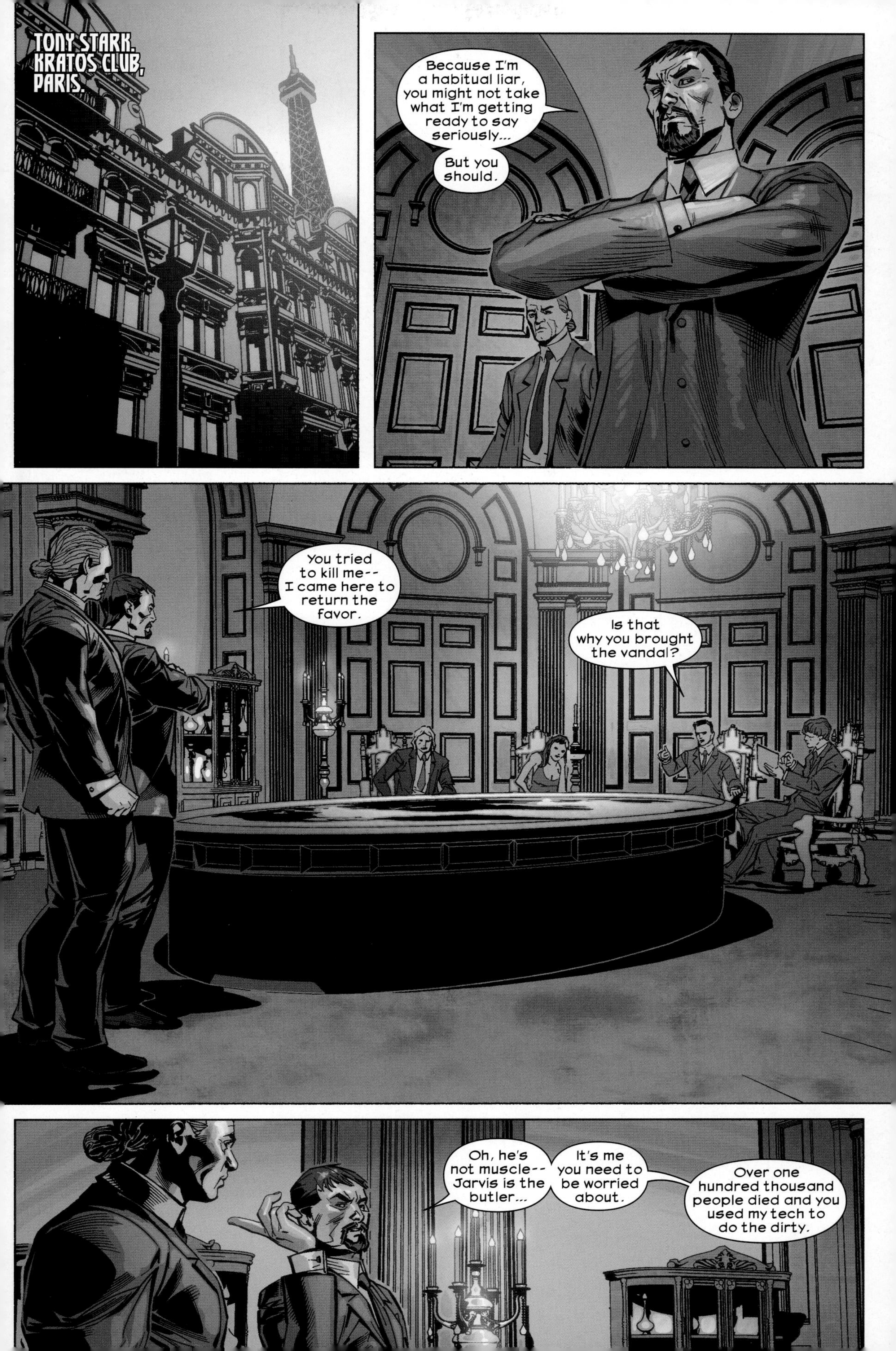
TONY STARK.
KRATOS CLUB,
PARIS.
Because I'm a habitual liar, you might not take what I'm getting ready to say seriously...
But you should.
You tried to kill me-- I came here to return the favor.
Is that why you brought the vandal?
Oh, he's not muscle-- Jarvis is the butler...
It's me you need to be worried about.
Over one hundred thousand people died and you used my tech to do the dirty.

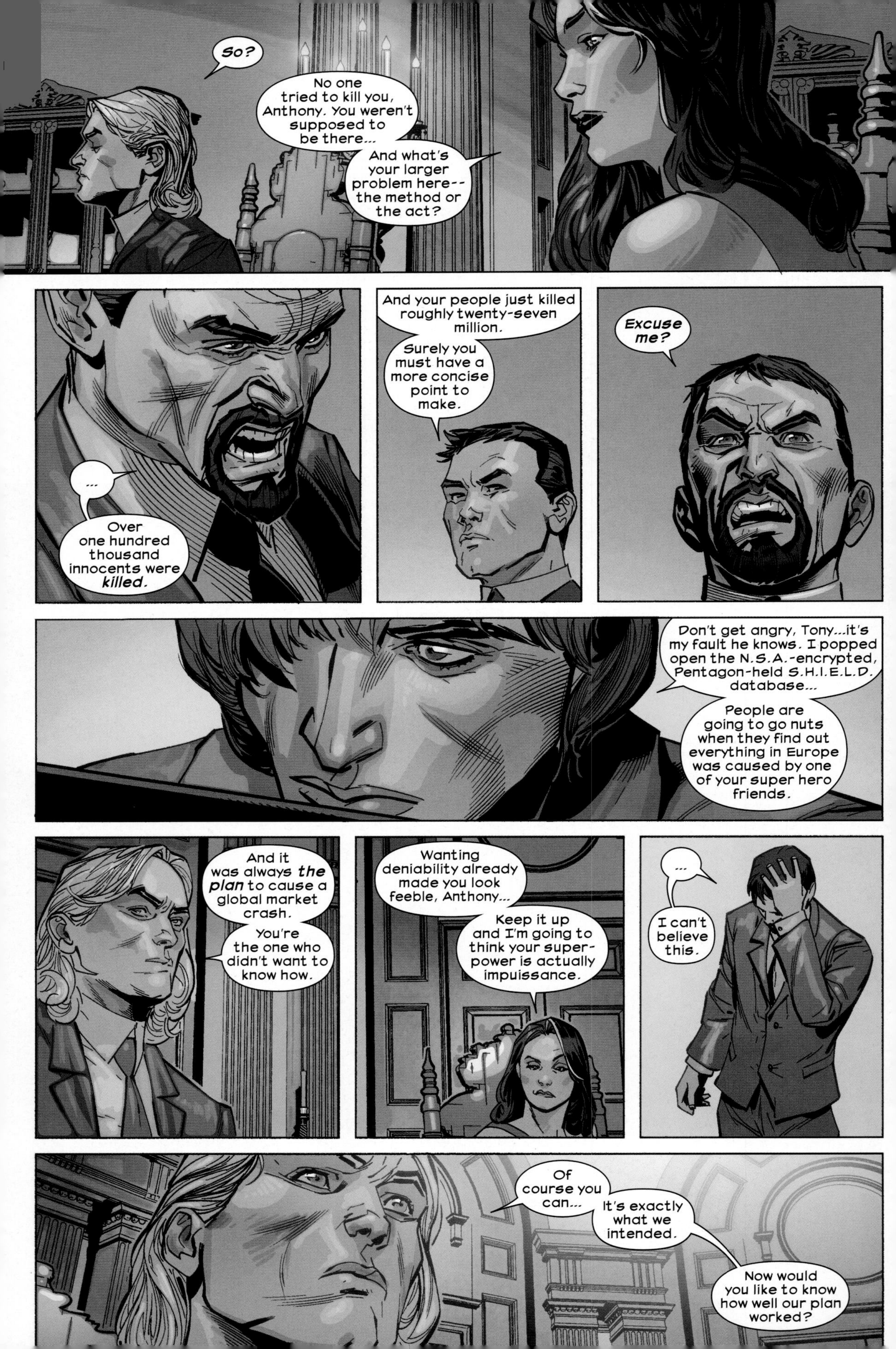
So?
No one tried to kill you, Anthony. You weren't supposed to be there...
And what's your larger problem here--the method or the act?
...
Over one hundred thousand innocents were *killed.*
And your people just killed roughly twenty-seven million.
Surely you must have a more concise point to make.
Excuse me?
Don't get angry, Tony...it's my fault he knows. I popped open the N.S.A.-encrypted, Pentagon-held S.H.I.E.L.D. database...
People are going to go nuts when they find out everything in Europe was caused by one of your super hero friends.
And it was always *the plan* to cause a global market crash.
You're the one who didn't want to know how.
Wanting deniability already made you look feeble, Anthony...
Keep it up and I'm going to think your super-power is actually impuissance.
...
I can't believe this.
Of course you can...
It's exactly what we intended.
Now would you like to know how well our plan worked?

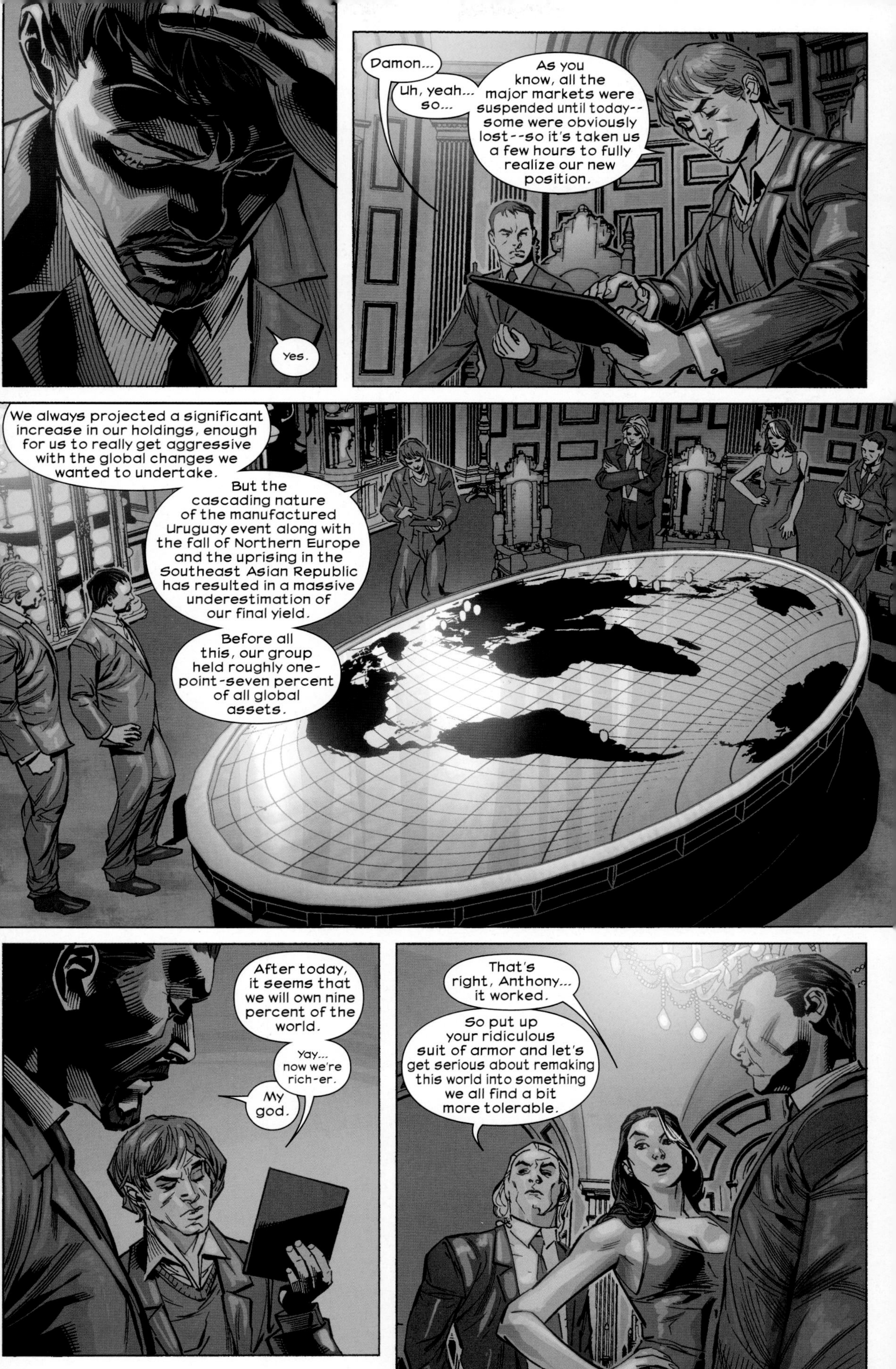
Yes.
Damon...
Uh, yeah... so...
As you know, all the major markets were suspended until today--some were obviously lost--so it's taken us a few hours to fully realize our new position.
We always projected a significant increase in our holdings, enough for us to really get aggressive with the global changes we wanted to undertake.
But the cascading nature of the manufactured Uruguay event along with the fall of Northern Europe and the uprising in the Southeast Asian Republic has resulted in a massive underestimation of our final yield.
Before all this, our group held roughly one-point-seven percent of all global assets.
After today, it seems that we will own nine percent of the world.
Yay... now we're rich-er.
My god.
That's right, Anthony... it worked.
So put up your ridiculous suit of armor and let's get serious about remaking this world into something we all find a bit more tolerable.

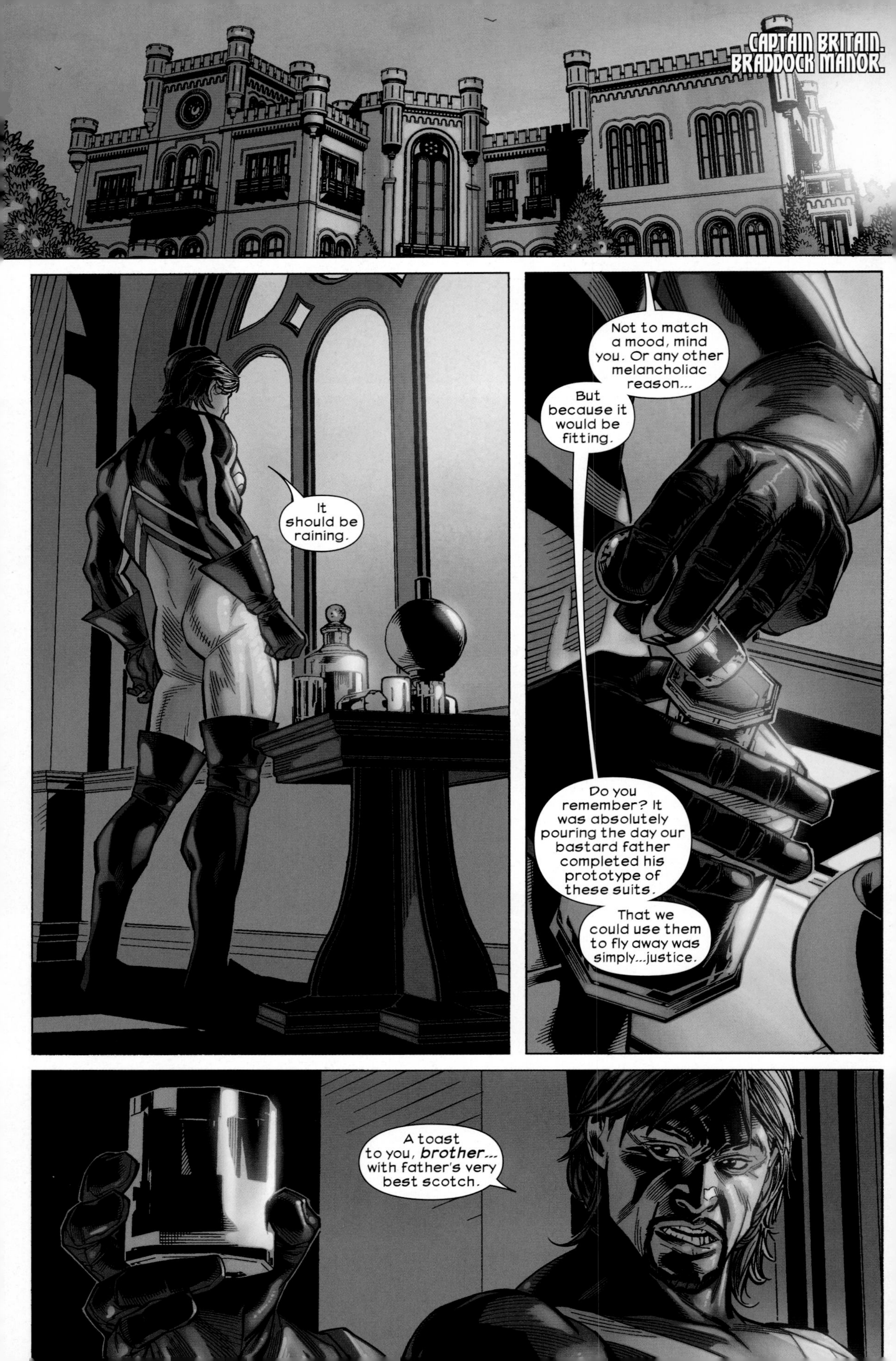
CAPTAIN BRITAIN.
BRADDOCK MANOR.
It should be raining.
Not to match a mood, mind you. Or any other melancholiac reason...
But because it would be fitting.
Do you remember? It was absolutely pouring the day our bastard father completed his prototype of these suits.
That we could use them to fly away was simply...justice.
A toast to you, *brother*... with father's very best scotch.

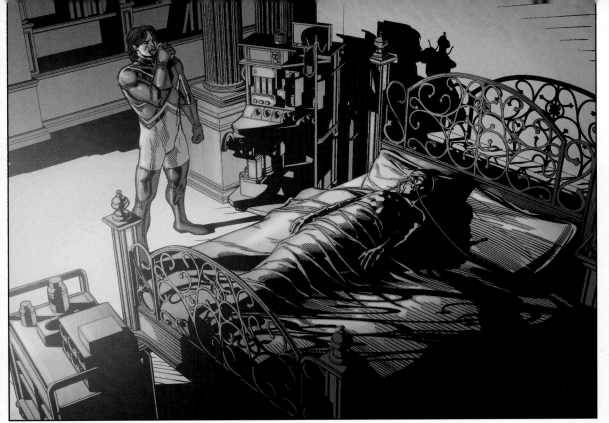

Get better soon, Brian.

When you are, we'll defile the sky together.

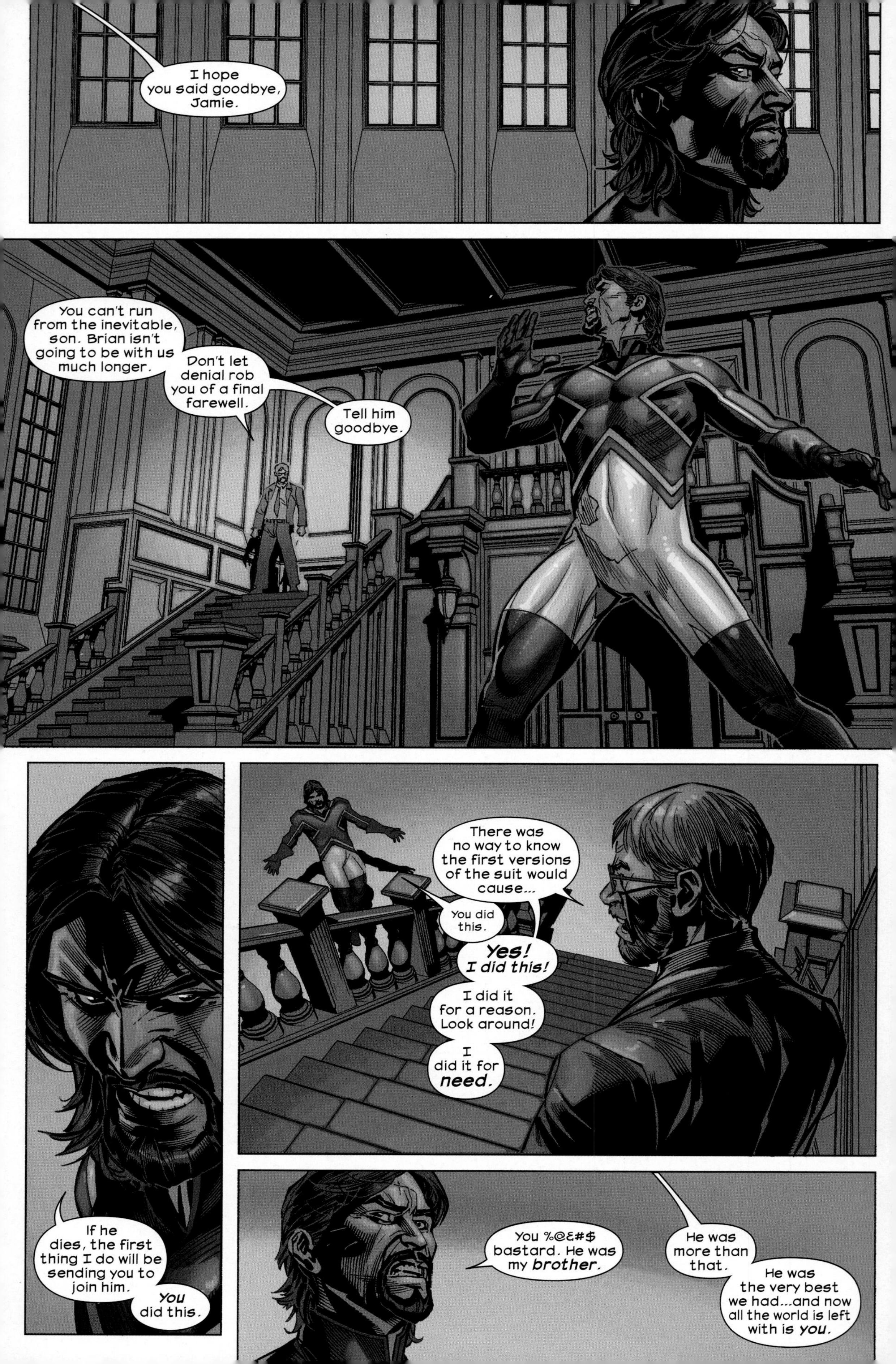
I hope you said goodbye, Jamie.
You can't run from the inevitable, son. Brian isn't going to be with us much longer.
Don't let denial rob you of a final farewell.
Tell him goodbye.
There was no way to know the first versions of the suit would cause...
You did this.
Yes! I did this!
I did it for a reason. Look around!
I did it for need.
If he dies, the first thing I do will be sending you to join him.
You did this.
You %@&#$ bastard. He was my brother.
He was more than that.
He was the very best we had...and now all the world is left with is you.

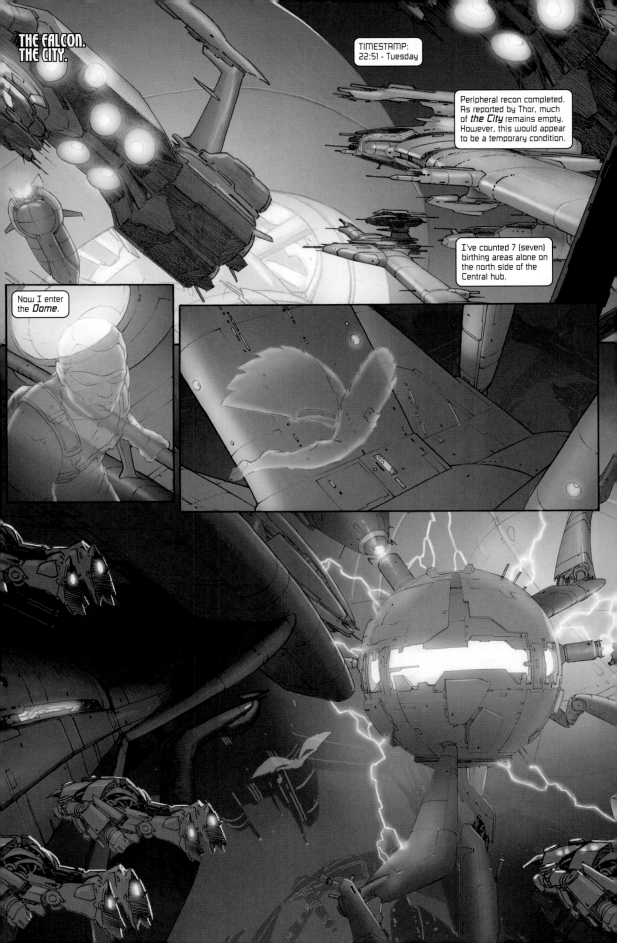

THE FALCON.
THE CITY.

TIMESTAMP:
22:51 - Tuesday

Peripheral recon completed.
As reported by Thor, much
of *the City* remains empty.
However, this would appear
to be a temporary condition.

I've counted 7 (seven)
birthing areas alone on
the north side of the
Central hub.

Now I enter
the *Dome*.

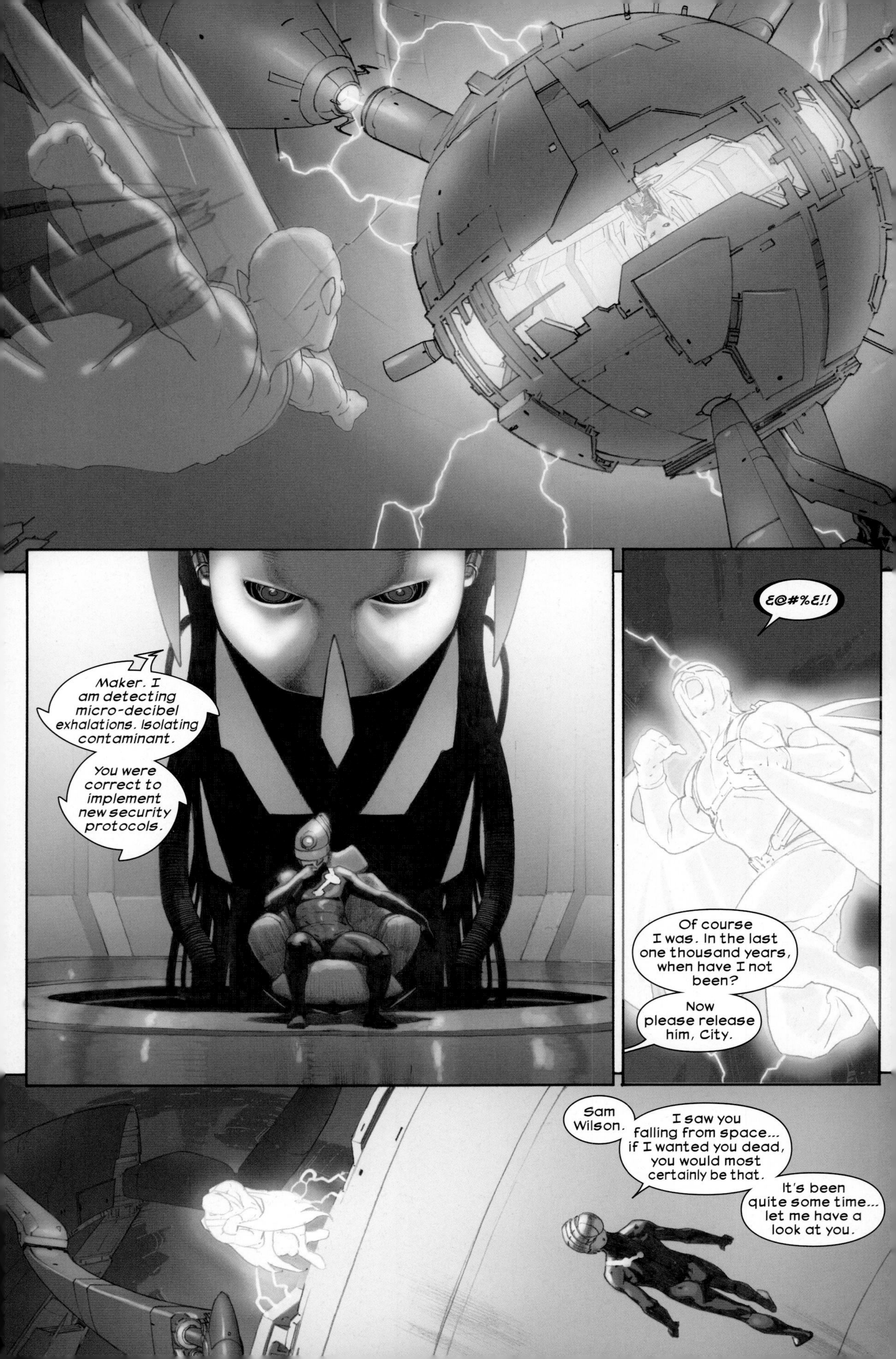

Maker. I am detecting micro-decibel exhalations. Isolating contaminant.
You were correct to implement new security protocols.
Ɛ@#%Ɛ!!
Of course I was. In the last one thousand years, when have I not been?
Now please release him, City.
Sam Wilson.
I saw you falling from space... if I wanted you dead, you would most certainly be that.
It's been quite some time... let me have a look at you.

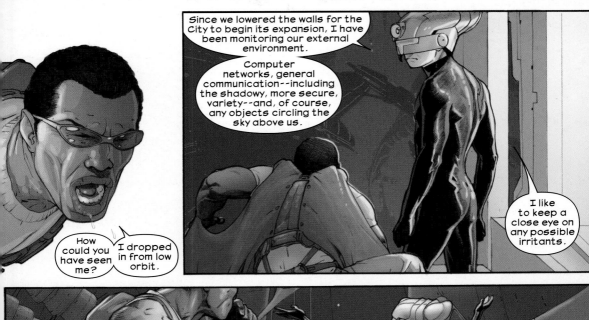

Since we lowered the walls for the City to begin its expansion, I have been monitoring our external environment.

Computer networks, general communication--including the shadowy, more secure, variety--and, of course, any objects circling the sky above us.

I like to keep a close eye on any possible irritants.

How could you have seen me?

I dropped in from low orbit.

See, what you have to understand is while *the Children* watch over *the City...*

I watch *the World*.

My god... that really is you, isn't it?

How are you alive, Reed?

Oh, longevity is a side effect of my enhanced abilities. I've lacked an entropy-based, naturally decaying biology since my transformation...

Only through great violence has my death been a possibility.

No...my cross over the past millennium has been evolution.

I have had to go to long, painful lengths to expand my intellect so that I could stay ahead of my perfect children.

Imagine the smartest neanderthal to ever live being faced with the simplest of modern men...

What good would he be?

Which brings us to your problem, Sam.

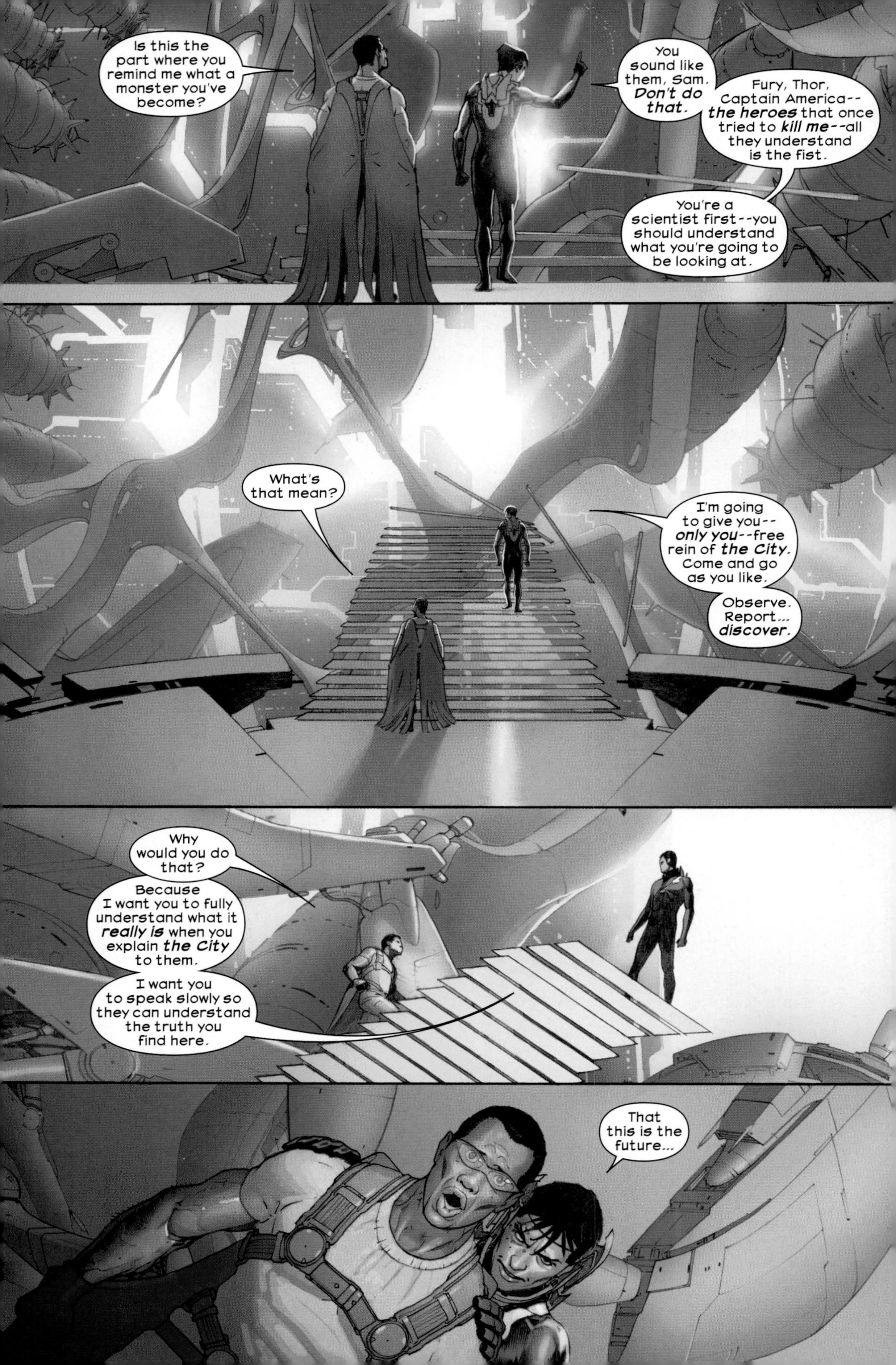
Is this the part where you remind me what a monster you've become?
You sound like them, Sam. Don't do that.
Fury, Thor, Captain America--the heroes that once tried to kill me--all they understand is the fist.
You're a scientist first--you should understand what you're going to be looking at.
What's that mean?
I'm going to give you--only you--free rein of the City. Come and go as you like.
Observe. Report... discover.
Why would you do that?
Because I want you to fully understand what it really is when you explain the City to them.
I want you to speak slowly so they can understand the truth you find here.
That this is the future...

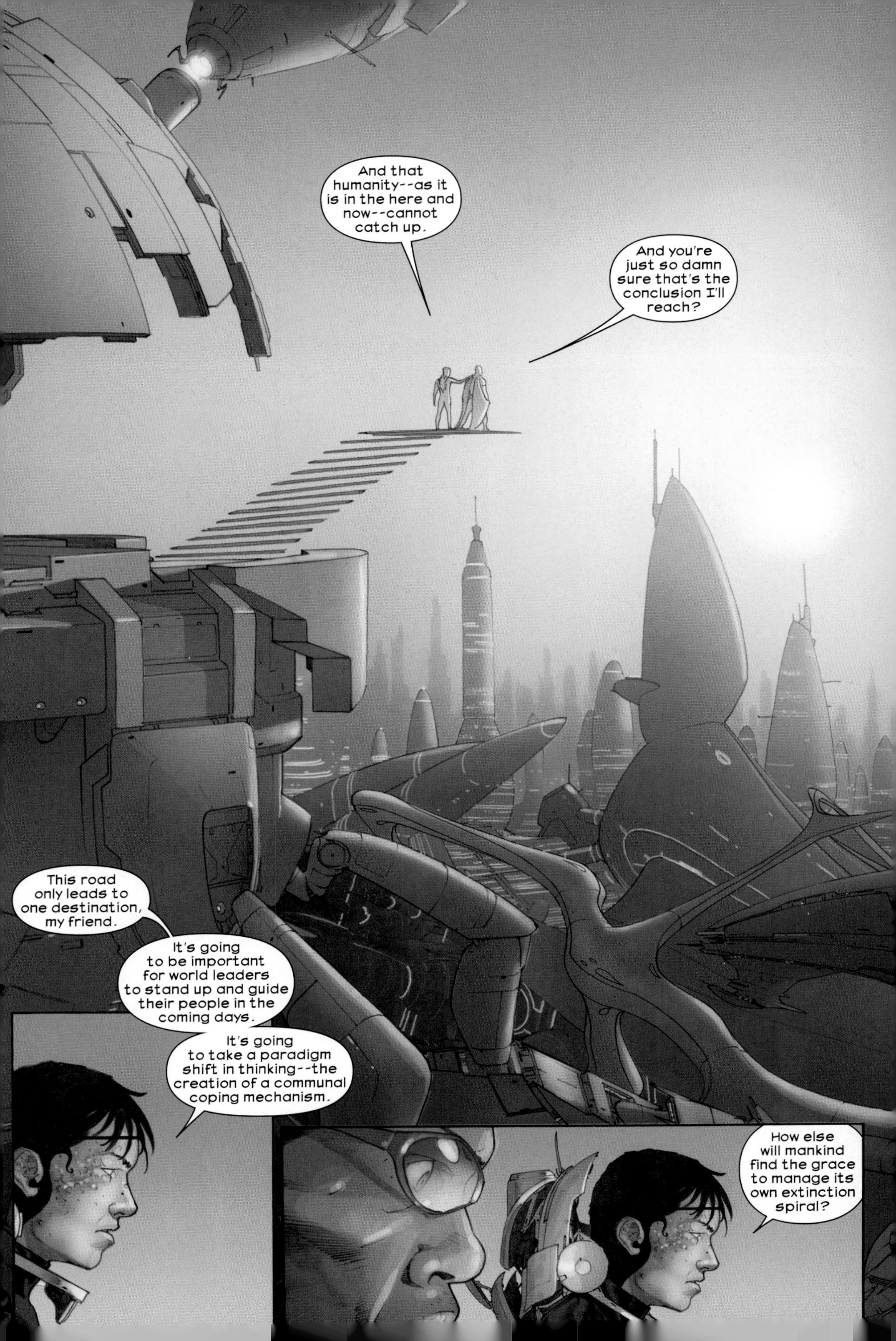
And that humanity--as it is in the here and now--cannot catch up.
And you're just so damn sure that's the conclusion I'll reach?
This road only leads to one destination, my friend.
It's going to be important for world leaders to stand up and guide their people in the coming days.
It's going to take a paradigm shift in thinking--the creation of a communal coping mechanism.
How else will mankind find the grace to manage its own extinction spiral?

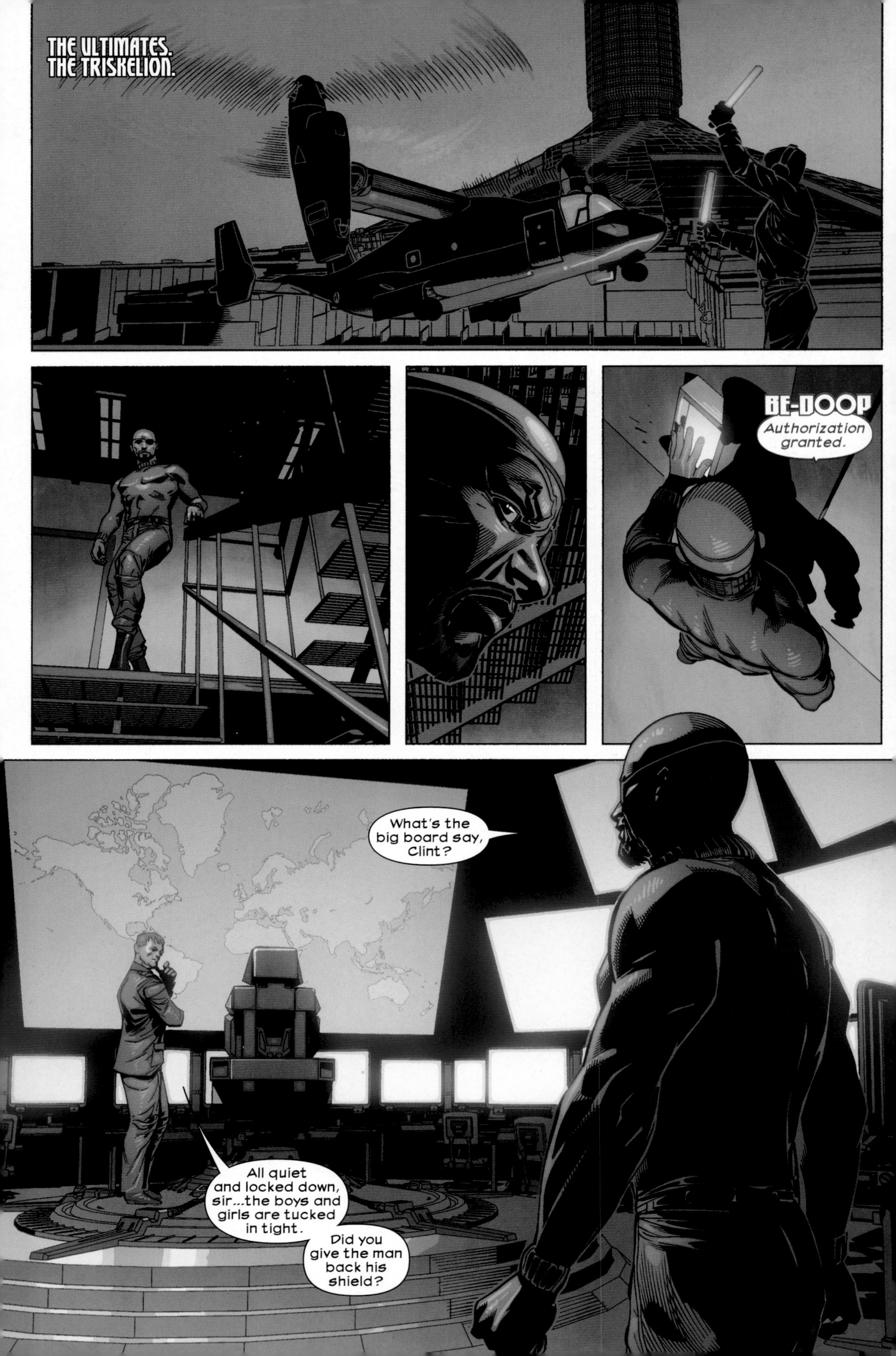
THE ULTIMATES.
THE TRISKELION.
BE-DOOP
Authorization granted.
What's the big board say, Clint?
All quiet and locked down, sir...the boys and girls are tucked in tight.
Did you give the man back his shield?

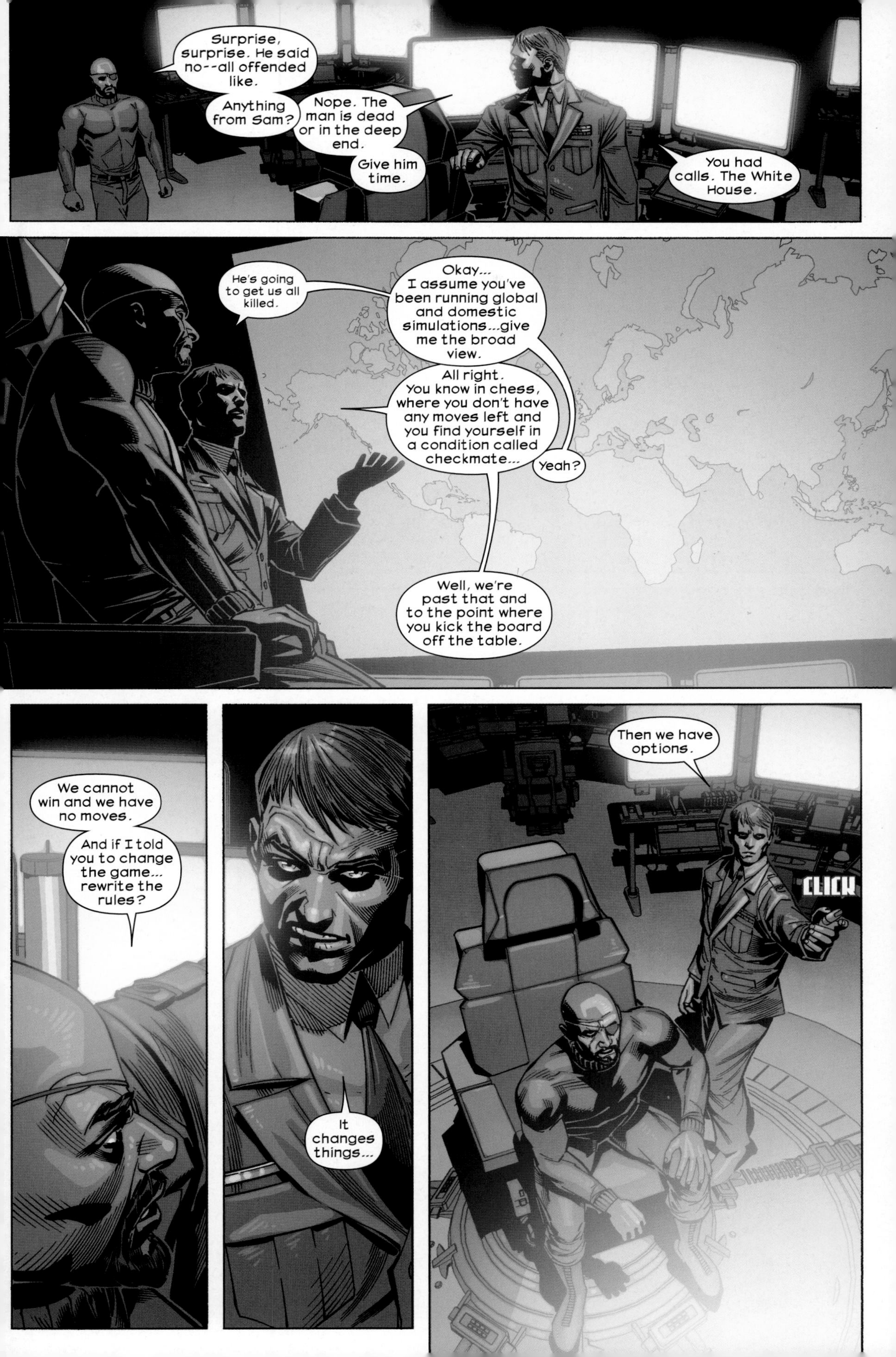
Surprise, surprise. He said no--all offended like.
Anything from Sam?
Nope. The man is dead or in the deep end.
Give him time.
You had calls. The White House.
He's going to get us all killed.
Okay... I assume you've been running global and domestic simulations...give me the broad view.
All right. You know in chess, where you don't have any moves left and you find yourself in a condition called checkmate...
Yeah?
Well, we're past that and to the point where you kick the board off the table.
We cannot win and we have no moves.
And if I told you to change the game... rewrite the rules?
It changes things...
Then we have options.
CLICK

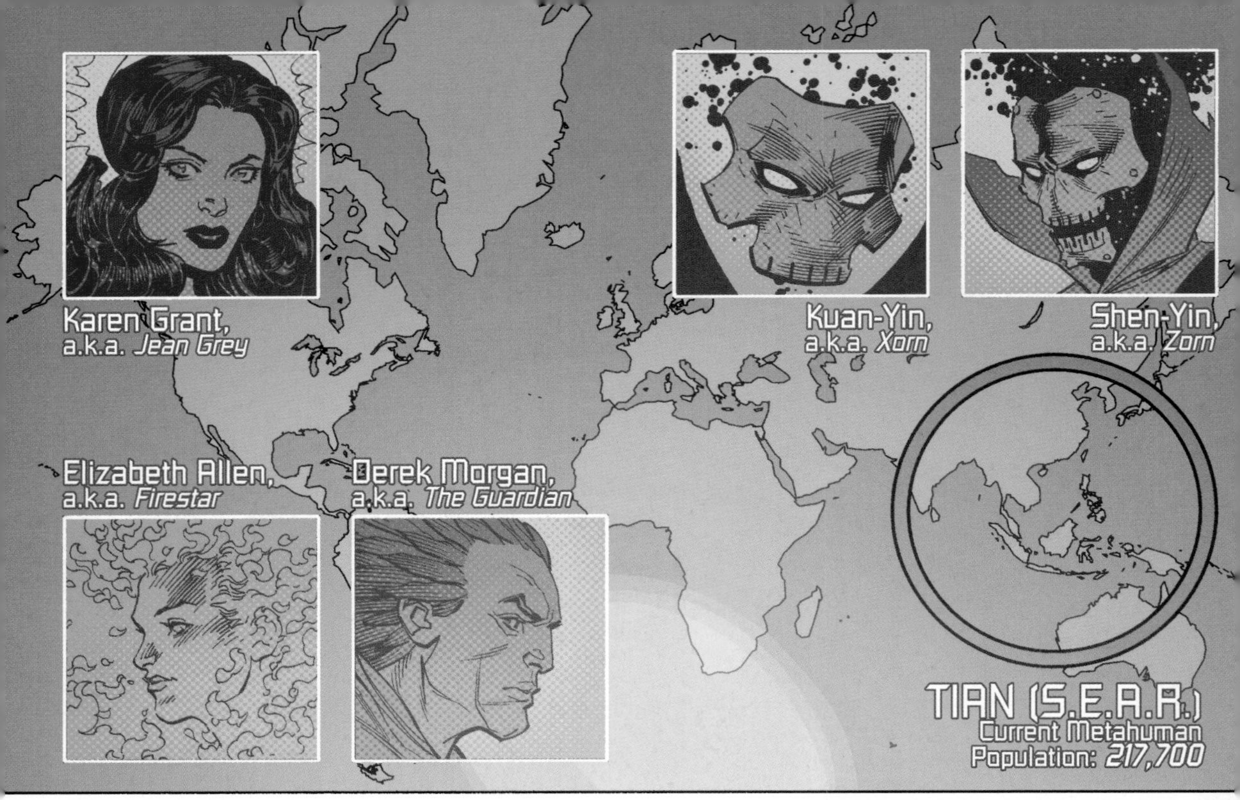
Karen Grant,
a.k.a. Jean Grey
Kuan-Yin,
a.k.a. Xorn
Shen-Yin,
a.k.a. Zorn
Elizabeth Allen,
a.k.a. Firestar
Derek Morgan,
a.k.a. The Guardian
TIAN (S.E.A.R.)
Current Metahuman
Population: 217,700

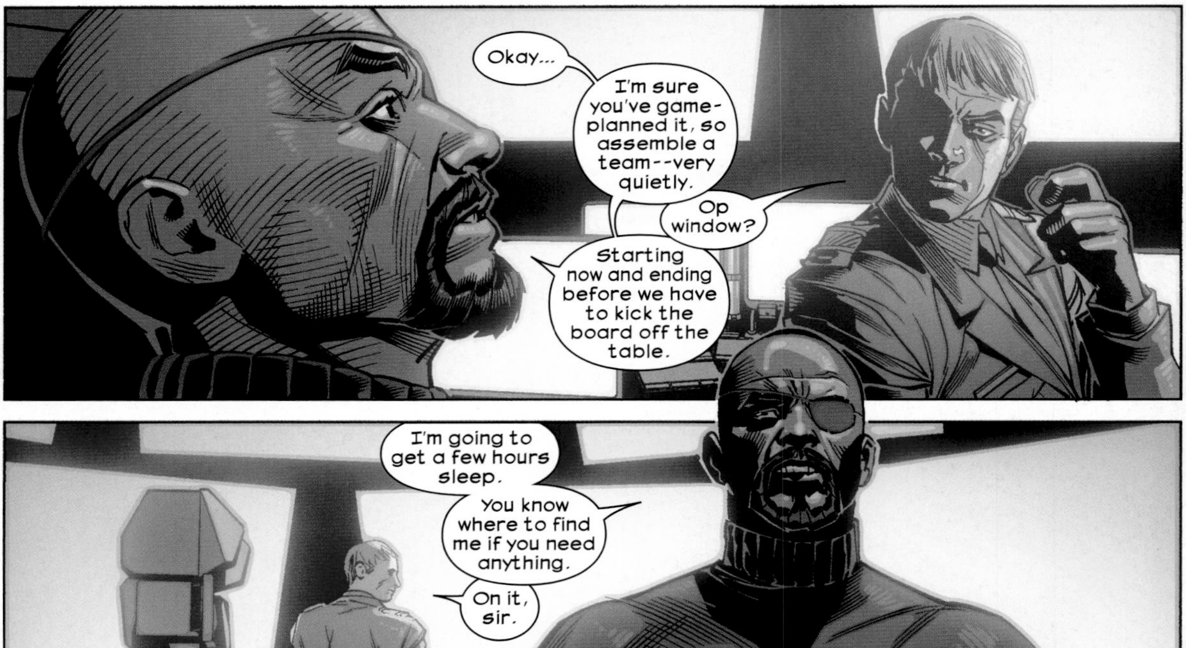
Okay...
I'm sure you've game-planned it, so assemble a team--very quietly.
Op window?
Starting now and ending before we have to kick the board off the table.

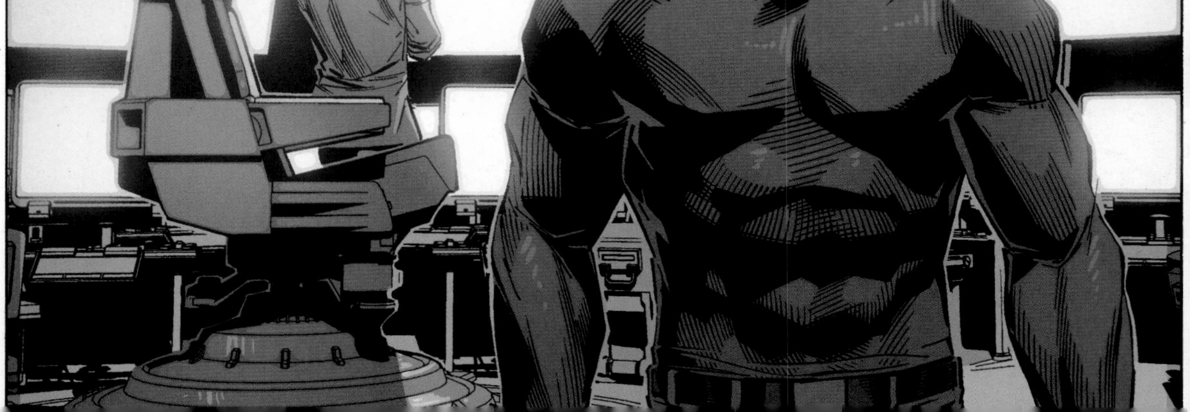
I'm going to get a few hours sleep.
You know where to find me if you need anything.
On it, sir.

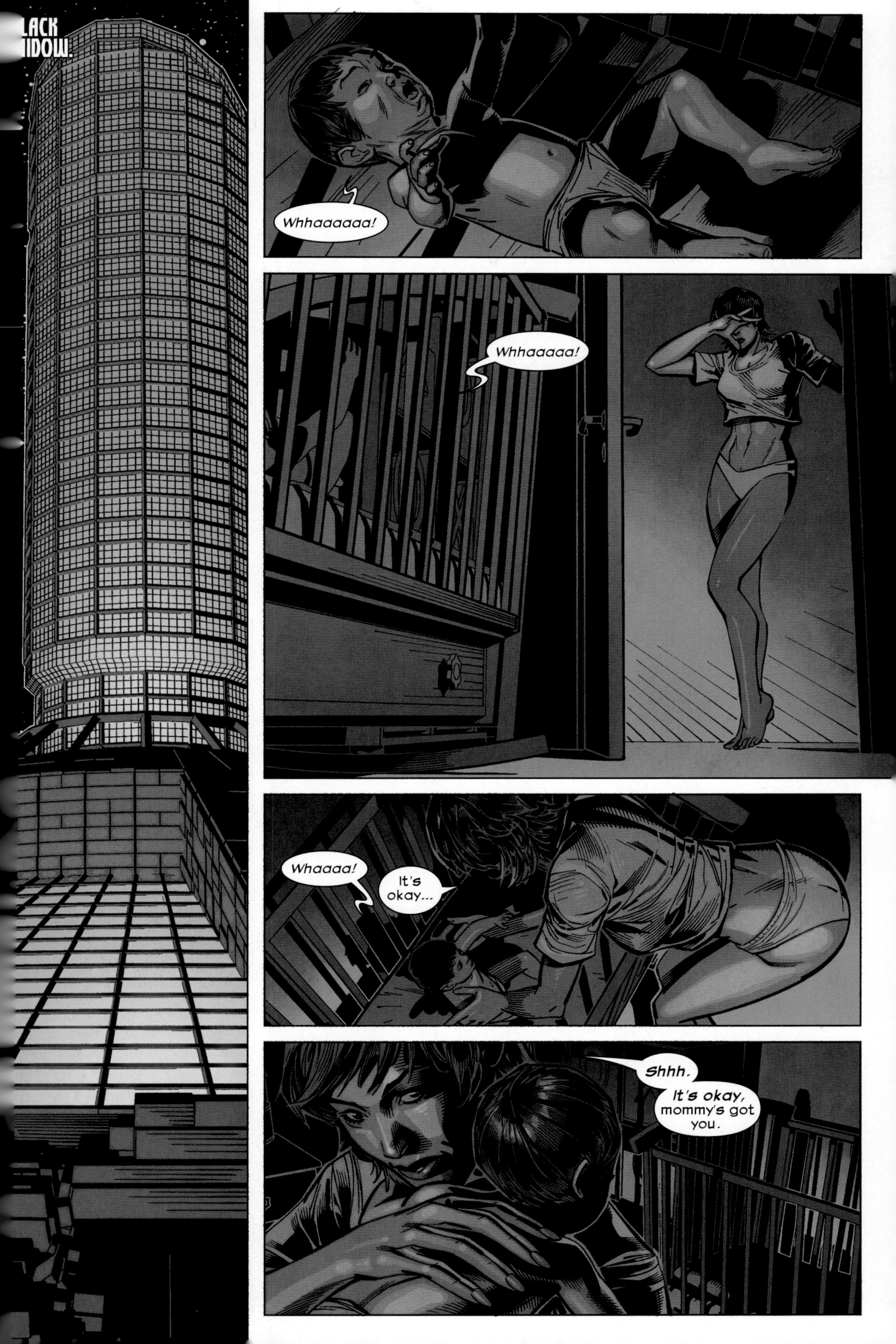
LACK
IDOW.
Whhaaaaaa!
Whhaaaaa!
Whaaaa!
It's okay...
Shhh.
It's okay, mommy's got you.

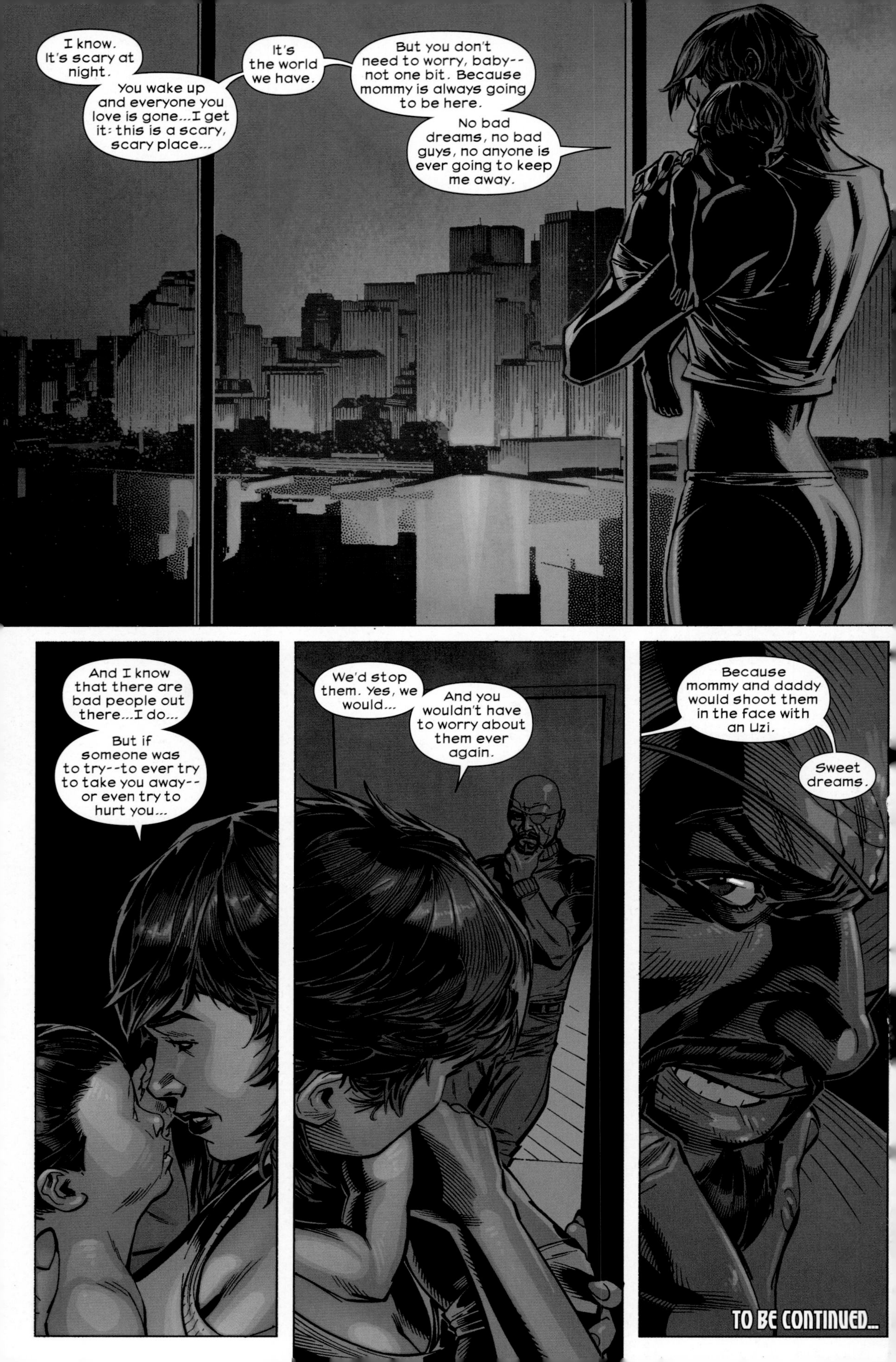
I know. It's scary at night.
You wake up and everyone you love is gone...I get it: this is a scary, scary place...
It's the world we have.
But you don't need to worry, baby--not one bit. Because mommy is always going to be here.
No bad dreams, no bad guys, no anyone is ever going to keep me away.
And I know that there are bad people out there...I do...
But if someone was to try--to ever try to take you away--or even try to hurt you...
We'd stop them. Yes, we would...
And you wouldn't have to worry about them ever again.
Because mommy and daddy would shoot them in the face with an Uzi.
Sweet dreams.
TO BE CONTINUED...